ONE SOLDIER'S WAR

ONE
SOLDIER'S
WAR

ARKADY BABCHENKO

Translated from the Russian by Nick Allen

GROVE PRESS
New York

First published in Great Britain in 2007 by Portobello Books Ltd.,
with the title *One Soldier's War in Chechnya*

Individual chapters were first published in Russian literary journals
during 2003–2006 and then in book form by Exmo in 2006

Printed in the United States of America

FIRST AMERICAN EDITION

ISBN-10: 0-8021-1860-7
ISBN-13: 978-0-8021-1860-8

Grove Press
an imprint of Grove/Atlantic, Inc.
841 Broadway
New York, NY 10003

Distributed by Publishers Group West

www.groveatlantic.com

08 09 10 11 12 10 9 8 7 6 5 4 3 2 1

Contents

Preface

It would be wrong to think that the war in Chechnya began the day the federal army was brought in. And there was certainly more than one motivation behind it. Chechnya is a complex tangle of factors and accidents, a whirlwind of events that the future historian will have difficulty sorting out.

The Chechnya conflict started in the early 1990s, soon after General Dzhokhar Dudayev came to power. He had been a pilot in the Soviet air force and fought in the Soviet–Afghan war. From the outset he followed the policy of political independence for Chechnya, and ultimately declared its cession from the Russian Federation.

In 1991 Dudayev expelled Russian army forces from the territory of Chechnya. When the army withdrew, a huge amount of ammunition was left behind. More than two hundred airplanes were abandoned in the airport of Grozny alone, together with tanks, armored carriers, artillery and even several 'Grad' rocket launchers. The amount of weaponry was simply astounding—whole ammunition depots, tens of thousands of units, were simply left behind.

Lawlessness and chaos set in after Dudayev had announced a 100 percent amnesty for all criminals, without exception, which led to a huge influx into Chechnya of all kinds of people who were in trouble with the law. The immediate result was an outbreak of banditry, and before long murder and robbery had become commonplace; more often than not, non-Chechens were the victims. A wave of Russian refugees flooded into Russia from Chechnya. It would be wrong to say that the genocide of the non-Chechen population was a state policy, but Chechens, whose society is based on a system of clans known as *teips*, were certainly better protected. (Chechnya's current president, Ramzan Kadyrov, belongs to the Benoi Teip, for example.) Since Russians have no *teip* system they found themselves completely defenseless: no one was going to avenge their deaths, and this made them easy prey.

Growing gangsterism and unemployment undermined Dudayev's authority and caused a split among the population. This conflict was exacerbated by the fierce struggle for domination going on among the *teips*. In November 1994, pro-Moscow opposition forces led by Umar Avturkhanov stormed Grozny and were defeated. Twenty Russian tanks were destroyed together with their crews, and the few surviving tankmen were captured. Moscow renounced them—President Boris Yeltsin, a despotic ruler, couldn't have cared less about individuals, and he was infuriated that General Dudayev had acted beyond his authority. In my opinion this was the real reason federal forces were sent into Chechnya.

The military operation to overthrow the Dudayev regime was launched on 11 December 1994. It was poorly planned—recall the then minister of Defense General Grachyov's announcement that he would 'capture Grozny with two regiments in two hours.' From the outset, the army was betrayed by the high command. Its soldiers were insufficiently trained, depressed and demoralized; they did not understand the aims of this war, and they were treated as cannon fodder.

That December in Grozny the Russian army bore huge losses. On New Year's Eve, the 131st Maikop brigade was almost completely wiped out. Various other units approaching the city from different directions were blocked and partially destroyed. People were killed in their thousands. To this day there are no official statistics for casualties in the first Chechnya campaign. Under the current Russian government we'll never know them anyway because they are catastrophic. But according to unofficial information, in January alone almost five thousand Russian officers and soldiers were killed in the Battle of Grozny.

The Chechen losses, not to mention the deaths among the civilian population, are not known and probably never will be— no one counted them at all.

I was drafted into the army as a second-year law student in November 1995, a year after the war began. I spent six months in a training unit in the Urals, and in May 1996 I was transported to the northern Caucasus together with fifteen hundred other conscripts. First I served at the frontline town of Mozdok, on the border with Chechnya, and then in Chechnya itself. Officially a truce had been signed by then, but shooting was going on all the time. This period is described in the chapters 'The Runway,' 'Mozdok-7' and 'The Summer of 1996.'

On 6 August 1996, Chechen fighters captured Grozny and held the city for two weeks. This was the second-heaviest battle, and it ended in yet another truce and the signing of the Khasavyurt Accords, by which Chechnya practically received independence within the Russian Federation.

In late August my father died and I was given leave. I barely made it to the funeral. That same day I fell ill with dysentery and was taken to the hospital in an ambulance. My leave expired before I was released from the hospital, and when I reported to the army authorities I was arrested as a deserter. I spent three months in the penal battalion (see the chapter 'Special Cargo').

Because of an absence of incriminating material—as if it were not clear from the start—the case was closed.

After Dudayev's death in April 1996, Aslan Maskhadov was elected president of Chechnya. Maskhadov was a reasonable and even-tempered man, and had been chief of GHQ under Dudayev, but his position was not secure; his army consisted of only two thousand men, and he was therefore powerless as president. In reality Chechnya was controlled by field commanders of fighters' units such as Ruslan Gelayev, Shamil Basayev, Arbi Barayev, and the Jordanian Khattab, to name but a few. Lawlessness reigned supreme, and people were kidnapped all the time. In the People's Friendship Square in the center of Grozny, there was a flourishing and perfectly open slave trade. According to official data, during the three years of Chechnya's 'independence' almost thirty thousand people were kidnapped, sold into slavery or executed in Chechnya.

After the demobilization, I completed the remaining two years at the Law Institute and graduated with a bachelor's degree. It was the autumn of 1999, and the second Chechen campaign was just beginning.

This time I volunteered to take part in the war. There were many thousands of us, ex-soldiers, who returned to that second war after the first. I have no answer to why I went there again. I don't know. I just couldn't help it. I was irresistibly drawn back there. Maybe it was because my past was there, a large part of my life. It was as if only my body had returned from that first war, but not my soul. Maybe war is the strongest narcotic in the world.

At any rate I couldn't just sit there—I had to do what I could. And yet there is no blood on my conscience, I know this for sure. My experiences of the second war are described in 'New Year's Eve,' 'Alkhan-Yurt,' 'The Storming Operation,' 'Argun' and 'Chechen Penal Battalion.'

The second war was quite different from the first. For Chechnya the first had been a war of liberation, a war for independence when the people were united and inspired; in the second it was not the Chechens we fought, but the rebel bands. By then the Chechens were tired of lawlessness and dislocation. The second war was even more incomprehensible and dirty than the first.

I spent six months in the second war and was demobilized in April 2000. I wrote an article about my firsthand experiences in Chechnya and took it to one of the Moscow dailies. I was offered a job, and that's how I became a journalist. It was at this time that I wrote 'Field Deception,' 'The Obelisk,' 'Lais,' 'A Soldier's Dream' and 'Traitors,' to name a few.

I did not mean to write a book; I did not even think about what it was I was writing—stories, memoirs or some other kind of text. It was not consciously a project; I just couldn't carry war within myself any longer. I needed to speak my mind, to squeeze the war out of my system. I wrote compulsively—on my way to work in the metro; during my journalistic assignments; at home at night—and some of the stories almost wrote themselves. Many of them were hard going, and I had to force myself to write them. But I was not writing a book: I was simply continuing those unfinished discussions with the boys. They stayed with me long after the war was over and I could not let them go. It was a form of madness.

This book is largely an autobiography—everything in it is true. A few stories have been compiled from several real episodes that have been compressed into a single period and shifted in time. Some events I did not witness personally but I can vouch for their veracity.

All the characters are real people—the names are real too. But in a few cases I have combined two or three persons into one character. I don't know why. Perhaps it was easier for me to write that way.

In the end it all added up to a book. Let that war remain in people's memories. It must not be forgotten.

Arkady Babchenko
April 2007

ONE

1/ Mountain Brigade

Only those who have spent time in the mountains can imagine what they're like. The mountains are as bad as it gets. Everything you need to live, you carry with you. You need food, so you discard all the things you can do without and stuff dry rations for five days into your knapsack. You need ammunition, so you load an ammo box of bullets and half a box of grenades into your pockets, backpack and cartridge pouches and hang them on your belt. They get in the way when you walk, rasping on your groin and hips, and their weight pulls on your neck. You chuck your AGS automatic grenade launcher over your right shoulder and the launcher of your wounded pal Andrei Volozhanin over your left shoulder. You string two belts of grenades in a cross over your chest, like the sailors in the old revolution movies, and if you have a spare hand you also grab a snail box of ammo belts.

Then there's your tent, pegs, hatchet, saw, shovel and what-ever else the platoon needs to survive. And the things you need for yourself—your rifle, jacket, blanket, sleeping bag, mess tins, thirty packs of smokes, a change of underwear, spare puttees, and so on—about 150 pounds in total. Then when you take your first step uphill you realize there's no way you'll make it to the top, even if they put a gun to your head. But then you take the second and third steps and start to clamber and scramble up, slide, fall, and start back up again, clinging tooth and nail to the bushes and branches. Stupefied, you sweat and sweat, thinking about nothing except the next step, just one more step . . .

The antitank platoon is scrambling alongside. They are even worse off: my grenade launcher weighs forty pounds, while their PTURs—guided antitank missiles—weigh ninety pounds. And Fat Andy whines: 'Commander, how about we dump one rocket, how about it?' And the commander, an enlisted lieutenant who also has tears of exertion in his eyes, asks: 'Come on, Andy, fat ass, what's the sense in us being up there without rockets? Our infantry are dying up there . . .'

Yes, our infantry are dying up there—we crawl and croak our way up, but we keep going.

Later we relieve the guys from the Buinaksk mountain assault brigade who have been living there in a daubed clay shepherd's hut.

After the luxurious apartments of Grozny, with their leather sofas and mirrored ceilings, this crummy barn seemed pitiful. Clay walls, a dirt floor and a small window that barely lets in any light. But this was their first real accommodation after months spent sleeping in rat holes and ditches. For seven months they trekked around the mountains, day in, day out, clearing the Chechens from the heights, sleeping where they dropped at night, too tired to get up, and when they awoke they'd go back up again. They became like Chechens themselves, bearded, unwashed, in soiled tank corps jackets, half crazed, full of hatred for everyone and everything. They looked at us with malice in their eyes—our arrival meant the end of their brief respite, that they had to leave their 'palace' and head back into the mountains yet again. Ahead of them lay a nine-hour march and then the storming of some strategically important hill. They talked about it lightly—nine hours isn't so long, usually the march lasts a whole day or even two. We realized that our torment had been a cakewalk compared with what they had to go through. We watched as they left and each one of us felt scared, because soon we would have to follow them. Our heights were already waiting for us.

2/ The River Argun

On 1 March they threw our platoon over to Shatoi. Our task was to hold the bridge across the River Argun. We had no water with us and so we took it from the river. It stank of rotten eggs and had the color of cement but we drank it anyway, telling ourselves that hydrogen sulphide was good for the kidneys. The river was to us what a desert spring is to the Bedouin. We washed and drank there and took its water to cook with. There were no rebels in this region and our lives assumed a calm, quiet rhythm.

In the mornings we would head down to the river like tourists, stripped to the waist, with flowery plundered towels thrown over our shoulders. We washed and splashed about like kids and then sat around on the rocks and sunbathed, our white bellies turned to the bright winter sunshine.

Then the first corpses floated down the Argun toward us. Farther upstream, two Niva jeeps carrying retreating rebels had fallen into the ravine. The bodies got washed out of the vehicles and swept downstream. But the first to float into sight was a captured Russian paratrooper, his black and white camouflaged smock contrasting against the murky water. We fished him out, then some officers came to collect him and drove off with him on the back of their truck.

But the water couldn't wash them all away, and a few Chechens were stuck in the twisted jeeps. The weather was warm and they would soon start to decompose. We wanted to get them out because they were ruining our water, but the ravine was too deep and steep so we stopped trying.

When I woke the next morning I went to the water barrel they brought to the kitchen each day. Usually it got emptied quickly, but this time it was full. Ladling out a mug I took the first sip, then realized the water had a tang of dead flesh to it— that's why no one was drinking it. I spat it out and put the mug down. Arkasha the sniper looked at me, took the mug, filled it with water, drank and gave it me.

'Come on, what's wrong with you? Drink!'

So we kept drinking it, this dead, sulphuric water, but no longer said it was good for our kidneys.

3/ Chechens

When we got back to the lookout post, Shishigin nudged me:

'Second floor, first window from the right, see?'

'Yes. You saw it too?'

'Yep.' He looked at me, biding his time. 'Chechens.'

We spotted them by the greenish tinge in the window from their night-vision sight.

Our respective lookout posts were in neighboring houses, located about 150 feet apart, ours on the third floor, theirs on the second. They were watching us through the night sight and we pinpointed them from the crunch of glass under their feet.

Neither side fired. By that time we had gotten to know their tactics pretty well, and sure enough they kept us under observation until daybreak, after which they fired a couple of rifle grenades and then pulled out. We couldn't scare them off, because of the comfortable apartment with its huge bed, down pillows and warm blankets that we had picked for our night quarters. Spitting on the war and ignoring security regulations as we hankered after comfort, we had chosen a mousetrap that afforded us no escape route. If it came to a shoot-out, one grenade through the small ventilation window would be enough to take care of us. So we had no choice but to wait and see if they opened fire. And if they did, then which way? Into the room where four of us were sleeping, or at the balcony, where one of us was always on lookout?

Russian roulette, with the Chechen sniper as the croupier, with odds of four to one on a quick end.

But they didn't shoot. Shishigin, who was standing on lookout at dawn, said he heard two short whistles and then the Chechens came down and left.

The next morning, as day finally broke, curiosity drew Shishigin and me over there. There in the thick layer of dust that covered the apartment were the imprints of army boots and sneakers. The booted one, the sniper, sat at the window all the time and surveyed our apartment while the other gave cover.

They didn't shoot because their Fly rocket launcher jammed. It happens. The Chechens had brought it in, aimed it and pulled the trigger, but it didn't work. It still lay there on the kitchen floor where they had discarded it. Another great Russian production flaw—the shoddy work of some metalworker who assembled the launcher had saved our lives.

Apart from the Fly launcher, there was a small stove in the kitchen. We didn't have one, so we decided to take this little trophy with us. As we were leaving the apartment building a flare rose from the Chechen side. They caught two inquisitive Russian idiots, and it looked like they were going to take us right there in the building's entrance. We skittered back to our house like mountain goats, covering the fifty yards in two steps, but we didn't dump the stove. Running into our house we began to laugh like mad, and couldn't stop roaring for almost half an hour. At that moment there was no one closer or dearer to me on earth than Shishigin.

4 / Chechens II

I have hardly taken off my boots when a shot rings out. I leap up, grab my rifle and run in my socks to the door, praying that they won't nail me through it. My heart is pounding like mad and my ears are thumping. I get to the doorway and slam into the wall, back first. I don't open the door, and wait. Silence. Suddenly I hear Shishigin's muffled voice:

'Come on you guys, get up one of you!'

With great difficulty, hopping on one foot, I try to put my boots on, but they resist, crumple up and won't slide on.

'Hold on, Vanya, I'm coming.'

What was probably only three seconds seemed to pass like an eternity, and then at last I somehow pull on the boots. Before opening the door I take a few deep breaths, as if preparing to dive into icy water, then I kick the door wide open with my foot and burst into the next room.

Empty.

'Vanya, where are you?'

'Here, here!' Pale as a sheet, Shishigin tumbles out of the toilet, buttoning up his pants as he comes, breathing out hoarsely and gasping: 'Chechens, below us, the same ones—I was on the can when I heard them whistle.'

'Shit! You might have thrown a fucking hand grenade at

them!' I am annoyed at him because now we'll have to go downstairs, where the Chechens are, and a cold fear contorts my stomach.

'I was on the can!' Shishigin says again and gives me the hunted look of a beaten dog.

Slowly, as quietly as possible so the glass doesn't scrunch underfoot, we go out into the corridor. Each step lasts forever, and in the time it takes to move down the ten-foot-long eternity of the hall it seems a thousand generations have been born and died on earth and the sun burned out and was born anew. At last we reach the staircase and I crouch down and poke my head around the corner, then whip it back. There doesn't seem to be anyone on the stairs. I take a longer look around the corner. No one. The trip wire I set yesterday between the third and fourth steps is undisturbed, which means they didn't come up. We have to go.

I motion to Shishigin to go to the opposite side of the stairwell and watch over the lower flight of stairs. He runs across, unslings his rifle and hisses:

'Arkasha, stay there!'

Moving carefully, my rifle trained on the staircase, I go over to the stairs, a single thought going through my head: 'Arkasha, don't go, don't go . . . ' I'm trying to convince myself, but then I take the first step down. 'Don't go!' I go down a few more steps and reach the corner. I am panting and my temples are pounding—this is scary stuff. 'Don't go, don't go, don't . . .' I burst into the apartment, boot open the door to the bedroom— empty. Then the kitchen, no one, and I go back, realizing that I have wasted time and now have none to spare. I lob a hand grenade into the gaping entrance of the apartment opposite, throw myself to the ground and wait for cries, moans, point-blank firing . . .

The blast thunders and then it's silent. There's no one there, they are gone.

I squat down and pull a pack of Prima cigarettes from my pocket, roll one in my fingers, light it and toss the empty pack. I'm incredibly tired.

A bead of sweat rolls from under my hat down the bridge of my nose, hangs for a moment from the tip and falls on the cigarette, extinguishing it. I stare dumbly, my hands trembling. It was stupid to go in there on my own, I know. I throw the cigarette away and stand up.

'Shishigin, give me a smoke. They've gone.'

5/ Yakovlev

Yakovlev vanished toward evening. He wasn't the first to go missing. A couple of weeks earlier two soldiers from the 8th company had taken a machine gun and tried to go home. No one would have looked for them but the disappearance of a machine gun in the battalion is a serious matter and the battalion commander, or Kombat, spent days scouring the fields for these two. The OMON paramilitary police found them when they showed up at a checkpoint to ask for food.

No one looked for Yakovlev. The storming of Grozny was under way, the 2nd battalion tried in vain for the third day to take the cross-shaped hospital, suffering high casualties, and we were bogged down for the third day at the first row of houses in the private district. The storming operation was faltering, and we didn't have time for Yakovlev. They listed him as a deserter, wrote off his rifle as lost in combat and closed the case.

Again it was the OMON who turned up our missing man during the night, while they were mopping up in the first line. In one cottage cellar they found a mutilated body. Yakovlev. The rebels had slit him open like a tin of meat, pulled out his intestines and used them to strangle him while he was still alive. On the neatly whitewashed wall above him, written in his blood, were the words *Allahu akbar*—God is great.

6 / The Cow

We inherited the cow from the Buinaksk brigade when we relieved them in the mountains. Painfully emaciated, it looked like an inmate of a Nazi concentration camp and was about to kick the bucket. She lay for a day, staring blankly at a point on the horizon, unable even to lick the wound on her shoulder left by a PTUR shell fragment.

On the first evening we put out a big pile of hay for the animal. Her nostrils twitched and her long tongue started to lick at the offering, looking up at us with one eye, unable to believe her luck. Then she began to crunch at the hay and she gorged on it for two days without stopping, not even sleeping. Before us, the paratroopers hadn't fed her at all. At first she ate lying down, then she stood up.

Three days later, when she was already walking, Murky managed to squeeze a mug of milk from her udders. It was thin and didn't taste too good, and it didn't have a drop of fat, but we drank it like God's nectar. We drank in turns, a mouthful for each, and were happy to have our cow.

The next day her nose started to bleed. She was dying, and without looking the cow in the eye we led her to the ravine to finish her off. She was barely able to walk on her weak, buckling legs, and we cursed her for dragging out her own execution like this.

Odegov led the cow on a rope to the edge of the ravine and turned around and fired at her somewhat hastily, sending the bullet passing through her nose. I heard bone break with a dull thump and crunch, like a side of raw meat being hit with the flat of a shovel. The cow staggered, looked at us, realized that we were killing her and lowered her head submissively.

Dark, clotted blood gushed from her nose. Odegov took aim a second time and suddenly lowered his rifle, turned around and started striding back up the hill. I caught up with him, took his rifle and came back and shot the cow point-blank between the ears. Her eyes jerked upward, as if following the bullet that killed her, then rolled in their sockets, and she slid down the gully.

We stood at the edge for a long time looking at the dead cow. The blood congealed on her nose and flies crawled up her nostrils and came out of the hole in the back of her head. Then I pulled Odegov's sleeve.

'It's only a cow.'

'I know.'

'Let's go.'

'OK.'

7 / To Mozdok

It had been raining for a week. The low gray sky was constantly covered with black clouds and the rain didn't let up for even a minute, only altered its intensity.

Our kit hadn't been dry for ages, everything from our sleeping bags to our puttees was soaked. And we were shivering from cold. The advent of the rain had replaced the 100-degree heat with a vile, muddy gunk, and the temperature fell to 60 degrees.

Our dugout flooded continually. We didn't have bunk beds and when we came back from sentry duty we would just lie in the cold, squelching mush and sleep all night in the same position: on our backs, trying to keep our noses and mouths above the water.

In the morning we crawled from the dugout as if from the bowels of a sunken ship. Making no attempt to shelter from the rain, we stomped through the puddles in our sodden boots, which were instantly caked with great clods of clay.

We stopped caring for ourselves, no longer washed, shaved or brushed our teeth. After a week without soap and water our hands cracked and bled continually, blighted by eczema in the cold. We hadn't warmed ourselves by a fire for a whole week because the damp reeds wouldn't burn and there was nowhere to gather firewood in the steppe. We began to turn wild as the

cold and wet and filth drove from us all feelings apart from hatred, and we hated everything on earth, including ourselves.
Squabbles flared over nothing and instantly escalated beyond
control.

And when I had almost transformed into an animal I was
summoned by the company commander.

'Get your kit ready. Your mother has come to see you. Tomorrow you'll travel with the column to Mozdok.'

These words instantly separated me from the others. They
would stay here in the rain while my torment was over. I was on
my way to see my mom in a warm, dry and clean place. And
nothing else bothered me about the life of the platoon, about
the lives of its men, apart from one thing I'd heard: that after a
brief cease-fire the Chechens had started to shoot up our convoys
again. As I spent my last night on guard duty and swallowed my
tasteless thin oatmeal in the morning, and as I promised Andy
that I would come back, all I could think about was that they
had started to shoot up the convoys again.

8/ The Ninth Neighborhood

Before dawn, at around six, the Chechens hit the area with grenade launchers as usual. We are deployed in the private sector, and the nine-story apartment buildings of the ninth neighborhood in front of us are occupied by allied Chechen troops commanded by the former Grozny mayor Bislan Gantamirov, who is fighting on our side.

They have it worst of all, and already four of them have been wounded, one seriously. They ran back to us and hammered on the gates. 'Hey, Russians, get up, give us a vehicle, we've got wounded!'

They lie in the snow on stretchers, covered to the chin with blankets and obviously in great pain, their faces bloodless, jaws clenched and heads tipped back. But they don't make a sound. Their silence is unnerving as we gently lift them onto our shoulders and we ask one of them, 'Are you alive?' He half opens his eyes, looks at us from tormented pupils. Alive.

We load them onto the armored carrier, the seriously wounded guy inside and the others on the top. I stand below and help them lift the stretchers. The deputy battalion commander injects them with his own promedol painkiller and two of the Gantamirov troops jump onto the vehicle with them.

'Come on, get a move on,' shouts one. 'Do you know where the hospital is in Khankala? I'll show you the way.'

Weaving between shell holes on the battered, deserted road, the lone carrier disappears into the dark, urgently racing along with no escort, jolting the wounded as it goes. I think to myself that the one who's badly injured will die on the way.

When it starts to get light we occupy the apartment buildings. They are empty and we take them without any fighting. The buildings stand in a square formation, forming an enclosed, protected yard inside. Only in one place is it vulnerable to snipers, and a bullet zips past my nose, taking a few chips out of a concrete wall. But elsewhere you can walk without hiding and stand up freely without needing to duck down as you move.

We savor this feeling and the elegant apartments with their red furniture, soft sofa beds and mirrored ceilings, savor having taken the houses so easily. The infantry disperses among the apartments, searching out the best ones to spend the night in.

Half an hour later we get shelled by self-propelled guns. I'm standing in the street with the company commander when the first house on the right suddenly shudders and starts to collapse in the center. A huge split spreads down from the ninth floor, balconies, girders and floor supports spew out and seem to hover in the air, turn over, and then drive themselves into the ground with a thud. Small debris scatters down into the yard after the heavy blocks.

We don't know what's happening and squat down instinctively, crawl behind a rusty, shrapnel-riddled garage and look all around us. Then we realize that it's friendly fire. The company commander fumbles for the headphones of the radio on my back and starts to call up the battalion commander, or Kombat. I crawl over to the spare radio that's standing on the open ground, with the commander scrambling after me, still wearing headphones. One after the other, him standing over my head and me crouched between his legs, we shout into the mouthpiece for them to cease firing. Tangled up in the wires and the headphones we forget about the shrapnel—all we can think about is reporting that we are here and that they should halt the shelling, that we must stop them from hitting our guys.

Infantrymen pour out of the house and stand dumbstruck on the porches, not knowing where to run. The company commander ignores their swearing and shouts at them: 'Take it easy, just don't panic, boys.'

The last to come out of the door is Gilman, lumbering calmly like an elephant.

'No one's panicking, sir. We have to get the guys out of here,' he says.

The commander tells them all to get back under cover. I take a dozen paces and turn around: he is still standing there, so I go back. I'm a radioman and I have to stay with him.

Huge 150-millimeter shells weighing more than 60 pounds roar through the air above us and blow up the upper floors. One blast erupts and a whole vertical section of the building vanishes, leaving just rusty steel entrails jutting from the shattered walls. Another shell flies down the middle of the yard and hits the house on the left before it explodes. We drop to the ground and crawl back behind the garage. Several apartments catch fire, the blaze crackles and it starts to get hot. Soon it becomes hard to breathe in the heavy, acrid smoke that rakes our throats.

Time loses its meaning. We lie behind the garage, pressing ourselves into the snow. How long this all lasts, I have no idea.

At last the bombardment dies down and helicopters start firing on our houses, but the shells are lighter caliber and it's not nearly the same sensation. Their NURS mini-rockets don't penetrate the houses and they burst outside in the yard. The helicopters empty their magazines and fly off. It's over.

The infantry return. Amazingly we don't have a single casualty, not even any wounded. Our armored cars aren't damaged. Despite standing right near the houses that took the brunt of the strike, they are only covered in light debris.

Once again Gantamirov's boys come off worse, with two seriously wounded. The shell that flew down the middle of the yard exploded right inside their headquarters while two men were there. The leg and side of one of them was blown to pieces and the other had both legs torn off.

Again we run the wounded to the carrier on stretchers and load them inside. Again they make no sound, except for when one opens his eyes and says quietly: 'Get my leg.' Sigai picks up the severed remnants of the leg and carries it along beside the stretcher. Five of them carry him, in pieces, four taking his torso and one his leg. When they load him into the carrier, the limb is placed beside him.

The other wounded man dies.

When the guys get back, Sigai comes over to me and asks for a cigarette. We light up.

I look at his hands as he rolls and loosens the tobacco with his thumb and then clenches the cigarette in his lips and draws on it. It seems to me that his hands, lips and the cigarette have bits of human flesh stuck to them, but it's just my imagination. His hands are clean, and there isn't even any blood on them.

We stand there, smoking. Then Sigai says: 'That's odd. When I went off to war, this was what I feared most, blown-off legs, human flesh. I thought it would be horrific. But then it turns out there's nothing horrific about it.'

9/ Sharik

He came to us when we had only two days of food supplies left. A handsome, smart face, fluffy coat and a tail that curled in a circle. Amazing eyes, one orange, the other green. He was well fed, but not as much as the other Grozny dogs that went out of their minds as they gnawed on corpses in the ruins. This one was good-natured.

We warned him. We talked to him like a person and he understood everything. Here, at war, everyone and everything seems to be at one with their surroundings, be it a person, a dog, a tree, a stone, a river. It seems everything has a spirit. When you dig a foxhole in the stony clay with an engineer's shovel, you talk to it as if it were a loved one: 'Come on my dear, just one more shovel, just a tad more,' and it yields to your entreaties, gives another chunk, hiding your body deeper. Everyone and everything understands and knows what their fate will be. And they are entitled to make their own decisions—where to grow, where to flow, where to die.

We didn't need to reason with him, just one word and it was all clear. We warned him and off he went. But later he came back anyway, because he wanted to be with us. It was his choice, no one forced him.

Then our food started to run out. We stretched it another

day, thanks to some beef given to us by the 15th regiment, which was stationed a little way off from us. Then it was all gone.

'I'll skin and gut him if someone else kills him,' said Andy, our cook, stroking Sharik behind the ear. 'I won't kill him. I love dogs, and all animals really.'

No one wanted to do it. We agonized for another half day while Sharik sat at our feet and listened to us discuss who would kill him.

Finally Andy took it upon himself. He led Sharik off to the river and put a bullet behind his ear. It killed him outright, not even a whimper, and his skinned body was soon strung from a tree branch.

Sharik had plenty of meat on him and the fat on his side glistened. 'That has to be cut off, dog fat tastes bitter,' Andy told us.

I did as he said and then cut up the warm flesh. We boiled it for two hours in a pot and then stewed it in some ketchup left from the dry rations. It tasted pretty good.

Next morning they brought us supplies of oats.

10/ The Apartment

I had an apartment in Grozny. Actually, I had lots of apartments in Grozny—plush ones, plain ones, ones fitted out with nice mahogany furniture and others totally smashed up, large and small, all sorts. But this one was in a class of its own.

I found it in the first neighborhood, in a yellow five-story building. From the front door, upholstered in cheap, fake leather, hung the keys. The owners didn't lock the door, as if imploring visitors to live here by all means, but just not to destroy the place.

It wasn't luxurious but it was undamaged. It still bore signs of life—evidently the owners had left just before the storming of the city. It was homely, quiet and bore no reminder of things military. Simple furnishings, books, old wallpaper, carpeted floor. Everything tidy, unlooted. Even the windowpanes were intact.

I didn't go in right away. And when I went back to the platoon I didn't tell anyone. I didn't want some stranger rifling through this little pocket of peaceful life, upsetting the order in the cupboards, looking at the photographs and rummaging in the drawers. I didn't want outsiders' boots trampling on things or their hands fiddling with the stove and ripping up the parquet floor for firewood.

This was peace, a fragment of quiet, calm life, a life that I once lived, free from war, with my family and with my girl, chatting over supper and making plans for the future.

This was my apartment, just mine, my very own home, so I thought up a game.

In the evening, when it got dark, I would come home after work and open my door with my keys. Boy, what a joy it is to unlock your door with your own keys, to enter your home and flop down exhausted in the armchair. To let your head loll back as you light up a cigarette and close your eyes . . .

She comes over to me, curls up on my lap and tenderly rests her little head on my chest. 'Darling, where have you been so long? I was waiting.'—'I'm sorry, I got held up at work.'—'Did you have a good day?'—'Yes, I killed two people.'—'Well done, I'm so proud of you!' She kisses me on the cheek and caresses my hand. 'Heavens, what have you done to your hands? Is that from the cold?' I look at them. Her small, slender hand with its smooth skin, scented with cosmetics, rests on my rough, dirty, cracked and bleeding paws. 'Yes, from the cold and dirt, eczema, but it's nothing to worry about, it'll pass.'—'I don't like your job,' she tells me. 'I'm scared here, let's move away somewhere.'—'We will move away, my love, I promise, don't worry, just be patient a little while longer. There, behind the ninth neighborhood, is my demobilization and peace. And you . . . We'll move, just be patient.' She gets up, goes into the kitchen, treading softly on the carpet. 'Go and wash your hands, supper's ready. I've made borscht, the real thing, not the half-cooked slop they give you at work. There's water in the bathroom, I brought it in from the well. It's cold now, but we can warm it up.' She pours borscht into the bowl, passes it over and sits down opposite me. 'What about you?' I ask. 'You tuck in, I've already eaten. Take off your chest harness first, silly,' she says with a peal of laughter. 'And don't dip your grenades in the soup, give them here, I'll put them on the windowsill. They're filthy, shame on you,' she says taking a cloth and wiping them. 'By the way, I cleaned your rocket launcher today, it was all dusty. I put it by the wardrobe, is that OK? I thought you might be cross at me. That thing scares me, when I was wiping it I was afraid it would go off. Will you take it to work with you, or can we maybe put it away in the cupboard?'—'Don't worry, I'll take it with me. I might need it tonight; there are some snipers in the high-rises.'—'Are you going now?'—'Yes, I have to go, I just popped in to see you.'—She comes over and puts her arms around my neck and presses herself against me. 'Come home soon, I'll be waiting. And be careful, don't get shot.' She fastens the top clip of my harness and finds a small hole on the shoulder strap. 'I'll sew that up when you get back,' she says, and kisses me good-bye. 'Go on, off you go now or you'll be late. Take care . . . Love you!'

I open my eyes and sit motionless for a while. My soul is empty, barren. The ash from my cigarette has dropped onto the carpet. I am seized with melancholy but I also feel good, as if it had all really happened.

I came a few times to the apartment, every day, and played the 'peace game,' albeit with a few aberrations like grenades on the windowsill, but still. Later, when we moved on, I dropped by one last time, stood on the threshold and carefully closed the door. I left the key in the lock.

TWO

11 / The Runway

We lie at the edge of the runway, Kisel, Vovka, Tatarintsev and I, our bare bellies turned up to the sky. They made us march over from the station a few hours ago and now we wait to see what will happen next.

Our boots stand in a row, our puttees spread out on top to dry as we soak up the sun's rays. It seems we have never been so warm in our lives. The yellow tips of the dry grass prick our backs and Kisel plucks a blade with his toes, turns onto his stomach and crumbles it in his hands.

'Look, dry as a bone. Back in Sverdlovsk they're still up to their necks in snow,' he marvels.

'It sure is warm,' agrees Vovka.

Vovka is eighteen, like me, and looks like a dried apricot—dark-complexioned, skinny, tall. His eyes are black and his eyebrows are fair, bleached by the sun. He comes from the south of Russia, near Anapa, and volunteered to go to Chechnya thinking this would take him closer to home.

Kisel is twenty-two and was drafted into the army after college. He's good at physics and math and can calculate sinusoids like nobody's business. Only what's the use of that now? He'd be better off knowing how to put on his puttees properly—he has white flabby skin and still manages to walk his feet to a bleeding mess because they are poorly wrapped. Kisel is due to be demobilized in six months and had no wish to be sent to Chechnya. All he wanted was to serve out his time somewhere in central Russia, near his hometown of Yaroslavl, but it wasn't to be.

Next to him sits Andrei Zhikh, fat-lipped and small, the puniest soldier in our platoon, which earned him the nickname Loop, after the little leather ring where you tuck the loose end of a soldier's belt. He's no more than five feet tall but he puts down enough food for four. Where it all goes is a mystery, and he stays small and skinny like a dried cockroach. What strikes you about him are those huge doughnut lips that can suck down a can of condensed milk in one go and which turn his soft Krasnodar accent into a mumble, and his stomach, which swells up to twice its size when Loop stuffs it with food.

To his right sits Vic Zelikman, a Jew who is more terrified than any of us of getting roughed up by the older soldiers. We are all afraid of this, but the puny, cultured Zyuzik, as we call him, takes the beatings particularly badly. In a year and a half of army service he still can't get used to the fact that he is a nonperson, a lowlife, a dumb animal, and every punch sends him into a depression. Now he sits thinking about how they will beat us here, wondering if it'll be worse than during training or not as bad.

The last member of our group, Ginger, is a quiet, sullen, stocky guy with huge hands and flaming red hair. Or rather he used to have flaming red hair before the barber got to him. Now his bald soldier's head looks like it's strewn with copper filings, as if someone filed a pipe over it. All he cares about is how to get the hell out of here faster.

Today we managed to eat properly for the first time. The

officer in charge of our group, a swarthy major who shouted at us all the way here, is sitting a good distance away in the middle of the field. We make the most of this and wolf down our dry rations.

Back on the train the only food the major had given us was a small tin of stewed meat for each day of the journey, and our stomachs were now pinched with hunger. When we halted briefly on spur lines to allow other trains through there wasn't enough time to distribute the bread and we were hungry all the time.

So as not to swell up from the pangs we swapped our boots for food. Before we left we had all been issued with new lace-up parade boots. 'I wonder where they think we'll be doing parade marching in Chechnya,' said Loop, who was the first to trade his pair for ten cabbage pies.

The women selling food at the stations took our boots out of sheer pity. When they saw our train pull in they swarmed around with pies and home-cooked chicken. They saw what sort of train it was standing on the line, started to wail and blessed us with crosses drawn in the air, and accepted boots and long johns they had no use for in exchange for food. One woman came up to our window and silently passed us a bottle of lemonade and a couple of pounds of chocolates. She promised to bring us cigarettes, but the major shooed us away from the window and told us not to lean out any more.

In the end they didn't manage to distribute all the bread and it simply went moldy. When we left the train in Mozdok, we walked past the bread car at the back just as they were throwing out sacks of fermented, green loaves. We grabbed what we could and managed to get more than most.

Right now our stomachs are full of stewed pork, although there was more fat than meat (Ginger assures us it's not fat at all but melted lubricant grease mixed with boot polish), and barley oats. On top of that, we had each tucked away a whole loaf of bread, and you could say life was looking pretty rosy just then. Or at least for the next half an hour it had taken on a clear definition, beyond which no one wanted to guess what lay in store. We live only for the moment.

'I wonder if they'll put us straight on regular rations today,' Loop mumbles through his doughnut lips and slips a spoon that has been licked to a clean gleam back into the top of his boot. With lunch safely in his gut he immediately starts to think about supper.

'Are you in a hurry to get there or something?' Vovka says, nodding at the ridge that separates us from Chechnya. 'As far as I'm concerned, it's better to go without grub altogether just to stay on this field a bit longer.'

'Or stay here for good, even,' Ginger adds.

'Maybe they'll assign us to baking buns,' Loop dreams out loud.

'Yeah, that would be right up your alley,' answers Kisel. 'The moment you're let loose on a bread-cutting machine you'll slip a loaf under each of those lips of yours and still not choke.'

'Some bread now wouldn't go amiss, that's true,' says Loop, a big grin on his face.

Back in training the swarthy major told us he was assembling a group to go and work in a bakery in Beslan, in North Ossetia. He knew how to win us over. To be assigned to a bakery is the secret dream of all new recruits, or 'spirits,' who have served less than six months of their two-year spell in the army. We are spirits, and they also call us stomachs, starvers, fainters, goblins, anything they like. We are particularly tormented by hunger in the first six months, and the calories we extracted in training from that gray sludge they call oatmeal were burned up in an instant on the windy drill square, when the sergeants drove us out for our 'after-lunch stroll.'

Our growing bodies were constantly deprived of nutrition and at night we would adjourn to the toilets to secretly devour tubes of toothpaste, which smelled so appetizingly of wild strawberries.

Then one day they lined us up in a row and the major went along asking each of us in turn: 'Do you want to serve in the Caucasus? Come on, it's warm there, there are plenty of apples to eat.'

But when he looked them in the eye, the soldiers shrank back. His pupils were full of fear and his uniform stank of death. Death and fear. He sweated it from all his pores and he left an unbearable, stifling trail behind him as he walked around the barracks.

Vovka and I said yes. Kisel said no and told the major and his Caucasus where both of them could go. Now the three of us lie on this runway in Mozdok and wait to be taken farther. And all the others who stood in that line are here too, waiting beside us, fifteen hundred in total, almost all just eighteen years old.

Kisel is still amazed at how they duped us all so well.

'Surely there has to be a consent form,' he argues, 'some kind of paper where I write that I request to be sent to the meat-grinder to continue my army service. I didn't sign anything of the sort.'

'What are you going on about?' says Vovka, playing along. 'What about the instructions for safety measures the major asked us to sign, remember? Do you ever even read what you sign? Don't you understand anything? Fifteen hundred guys uniformly expressed a wish to protect the constitutional order of their Motherland with their lives, if need be. And seeing how our no-ble sentiment so moved the Motherland, we made it even easier for her and said: No need for separate consent papers for each of us, we'll go off to war by lists. Let them use the wood they save to make furniture for an orphanage for Chechen children who suffer because of what we do in this war.'

'You know what, Kisel?' I say with irritation. 'You couldn't have signed anything and still end up here. If the order comes for you to go and bite it, then you go—so why are you going on about your precious report? Why don't you just give me a smoke instead?'

He passes me a cigarette and we light up.

There is constant traffic on the runway. Someone lands, someone takes off, wounded soldiers wait for a flight, and people crowd around a nearby water fountain. Every ten minutes low-flying attack aircraft leave for Chechnya, groaning under the weight of munitions and then later they return empty. Helicopters warm up their engines, the hot wind drives dust across the runway, and we get jumpy.

It's a terrible mess; there are refugees everywhere, walking across the field with their junk and telling horrific tales. These are the lucky ones who managed to escape from the bombardments. The helicopters aren't supposed to take civilians but people take them by storm and ride standing, as if they are on a tram. One old man flew here on the undercarriage; he tied himself to the wheel and hung like that during the forty-minute flight to Mozdok from Khankala. He even managed to bring two suitcases with him.

The exhausted pilots make no exceptions for anyone and indifferently shout out the names on the flight roster, ticking people off list by list. They are beyond caring much about anything any more. Right now they're making up passenger lists for flights to Rostov and Moscow, which might leave the day after tomorrow if they aren't canceled.

Any remaining places are filled with the wounded. Apart from cargo, each flight can take only about ten people, and the seriously wounded get priority. Lying on stretchers, they are packed in between crates, rested on sacks or simply set on the floor, crammed in any old how just as long as they're sent off. People trip over them and knock them off their stretchers. Someone's foot catches a captain with a stomach injury and pulls out the drain tube, letting blood and slime run out of the hatch and onto the concrete. The captain screams, while flies descend instantly on the puddle.

There aren't enough flights into Chechnya either. Some journalists have been waiting almost a week, and builders sunbathe here for the third day. But we sense that we will be sent today, before sunset. We aren't journalists or builders, we are fresh cannon fodder, and they won't keep us waiting around for long.

'Funny old life, isn't it?' muses Kisel. 'I'm sure those journalists would pay any money to get on the next flight to Chechnya, but no one takes them, while I would pay any money to stay here, where it's better by a mile. Better still would be to get as far away from here as possible, but they'll put me on the next flight. Why is that?'

A 'Cow' Mi-26 cargo helicopter lands. Our guys stormed some village and all day long they have been evacuating dead and wounded from Chechnya. They unload five silvery sacks onto the runway, one after the other. The shining bags gleam in the sun like sweets, and the wrappers are so bright and pretty that it's hard to believe they are filled with pieces of human bodies.

At first we couldn't work out what they were.

'Probably humanitarian aid,' Vovka guesses when he sees the bags on the concrete, until Kisel points out that they take aid in there, they don't bring it back.

It finally dawned on us when a canvas-backed Ural truck

drove up on the runway, and two soldiers jumped out and started loading the sacks. They grabbed them by the corners, and when the sacks sagged in the middle we realized that there were corpses inside.

But this time the Ural doesn't come and the bodies just lie there on the concrete. No one pays any attention to them, as if they are a part of the landing strip, as if that's the way it should be, dead Russian boys lying in the arid steppe in a strange southern town.

Two other soldiers appear in long johns cut off at the knees, carrying a bucket of water. They wipe down the Cow's floor with rags, and half an hour later the helicopter carries the next group to Chechnya, filled to the gills once again. No one bothers to spin us any more fairy tales about baking buns in Beslan.

None of us says so, but each time we hear the heavy bee-like droning over the ridge we all think: 'Is this really it, is it really my turn?' At this moment we are on our own, every man for himself. Those who remain behind sigh with relief when the Cow carries off a group without them on board. That means another half an hour of life.

Carved into Kisel's back are the words I LOVE YOU, each letter the size of a fist. The white scars are thin and neat but you can tell the knife went deep under the skin. For the past six months we have been trying to wheedle the story out of him but he tells us nothing.

Now I sense he will spill the beans. Vovka thinks so too.

'Go on, Kisel, tell us how you got that,' he tries again.

'Come on, out with it,' I say, backing him up. 'Don't take your secret to the grave with you.'

'Idiot,' says Kisel. 'Keep your trap shut.'

He turns over again onto his back and shuts his eyes and his face clouds over. He doesn't feel like talking but he might be thinking he could really get killed.

'My Natasha did that,' he says eventually. 'Back when we first met and hadn't yet married. We went to a party together, dancing and stuff, and a lot of drinking of course. I got well tanked up that night, dressed up like a Christmas tree in my best gear. Then I woke up next morning and the bed and sheet were covered in blood. I thought I'd kill her for doing that, but as you see, we got married instead.'

'That's some little lady you have!' says Vovka, who has a girlfriend three years younger than him. They ripen fast down there in the south, like fruit. 'You should send her down our way, they'd soon whip her into shape, literally. I'd like to see my girl try something like that. So what, you can't even come home drunk without getting a rolling pin in the head?'

'No, it's not like that. My wife is actually gentle, she's great,' Kisel says. 'I don't know what got into her, she never pulled another stunt like that again. She says it was love at first sight for her, and that's how she wanted to bind me to her. "Who else will want you now I've put my stamp on you," she tells me.' He plucks another blade of grass and chews it pensively. 'We'll have four kids for sure ... Yep, when I get home I'll rustle up four for us,' Kisel says and then falls quiet.

I look at his back and then think to myself that at least he won't remain unidentified and lie in those refrigerators we saw today at the station. That's assuming his back stays in one piece.

'Kisel, are you afraid to die?' I ask.

'Yes.' He is the oldest and smartest among us.

The sunlight shines through my eyelids and the world becomes orange. The warmth sends goose bumps fluttering across my skin. I can't get used to this. Only the day before yesterday we were in snowbound Sverdlovsk, and here it's baking. They brought us from winter straight into summer, packed thirteen at a time into each compartment of the railroad cars, surrounded by a stinky must, bare feet dangling from the upper births. There wasn't enough room for everyone, so we even took it in turns to sleep in pairs under the table, day and night. Wherever you looked there were piles of boots and overcoats. It was even good that the major didn't feed us; we rode sitting for a day and a half, doubled up like fetuses, and if we had eaten our fill even once, we'd all have gone down with acute intestinal blockage. In Rostov-on-Don our train stopped opposite the station building. We came to a halt on the first line, right by the main entrance, and people averted their eyes as they passed us.

Here on the field, under a poplar, some lightly wounded soldiers are drinking vodka they got by exchanging goods in the boiler house. They try to drown the fear they experienced over the ridge, their faces gray and eyes wild. An hour ago they were being shot at and some of their mates were being killed and now they are drinking vodka and don't have to duck any more, and it hasn't sunk in yet. They shriek and sob as they down the booze by the bucket. We can hardly bear to look at them.

We aren't the first on this field. There were tens of thousands before us, awaiting their fate just like us, and the steppe has absorbed their fear like sweat. Now this fear oozes from the poisoned ground, flooding our bodies and squirming somewhere in the pit of our stomachs like a slimy worm, chilling us in spite of the burning sun. It hangs over the place like fog, and after the war they will have to purge this field of the fear, like they would radiation.

Not far from us lie little clusters of civilian builders and the nearest ones are drinking grain alcohol, helping it down with transparent slices of salted pork fat. There's a woman with them, young, with a red, woozy face and full lips. We already know she's called Marina. We have become so unused to civilian life and women, and we steal glances at her. Marina is large-breasted and has an ample bottom, which gets Loop very excited, groaning and murmuring through his own pudgy lips. You aren't a real soldier if you don't letch at the girls, so we all act like veteran skirt chasers, although in reality few of us had even kissed a girl properly before the army, and only Kisel had actually been with a woman. Marina offers Loop a drink. He accepts, full of bravado, and knocks back a glass. Five minutes later he is sprawled unconscious on the ground and we carry him off into the shade. She offers us a drink too but we politely decline.

'I wonder why they're here?' says Vovka.

'They're going to rebuild Grozny,' answers Kisel. 'They called a truce and the fighting will soon be over.'

'But they're still bombing the place, look at those attack planes,' says Ginger, nodding at another pair of SU-25 taxiing onto the strip.

As they stop and flex their flaps up and down, Vovka says they look like the rear end of a worm taking a dump. Now, I don't know where he ever saw a worm doing that, but he had us convinced.

'What makes you think the planes are heading for Grozny?' Kisel asks Ginger loudly. 'And what do the builders care? The more the place gets bombed, the more work for them, and on triple time, too. There's an armistice on now, no fighting, so they take them in to do some building while the going's good.'

'How do you know there's an armistice?'

'I saw it on TV.'

'So what, they show a lot of stuff on TV.'

'There won't be any more fighting,' Kisel carries on, but now he's poking fun. 'The rebel forces have been broken up, constitutional law has been restored and peace with all its bounty has descended on this long-suffering Caucasus soil.'

'Amen,' I add.

'So why are they taking us there if there's an armistice?' Ginger asks in puzzlement. 'And there are tanks back at the station, a whole column, I saw them myself. And they'll all get killed there,' he says, nodding toward the builders.

'I don't get it either,' I say. 'If there's an armistice, why are they bringing out bodies? As far as I know there are either bodies or peace, you don't get both at the same time.'

'Sometimes you do,' replies Kisel. 'Anything can happen in our country.'

The next Cow sets down heavily on the concrete. Once again they unload the wounded, put them on stretchers and run them off to the field hospital set up right by the camouflaged helicopter pens.

They carry one past us, a fair-headed boy. His leg below the knee is dangling on the tatters of his pants and on threads of calf muscle, his foot still in a cut-off army boot. Bone protrudes from the flesh and light shines through the hole in his leg. The strides of the soldiers jerk the stretcher around, and every time it lurches upward the dangling leg jerks downward, up, down, looking as if it will rip off at any moment. I even reach out to catch it if it should fall beside me. The flesh is turned inside out and dotted with bits of dirt.

The wounded man is pumped full of promedol and doesn't feel a thing. He stinks of smoking cloth and puttees and freshly butchered meat.

From time to time inarticulate inhuman screams rise from the field hospital. Sometimes they carry out bloody, pus-covered bandages and chuck them on a garbage heap, and fat flies immediately rise from the trash in a thick cloud.

After the wounded they start lifting those pretty silver sacks from the chopper. Two half-naked soldiers add eight more sacks to the five still lying there. A Ural truck drives up. It's hot and they are wearing only long johns and slippers as they go about their business, just another day's work for them. Heat, a runway piled up with corpses and two soldiers in cut-off long johns loading dead people in sacks, like potatoes.

They lay out the bodies on the back of the truck, starting from the sides, and when there is no more room on the floor they stack them in a second layer. They plonk the last one down in the middle and jump in with it and the truck sets off for the station. This morning we saw refrigerator cars in the sidings. Now we know what those are for.

The sacks lurch with the Ural as it jolts across the ruts and the soldiers use their feet to keep them pressed to the floor.

Meanwhile, they fill the helicopter with a fresh load of cannon fodder, still dressed in crisp new winter uniforms. The young soldiers run into the Cow's cargo bay in close file, getting tangled in the flaps of their overcoats. One guy's backpack comes undone, scattering packs of cigarettes on the ground. The last thing I see in the chopper's dark belly are the soldiers' dismayed eyes looking straight at me.

The helicopter blades howl; it takes off, heads toward the ridge and flies on into the war. This conveyer belt works from the early morning, for as long as we are here, bringing bodies out of there and taking in soldiers in new overcoats. Everything runs smooth as clockwork and we realize that the choppers have been doing this run for more than a day, and probably more than a month.

'Fuckers,' says Kisel. 'Fuckers, all of them.'

'Yep,' I say.

'Fuckers,' agrees Vovka.

I scrounge another smoke off Kisel, one of those vile Primas made in Kremenchug that hardly burn. Vovka says the tobacco is mixed with horse dung. The pack and his stable back home stink the same and his horse craps out the same clumps of straw we find in the cigarettes, he tells us. My mouth dries up after two puffs. Vovka stubs his out on the ground and winds on his puttees.

'I'm going to get some water. Give me your flasks.'

We hand him seven water bottles, including the spare one I stole from the storage shed in Sverdlovsk.

Vovka is away for half an hour; there's a crowd at the water fountain and a long line to get a drink.

On his way back I watch him pass the major, who is sitting on the ground in the middle of our group, and see him look over his shoulder at the papers he's holding in his hand. These are our dossiers. The major lays them out in two piles like he is the very Lord of Fate. One pile is large, the other is small, and it's clear that those in the smaller one will now be loaded into the Cow and flown to Khankala, the main base outside Grozny, or Severny, and the others will stay here. Maybe not for long, possibly a few hours, just until the next flight, but here nonetheless. Each one of us hopes that his own fate lies in the big pile; we all want to stay here a bit longer.

I put out my cigarette, lie on my back and shut my eyes.

'Kisel,' I say. 'You promised to give me the chords for that Aguzarova song "Old Hotel."'

'OK, write them down then.'

I get a pen from my breast pocket and a red, homemade notebook cut from a thick exercise book. Kisel dictates. '*City swimming in a sea of night light* . . . That's Am Chord . . . *City alive with its people's delight*—Dm, E, Am—*Old hotel, open your doors, Old hotel, at midnight I'm yours* . . . '

I scribble it down.

The sun is shining brightly, the birds are singing and the steppe overwhelms with the scent of lush grass and apricots. This is real life, bright, sunny, brimming with vitality, and everything should be just great, wonderful as we begin to wake. It's inconceivable that on this beautiful day those damned helicopters keep landing on the runway and people unload bodies and lay them out in a row in the sun. You just want this to be a place where people love, have families and don't butcher each other. War should happen in rotten places, not where it's good. War should happen inside the Arctic Circle where life is dark and gloomy and where there's no sun for half the year. We can't believe that they brought us to the edge of paradise, with its tang of apricots, only to wrap us in silver sacks.

Vovka comes back, stops with the filled flasks in his hands and looks at me without speaking.

'What are you standing around for, give us some water. I'm thirsty as hell,' I say. He passes me the wet flask without looking at me. The water is warm, foul tasting and stinks of chlorine. As soon as you drink perspiration breaks out immediately under your arms.

Vovka sits down next to me without catching my eye and digs at the ground with his boot. I understand that something changed over there by the major.

'They're taking you,' he says finally.

'On my own? What about you—how can I go without you?' I ask.

'They're sending you, and Kisel and I are staying.'

I look at Vovka and think he's winding me up. Yes, he's joking of course, no one is going to split us up! We were never on our own, we were always together and we'll stay together right to the end, until they demobilize us. They can't separate people on this lousy field, just a step away from the war, because here and now is where we come together as a combat unit, where we become brothers, where we experience fear together for the first time, sadness, uncertainty and waiting. And we start to feel certain that we will survive, despite being faced with the stark finality of death.

But Vovka isn't joking. Christ, why did I volunteer to come here? What are we doing here anyway? Why do I now have to get up, put on my boots and go and die, leaving nothing of myself behind except a look of dismay as the Cow's belly claps shut. This is all wrong—it won't happen like this, it can't.

I painstakingly wind on my puttees and try not to look at Kisel, who stands there in just his pants, wiggling his bare toes, or at Vovka sitting beside him.

We are all thinking the same thing. I'm being taken away and they are staying.

I suddenly feel a surge of anger toward Kisel and his chunky white feet, the scars on his back, his hands stuffed into his pockets, like he's betrayed or abandoned me. I know it's not his fault but I'm angry just the same, I can't help it. He was the oldest among us, the most experienced, he always gave the most sensible advice and made the smartest decisions, and we always felt like he was our elder brother and we were in his care. And now he is staying in the rear while I fly off without him.

We look at each other. We are no longer together. I'm on my own.

'Well, Kisel, see you then,' I say, offering my hand.

He suddenly starts to throw his clothes on.

'I'm coming with you. I'll go and ask the major to send me too. We should stay together. Wherever you go, I go too. I'm not going to stay here.'

'Don't Kisel,' I implore. 'You don't want to get on that helicopter. Maybe you really are going to bake buns in Beslan.'

'No, no,' he stammers and starts to babble. 'Don't you see, no one will stay, we're all going there, every last one of us. Forget about buns, there are fifteen hundred of us here, what are we going to do, swamp the country with buns? This is a transit field, either in or out, and they brought us here today to send us to Chechnya. We were born and raised to be sent there today and I want to be with you when we go.'

'Me too,' says Vovka. 'I'm coming with you to see the major.'

Kisel, smart cookie that he is, had it all sorted out in his head in a moment. I sniffle unexpectedly and my eyes moisten. It's good that we are together again.

The three of us approach the major who is still sitting on the ground and laying out files. Another small pile lies separately from the bulk of them, maybe five at the most, and I spot my name on one.

I report to the major. Without raising his head he barks: 'A team of five people are to be posted in Mozdok as I said. Wait here, an escort officer will come for you. That will be all.'

Just like that, the major had switched everything around. Now it seems I am the one staying. I've had enough of all the confusion.

'Comrade Major . . . Comrade Major, permission to speak. There are three of us.'

'What?'

'There are three of us—me, Tatarintsev and Kiselyov.' I realize that the major won't change anything now, and that he couldn't care less who flies and who stays, but maybe he could find a way to replace me. I'm not asking to go to the rear, on the contrary.

'This is nonsense,' he says. 'I spent plenty of time with you soldiers and I know that friendship means nothing to you. The only people you really care about are the ones from your home region, and you don't have any here, Babchenko. There's just you, so why should you care where you serve?'

'Comrade Major, please . . .'

'Is there something you don't understand, soldier? You'll remain right here in the unit where I have put you! Stand down!'

'But sir . . .'

'Not another word!'

Kisel and Vovka hover nearby on the prickly grass, looking like little kids in the middle of this field. They are downcast, and maybe for the first time ever Kisel is at a loss for words. I go over and hug him.

'Bye, Kisel.'

'Bye,' he says. 'I'm glad I managed to give you those chords. At least you have something to remember me by.'

Vovka unpins the badge from his chest, a blue shield with an oak sprig and the number three in the center, and hands it to me.

'Here, have this. You may as well hang on to it.'

I give him my own badge.

'Pity it worked out like this,' I tell them.

'Yes it is,' says Vovka.

'Yep,' says Kisel.

I feel an acute sense of loneliness. What will I do without them?

Another helicopter comes in to land above us. Lowering our heads, we watch it descend. It's probably ours, or rather theirs. Now they'll get on it and fly away, and I'll be left here, all on my own.

I walk away, looking back at them as they stand on this field, hands in their pockets, heads bowed—big, stocky Kisel and sunburned, skinny Vovka. I know we won't see each other again. It's all some kind of a crime.

We are led to a truck and we line up in pairs facing the back of it, waiting for the order to climb on.

'It's the same Ural,' says Loop, who is standing at the front. 'Guys, it's the same truck they use to collect the bodies.'

He turns around and looks wide-eyed at each of us, like he's waiting for us to mutiny, or call off the whole trip and send him home. He still hasn't sobered up from the booze he drank and his drowsy eyes now seem extra large.

'How do you know?' someone asks.

'I remember that hole in the canvas,' he replies, pointing at a large rip like a starfish. 'There's no mistaking that.'

We look at the rip and stand there not knowing how to react. Our escort officer strides up.

'All aboard!' he commands without stopping, and we climb into the Ural.

I seem to detect the stench of death but really it's just a normal truck smell of diesel and grease, nothing else.

The tarmac suddenly slips away behind us as the truck drives off and the runway recedes steadily into the distance until it is hidden behind some trees.

Suddenly, through a gap in the leaves, I think I can see Vovka and Kisel, still standing in the middle of the field and waving. Just in case it's them I wave back, but it does little to comfort me. They were my friends and now they are gone. And so is the runway and the waiting, and that fear bearing down on me and seizing my throat. Now there's no more war. I have left it all behind and that is that. I feel sorry for Kisel and Vovka but it's more of an abstract sense of pity, like childhood memories, not really pity even, more like a kind of melancholy.

I feel like a deserter but it's as if a weight has lifted from my shoulders. My God, I'm not going to be loaded onto that heli-copter! The worst part is over and now the main thing is to get as far away as possible from that runway. I hold on to the metal canopy arch, trying not to fall to the floor where dead people have lain.

12/ Mozdok-7

The truck door slams and the driver's feet scrunch on the gravel.

'We're here, get out,' he says, opening the tailgate.

There are six of us in the back. Me, Loop, Andy, Osipov, Ginger and Vic Zelikman. We had got settled in beneath the dark tarpaulin and we didn't want to get out.

'What are you sitting around for, assholes!' the driver yells. 'Do I have to throw you out myself?'

We do as we are told and I jump out first. Our truck is parked in the middle of the parade ground. Everything is as it always is: a rostrum, barracks around the edge, a canteen and a few scrawny trees. A few older conscripts study us as they stand smoking on a porch. It's baking hot.

At the side of the parade ground soldiers are working away, dressed like our grandfathers were in the Second World War, in khaki tunics and broad riding pants. There are lots of them, shoveling out gravel, their faces stupefied and submissive as they work away steadily, like prisoners of war in a concentration camp. A pall of dust rises in the air and settles on their bare feet. Some of them have toes streaked in blood; clotted trickles run across their dusty skin and coagulate on the ground. But no one looks up from his work and the only sound is the *swish-swish* of the gravel.

We stand in the middle of the parade ground, the dust settling on our new uniforms and shining boots. I notice this out of the corner of my eye and think to myself that from this point on my boots will always be white.

'Why are they barefoot?' Ginger asks. 'Guys, why are they barefoot?'

'Fucking hell, what is this place?' whispers Zelikman. 'Is this the army?' Zelikman is short-sighted and looks like a small cowering pony, so terrified is he of being knocked about; during the six months of training he hadn't got used to beatings and to his status of trash. And we were going to get beaten all right, well and truly; you could tell right away that the army practice of *dedovshchina*, the violent bullying of new recruits by older soldiers, was ingrained here. Back over the ridge in Chechnya something awful was happening, and the fate of these soldiers here bothered no one.

'What did you expect? This isn't a training camp but a regular service unit,' Loop says, looking around him, clearly ill at ease.

A captain comes over to us.

'Let's go,' he says and leads us along the parade ground.

We follow him silently in pairs while the barefooted soldiers keep shoveling gravel. The captain takes us to headquarters, beyond the barracks in the far corner of the grounds.

Eight 'Butterfly' staff vehicles covered in camouflage netting form a small thoroughfare and the place is pretty crowded. There are some lightly wounded soldiers in fresh bandages, and we hear them talking about combat bonuses, travel expenses and death payments. One lieutenant with his arm in a sling is trying to find out something about one-off disbursements for wounds. He grabs everyone who passes him by the sleeve, almost shouting and stammering heavily from shell shock, a tuft of cotton wool crusted brown with blood protruding from his ear. But each time he is unable to finish his question, waves his hand and wanders off. He seems drunk, his eyes have a crazed, vicious look and sometimes he stumbles sideways. Dirty fingers with uncut nails stick out from under his bandages, and the lieutenant rubs and flexes them, his face creasing with pain.

The captain takes us to one of the Butterflies where they will add us to the list of the unit's personnel so that we'll get our food allowance.

'Look,' says Loop, touching my sleeve.

In the open area between headquarters and the parade ground there are two light tanks hidden by tarpaulins. One isn't completely covered, and we see a broken caterpillar track dangling and scorched roller wheels, their black rubber curled up like bits of pork crackling. The turret has been torn off altogether.

'Did you see?' Loop asks me. 'Do you think they . . .?'

I don't think anything. I start to feel sick.

Night falls. We have been sitting on stools by the open window of the barracks since the captain brought us here from headquarters and told us to wait. No one else comes for us and so that's what we do, but we have no idea what we're waiting for. Probably the order to turn in—it's already nine thirty in the evening. Apart from us the barracks are empty, no soldiers, no officers.

'Man, am I hungry,' says Osipov. 'I wonder if they'll give us breakfast tomorrow.'

'They aren't supposed to give us anything,' answers Loop, all-knowing in matters of army food. 'We get our allowances only a whole day after we arrive, so that will be suppertime tomorrow.'

We have no idea what they are or aren't supposed to give us, but we are so hungry our navels feel like they are stuck to our backbones.

A strong smell of grass wafts through the window and cicadas chirp rhythmically. The steppe starts right by the barracks and reaches almost to the ridge, which we can hardly see now against the black sky. During the day helicopters flew there in pairs, and now heavy attack planes are heading off on night bombing raids. They are bombing Chechnya around the clock and the sound of the explosions is audible even here. Sometimes we can see the flashes too.

Loop sees planes taking off at night for the first time in his life and he's spellbound. The nozzle lights shoot faster and faster along the strip, the roar drowns out everything else and the plane takes to the air; it circles over Mozdok, waiting for the wingman, and sets off for Chechnya. I think to myself that that's someone's death taking flight; all of these pilots must have killed at least one person and they will kill many more, maybe now, maybe tonight.

The evening 'stroll' begins in the regiment. One lone company, obviously undermanned, maybe forty men at most, leaves its barracks and marches up and down the square. It's the same guys who were shoveling gravel barefoot earlier. They still don't have boots; instead they are wearing army issue slippers, a piece of rubber with two synthetic straps sewn together in a cross shape. They are very uncomfortable, and since they are not meant for marching they rasp your feet raw.

'Company!' commands the drill sergeant and the company marches three steps forward in response. Their slippers slap weakly on the square and give no clear marching rhythm, flying off the feet of some of the soldiers and landing on the edges of the square, leaving them to carry on barefoot.

'Halt!' yells the sergeant. 'Don't you pricks even know how to march in time? Well now I'm going to teach you . . . Company!'

Once again they take three steps and again it's a mess. Half of them are now barefoot and the soldiers stamp with their bare heels on the tarmac.

'Company!' the sergeant shouts again, and the soldiers stamp their heels on the square with all their might, grimacing from the pain.

'The swine, they'll rip their feet to shreds like that,' says Osipov. 'The bones will rot and it won't heal later.'

He knows what he's talking about; his feet have been rotting for six months and each fresh issue of underwear is a torment for him. His long johns stick to his flesh and he has to tear them off. By the evening half a cup of pus and lymph has collected in his boots. But they won't put him in the hospital because we all have it, rotten feet are part of army life, and streptodermatitis is a constant torment. Zelikman, Loop and I have pusy sores all over our feet, but Osipov has no skin left on his at all, from his heels up to his knees.

'Why are there so few of them?' Zelikman asks.

'There'll be even less soon,' Osipov mutters darkly. 'That bastard will land half the company in the hospital.'

'Sing!' the sergeant orders, and from the ranks a beautiful voice rises above the marching company. The boy sings well and obviously has talent, and it's odd to hear this perfect voice in the middle of the deserted square with half a company of tattered, barefoot soldiers marching.

'Shall we go for a quick march too?' Zelikman asks. 'What if they've lost us? What if the regiment commander appears now for evening roll call?'

Since there are hardly any officers in the regiment right now, it seems very unlikely that anyone might be even remotely interested in us. But just in case, we decide to go down to the square, on the off chance that someone is keeping an eye on the evening stroll from headquarters. The five of us march for a few minutes on the square, which is empty now that the infantry company has finished.

'Hey, you guys, come here,' someone calls from a doorway.

'Now we've gone and done it!' Loop hisses at Zelikman. 'Now they are going to string us up. We should have stayed put and kept our heads down! We aren't going anywhere, turn back toward the barracks.'

We ignore the shouts, pretending we think they are meant for someone else, and we quickly go back to the barracks. We hear laughter behind us.

We run up to the second floor, wash quickly without switching on the light and bed down for the night. There are no sheets under the blankets and no cases on the pillows, and the mattresses are so dusty that our arms and faces are immediately covered in grime.

I dream about helicopters circling silently in the air above Moscow, over my home in the Taganka district, and showering down clouds of silvery packets. People excitedly reach up to catch them and my mother is also standing on the balcony with her arms outstretched. She wants to catch one with my face on it but it keeps jumping around like a butterfly, and I flutter off to the side. I smile. 'Mom, what are you doing? Those aren't packets, those are bags with bodies in them. Can't you see how many of us dead guys there are? There's a war going on down there and you don't even know—why's that?' I ask. 'I do know,' she says. 'You got killed already.'—'No, I'm still alive. Remember I wrote to you that I was still alive and that they weren't going to kill me? I'm still in the barracks, Mom, I'm fine. There are lots of us here, I'm not on my own, and everything is OK, see for yourself.'

The barracks fill with noise, doors slam and people go to their billets, switching lights on, fiddling with weapons. I sense all of this through my sleep and think it must still be a dream. 'You see Mom, these ones are all dead, they were in Chechnya. But I'm still in Mozdok, I'm alive . . . '

The next moment someone kicks me off the bed and I land on the floor. Osipov lands on top of me right after.

'Get up, bastard!' someone shouts above us.

We leap to our feet like madmen and draw ourselves to attention. Osipov immediately gets punched in the jaw and I get a kick in the ear. As I fall I manage to glimpse Zelikman having his head smashed against the bed frame, then I get punched in the solar plexus and I hit the floor, completely dazed and gasping for air.

The first time I really got beaten up was on 9 May. Victory Day. All hell was let loose in our barracks that time. The reconnaissance boys kicked us out of our beds and beat us the whole night. Toward morning they got tired of that and ordered us to do squats on the floor. 'You, count,' Boxer told me, and I started to count aloud. Osipov and I did more than the others— 384. We sat down, pressed up tightly against each other, and our mingled sweat ran down our legs, dripped onto the bare floorboards and soon formed a pool beneath us. Andy also dripped pus and blood into the mix as his sores opened up again. We carried on for an hour until Boxer got bored of this and knocked us down with two sharp punches.

From that day onward I got beaten by everyone, from privates to the deputy regiment commander, Colonel Pilipchuk, or Chuk, as we called him for short. The only person I didn't get beaten by was a general, maybe because we didn't have any in our regiment.

It's night. I am sitting on the barracks porch, smoking and watching the attack planes accelerating and taking off on the runway. There's no way I can go back to the barracks—by evening I'm supposed to bring Timokha 600,000 rubles that I don't have and have no way of getting. I get 18,000 rubles a month, but the most I can buy for that is ten packs of cheap cigarettes. Inflation is rampant in the country and money is worth less and less all the time, just as our lives are.

Yakunin and Ginger know where there are 600,000 to be had but they won't tell. They'll get out of here soon; anyone who manages to lay his hands on money will get away from this regiment, this lousy runway where smoke-scorched helicopters land all the time. We are inseparable from this field and I have already realized that sooner or later we will all end up on it, waiting to fly to Chechnya.

Fourteen members of our company are AWOL, absent without leave. Young conscripts flee in droves, heading straight from their beds into the steppe, barefoot and wearing only their long johns, unable to withstand the nightly torment any longer. Even our lieutenant, who was called up for two years after he graduated from college, went AWOL. There are only eight of us left, us five and three local boys—Murky, Pinocchio (or Pincha) and Khariton. We live together in the reconnaissance company, and the recon regard us as their personal slaves and do what the hell they like with us.

I spit a tobacco grain onto the asphalt. My spit tastes of salt and blood; my teeth were busted loose ages ago and wobble in my mouth. I can't eat solid food and have trouble even chewing bread. When they give us rusks in the canteen I only eat the soup. We're all the same. We can't chew and we can't breathe in properly because our chests have been so battered by the fists of the *dembels*—the recruits on their last six months before demobilization—that they became one huge bruise. We inhale carefully, taking only quick short breaths.

'Only the first six months is tough in the army,' Pincha says. 'After that you don't feel the pain.'

They brought us to this unit only three weeks ago, but it already seems an eternity.

Damn, if I had only been able back then to persuade the major to put my dossier in the other pile, everything would be different! But the major put it where he did, and here I am. Maybe it's for the best. Maybe Kisel and Vovka are already dead, while I am still alive. I lived three more weeks—that's a hell of a long time, that much we do know by now.

The next pair of attack planes accelerates on the runway. I wonder why the pilots fight? No one forces them. They aren't me—they're free. There is no way I can leave here; I have another eighteen months of national service. So I sit on the porch watching the planes accelerate, and I think what I can tell Timokha so he doesn't beat me too badly.

The planes take off with a roar that shakes the barracks windows and disappear into the night, the twin dots of their exhausts twinkling. I take a final drag on the cigarette, stub it out and go up to the second floor.

'Well, did you bring it?' asks Timokha, a tall, swarthy guy with big cowlike eyes. He is sitting in the storeroom, his feet up on the table as he watches TV. I stand in front of him, staring silently at the floor.

I try not to annoy him. When you're asked why you haven't done something, the best thing you can do is to stand there and maintain meek silence. We call this 'switching on the fool.'

'Has the cat got your tongue? Did you bring it?'

'No,' I reply, barely audibly.

'Why not?'

'I haven't got any money.'

'I didn't ask you if you've got any money, dickhead!' he roars. 'I don't give a damn what you do or don't have. I'm asking you why you haven't brought 600,000 rubles.'

He gets up and punches me in the nose, from below, hard. The bridge of my nose crunches and my lips become warm and sticky. I lick the blood from them and spit it out on the floor. The second blow hits me under the eye, then I take one in the teeth. I fall with a moan. I can't say it hurt that much, but it's best to moan loudly so the beating stops sooner.

This time it's no joke the way Timokha gets worked up. He kicks me and screams: 'Why didn't you bring the money, fucker? Why didn't you bring the money?'

He makes me do push-ups and when I'm on my way up he kicks me in the teeth with a dirty boot. He catches me hard and my head snaps right back. I lose my bearings for a moment, my left arm collapses under me and I fall on my elbow. My split lip gushes onto the floor, and I spit out blood and the polish that I had scraped off Timokha's boot with my teeth.

'Count!' he yells.

I push myself up again and count out loud. Spurts of blood fly onto the floor. There's a news report on the television, something about Chechnya. The army commander has arrived for an inspection in Vladikavkaz. He is satisfied with the state of battle readiness and discipline in the forces. Tomorrow the commander is due to visit our regiment and check the discipline here. He'll probably be satisfied with the disciplinary readiness of our regiment too.

Timokha eventually tires. He orders me to get a cloth and

clean up the blood. I wipe the boards but the blood has already soaked into the wood and left a noticeable stain.

'What are you trying to do, asshole, get me in trouble?' Timokha hisses and hits me in the forehead with his palm. 'What the hell do you think you're doing splashing your filthy blood here, moron? Now wipe that off! I'll give you one more week to get the money, understand? I'm going on leave in a week. If you don't get the money by then I'll come back and kill you. The clock's ticking.'

I go back to my billet and sit on the bed. I have to last one more week. Timokha will get back from leave in two or three months, no sooner. No one comes back earlier, and three months is a long time, almost half a lifetime, anything could happen.

I crawl under my dusty, dirty blanket. Of the sixty beds in the empty barracks only four are made up, for Zyuzik, Loop, Osipov and Yakunin. Ginger is gone.

'Did he beat you?' Loop mumbles from under the blanket. His lips are now like two purple dumplings from his share of knocks.

'Yes,' I reply, smearing toothpaste under my eye.

We learned this trick back in training, a tried and tested treatment for black eyes. If my eye swells up the next day, Timokha will beat me even harder; he'll tell me I'm a snitch and that this is how I'm trying to turn him in. Even though there isn't a single new guy in the regiment who still has an unmarked face.

My split lips ache even in my sleep.

I am on orderly duty and wash the floor. The officers have been drinking in the storeroom all evening. The commander of the recon company, Lieutenant Yelin, is now seriously drunk; his corpulent face is sunk into his shoulders and his eyes are dazed and empty apart from the glow of hatred in his pupils.

Alternately resting his rifle on his knees, Yelin is methodically firing at the ceiling. That's a habit of his. When he gets drunk he sits in this armchair and fires at the ceiling. It's probably because of his shell shock—they say he used to be a cheerful, smiley man. Then half of his company got killed near Samashki, and later he got blown up in a carrier. Then I heard the same thing happened again. These days Yelin is the craziest officer in the regiment; he hardly talks to anyone, he uses his fists to give orders and he couldn't give much of a damn about anything, not the lives of the soldiers, or the Chechens, or even his own. He doesn't take prisoners; instead he slaughters them himself, the same way they slaughter our soldiers, by pinning their heads to the ground with his foot and slitting their throats with a knife. The only thing he wants is for the war never to end so that there is always someone to kill. The whole ceiling of the storeroom is riddled like a sieve with bullet holes and the plaster showers down on Yelin like rain, but he pays no heed and just keeps firing upward.

Next to him sits a small Armenian, Major Arzumanyan, commander of a tank battalion. He's also suffering from mild shell shock. Vodka doesn't affect him, and he loudly tells Yelin about a battle in Bamut.

'Why didn't they let us totally flatten that shitty little village? Who set us up, who was it? We had already driven them out into the mountains, all we needed was just one more push, a last dash, and suddenly we get told to pull out! Why? Why? We had two hundred yards to go to the school. If we'd taken it the village would have been ours! Who bought up this war and who's paying for it? Three of my vehicles are burned out, and I've got thirty dead men! Now I'm going to pick up some more, choose a new batch of greenhorns and send them off to the slaughterhouse, all over again. All they're good for is biting it in big bunches. And who's supposed to answer for that?'

Yelin grunts and shoots at the ceiling. They pour another round and the cold vodka glugs into the glasses. I can smell it, the tang of raw vodka. They make this stuff here in Mozdok, at the brick factory, and it's dirt cheap. Every soldier knows a few houses in the village where you can buy this cheap stuff stolen from the factory. It was me who went and got them this bottle.

I am washing the floor by the open door of the storeroom and try not to make a noise and catch their attention. The main thing in the army is not to be noticed; then you get beaten less and you're pestered less. Or is it best to get out of here altogether like Ginger, who hasn't been seen in the barracks for several days. He's living out in the steppe somewhere like a dog, and visits the regiment only to get some grub. I've seen him a couple of times at night, near the canteen.

They notice me all the same.

'Hey, soldier,' Arzumanyan says. 'Come here.'

I do as I'm told.

'Why do you pricks go and get killed like flies? What do they bother training you for if all you can do is die? What did they teach you there? Do they teach you to shoot at all?' he asks.

I say nothing.

'Well, you dumb fuck?'

'Yes,' I say.

'Yes . . . So how many times did you fire a weapon?'

'Twice.'

'Twice? Pricks. Want to join my tanks? Come on, tomorrow you'll fly with me to Shali where they'll have you for breakfast. And me. Well, are you coming? Yelin, let me have him.'

I stand in front of them, drenched in sweat, with wet, rolled-up sleeves and a rag in my hand. I hang my head and say nothing. I have no wish to fly with the shell-shocked major to Shali and get eaten for breakfast. I want to stay here, get my bruises but remain alive. I'm afraid that Yelin really will hand me over. I'm not one of his men, but they won't look into it if he does. One wave of his hand and it's done.

Yelin blearily looks up at me from under his lowered brow, struggling to take everything in. Now they're going to give me a beating.

The tank officer suddenly deflates. The spring in him unwinds and he slumps back in his armchair.

'Get the hell out of here,' he says with a wave of the hand. 'You wouldn't fit in a tank anyway—too tall.'

I leave and creep out of the barracks before Yelin can stop me.

I sit down on the porch, light up and look at the take-off strip. I wouldn't mind sneaking into the cockpit with them and flying the hell out of here. Or even better, I could get transferred to the pilots corps. Now *they* have it good! In their barracks there are just officers and two dozen soldiers. The pilots don't beat the soldiers; they feed them well and the only work there is making the beds and washing the floor.

But I have no right to complain. I had a lucky night tonight; I didn't get beaten or whisked off to Shali.

Ginger and Yakunin did come up with some money in the end. They took a high-pressure fuel pump off one of the wrecked BMP tracked carriers and sold it to the Greek. The Greek is a builder who lives on the construction site and plasters the barracks. Apart from that he's the link between the soldiers and the market outside, and does a bit of business on the side, just like everyone else in this war.

A fuel pump is a much sought after item; you can put them on normal diesel trucks as well as army vehicles. In the regiment you can get hold of one for half the usual price.

Ginger sold the pump to the Greek for exactly 600,000 rubles. He won't give this money to Timokha. After lunch they are going to go AWOL and they start to persuade Loop to go with them. He agrees immediately.

We stand in the line outside the canteen, waiting for them to let us in. Loop is next to me; he doesn't tell me anything but I know that after lunch Yakunin and Ginger will be waiting for him beyond the runway. They vanished from the regiment in the morning and didn't even show up for breakfast.

'Don't leave me here, Loop. Don't leave me alone, I'll get beaten to a pulp here, do you hear?' I tell him. 'There's only you and me left. Kisel's gone, so has Vovka, don't you go and leave now. Let me come and hoof it with you guys. I'll find some money. Don't abandon me here, we should stick together, otherwise they'll tear us to pieces. Why are you deserting? Let's get together and give the recon a good thrashing, what do you say?'

I grab his sleeve and spout all sorts of nonsense. I'm terrified of staying here on my own. As it is now they beat all six of us and it's easier to put up with the torment together.

'The plane leaves tonight,' says Loop, pulling his arm away. 'You won't manage to get the money together.'

Loop is unbelievably lucky. Yakunin and Ginger are just taking him along, he hasn't done anything, he didn't have to get the money. We are all trying to get away from this regiment and he manages it without the slightest effort. I have no idea how I'll get by here on my own. We can forget about Zyuzik. Andy, well, he's still here, but two isn't enough. He's not in my detachment and I feel an incredible solitude.

Yakunin and Ginger go on their own. They don't take Loop in the end; there isn't enough money for them all. We stay.

Now Timokha demands money from me and Zyuzik. We are

sitting on the porch. I'm smoking and Zyuzik is scraping off the freshly fitted tiles with a twig. The afternoon sentry muster is starting the drumbeat on the square, and the regimental duty officer is quizzing the assembled soldiers about the duties of an orderly.

We have to last two more days. Timokha is going on leave the day after tomorrow. Two days is a hell of a long time if you measure it in smashed faces.

'So what are we going to do?' Zyuzik asks.

'I don't know. We'll have to sell something.'

'What?'

We have absolutely nothing to sell. We don't have any equipment or weapons, and we can't steal anything either because we don't know where there is anything worth taking.

'I don't know. Let's sell some cartridges.'

'Where are we going to get them?' he asks. 'We only have guard duty tomorrow, and Smiler won't open the armory till then.'

The armory is locked with a simple padlock and the duty soldier has the keys. Today it's Smiler. He can take as much weaponry as he sees fit. No one monitors the ammunition, the bullets are simply heaped in the corner and no one has ever so much as counted them. Tomorrow, when I get guard duty, we can sell as many as we like. But the problem is that we need the money by tomorrow morning.

'Listen, maybe Sanya has some in his carrier,' I say.

Yesterday bowlegged Sanya made me wash his carrier and under the turret I saw a sports bag stuffed with cartridge belts that he had put aside for himself. It's risky, of course—he'll kill us if he finds out, but we have no other choice.

We wait till lunchtime, and when the recon go to the canteen

I climb into the vehicle. The bag is under the turret, where I left it. He'll guess immediately who took it.

I open the bag and swear under my breath. It turns out that it doesn't hold machine-gun belts but shells for a rapid-fire BMP cannon. They are much bigger and there's no real demand for them. The Chechens don't have many armored cars so there's no one to sell them to. But I take two of them just to try, one explosive shell and one incendiary.

In the evening we go into Mozdok. There's no fence around our regiment and it's easy to slip away, straight out of the barracks. The soldiers wander around the steppe like stray dogs— no one counts them or guards them. You can be absent from the barracks for weeks and no one will be after you. You may get murdered, or abducted and sold into slavery, and no one will know. In this regiment we are left to our own devices; the commanders pay little attention to such trifling matters as what the soliders are up to.

We walk along the streets in the evening, offering the shells to everyone we meet. No one is the least bit surprised at this since everyone sells weapons down here. The locals shake their heads. A couple of people ask what kind of rounds they are but when they hear BMP cannon they carry on. One boy of about twelve asks us if we can get Fly rocket launchers, he'll give a million rubles for each one. We agree to meet him again in two days.

We don't manage to sell the shells. We stand at the bus stop as the streets begin to empty and the town gradually goes to sleep. No one walks around here at night; it's too dangerous. The explosive shell weighs heavily in my pocket, so I take it out and toss it into the bushes behind the bus stop. Zyuzik dumps the incendiary shell there too.

'So what do we do?' I ask.

'I don't know.'

We have no intention of going back to the barracks without the money. We are prepared to stand at this bus stop for two days until Timokha goes on leave, just so as not to go back. He won't let us sleep today anyway; he'll come harassing us for the money. The closer he gets to his leave the crazier he gets, and he keeps close tabs on our search for cash.

In the station a train begins to move, a passenger train heading not toward Chechnya but home, to the north. We wander around just for the hell of it, without any particular aim. A car stands parked alone in one of the house yards. It has a stereo system and a plan immediately formulates in my head.

'Listen, Zyuzik, go and keep watch.'

'What are you going to do?'

'Nothing. Go and keep watch.'

He runs to the corner of the house.

I pick a stone up from the ground and throw it at the side window, which instantly fractures into a web of cracks and falls into the car with a crunch. I quickly put my arm through, open the door and get inside. I have no idea how you steal a car stereo, in fact I have never stolen anything before in my life, but I work quickly and surely as if I had spent an entire lifetime thieving.

'The speakers, get the speakers!' Zyuzik hisses at me from the corner. I rip the speakers out with all the wiring and we grab our loot and run across the road through more yards.

'This is stealing!' Zyuzik informs me as we try to regain our breath in a doorway where we stop to stuff the stolen gear into our clothing.

'If they catch us we'll get locked up for this.'

'Yep. And they'll make us stand in the corner,' I answer.

I hide the stereo inside my jacket, he takes the speakers and we keep going. We rob three more cars that night. By my calculations that should be enough.

Today Timokha doesn't kick me out of bed as usual, but shakes me by the shoulder.

'Come on, open up the armory.'

'Timokha, I don't have the money,' I say sleepily. I've only had about an hour and a half of sleep tonight, no more. 'I'll get it tomorrow and bring it to you, honest.'

'Yeah, yeah, you'll bring it tomorrow. Go on, open up.'

I'm the company's duty soldier and today I have the armory keys.

'What, do you want me to issue you with a weapon? Are you going to Chechnya?' I ask, finally understanding what's going on.

'Yes, to Chechnya, open up.'

Generally the armory room should be opened up only in the presence of an officer and strictly only with the authorization of the regimental duty officer. If you need to draw or deposit weapons the duty soldier calls headquarters and says: 'Requesting permission to open the armory room for such and such.'

'Permission granted,' replies the duty officer, who deactivates the alarm system on his control panel. Then he sends an officer who, together with the duty soldier, enters the room with the weapons. That's how it's supposed to be, but we have no alarm system, the armory is secured with one simple padlock and the keys are always with the duty soldier. No officer ever comes to check.

The armory is a small room in the middle of the barracks, stuffed with crates full of weapons and ammunition. Whenever we take over watch duties from each other we're supposed to count the number of weapons and sign for them. Today I'm in charge of the entire arsenal. The crates hold forty-eight assault rifles, thirty disposable rocket launchers, twelve sniper rifles, four RPG-7, grenades, bayonets, tightly stuffed bullet belts, silencers and other military junk. Packs of cartridges lie piled in the corner, uncounted, but every time we sign for 12,627 rounds. Yesterday I too signed for all this weaponry allegedly received from Smiler but it means nothing; any older conscript can get the keys from me and take whatever he wants from the armory.

Timokha, bowlegged Sanya and a few other guys go into the armory with me. I sit down behind the table and open the logbook for weapons issue. I am ready to enter the number of weapons they'll take out on their assignment.

But no one wants anything issued. The recon fuss around, open up all the crates in turn, put two Fly launchers on the floor, a few ammo belts, some grenades and packs of 5.45-caliber rounds. They stuff it all in a duffel bag, two of them carry it between them by the handles and they quickly take it out of the barracks. Only Timokha and I are left in the armory.

'You didn't see anything, got it?' he says.

'Yes,' I say, but I haven't really got it and I pass him the book. 'Here, sign, I'll add the serial numbers of the Fly launchers afterward.'

Timokha gives me a sharp punch to the jaw, then kicks me in the stomach and I double up.

'Idiot,' he spits. 'You didn't see anything! You write these Flies down as combat issue, you know how to do that?'

'Yes, I know,' I groan back at his boots. He hit me so hard I can't straighten up. He leaves. Panting, I crawl behind the table and open the issue book. I look for blank lines for the previous days. I find one and enter the two stolen launchers into the space. Now it looks as though these launchers went to Chechnya on 10 February, and beside the entry is Yelin's signature; he took receipt of them. No one will try to ascertain what happened to them after that, and someone could have fired them already. Either way, Smiler will take over the armory from me tomorrow, and the day after tomorrow I'll take it back from him.

I don't bother about the cartridges and grenades. I shut the book and leave the room.

No good came of trying to sell those bullets. When Smiler and Khariton carried their bag of stuff into Mozdok they ran straight into Chuk's enormous belly. He bundled them into the corner of a Butterfly and gave them such a hiding that they had trouble remembering their own names.

Smiler came off a lot worse. Chuk beat him and screamed: 'OK, this piece of shit is a radioman, but you are in recon!' He yelled. 'Why did you run into me? Are you mad? What if there'd been a regional commission here, what would you have done, walked slap-bang into the commander? Or if you ran into Chechens? How are you supposed to go on a recon mission? How will you fight, you asshole?'

Even the commanders don't regard us radiomen as people: the communications company of the 429th motor-rifle regiment is the most shit-upon unit in the whole of the North Caucasus military district. You can use us to carry water, kick us black and blue with your boots, make us conjure up money, break our jaws, fracture our skulls with stools—there's no end to the fun you can have with us. We just groan and do what we are ordered.

Back in civilian life, when people used to tell me stories about army bullying, I thought I couldn't live like that, I'd never survive it. Ha! What choice do I have anyway? You either hang yourself or take it in the face—that's your entire choice.

Now Khariton and Smiler are sitting in headquarters writing

a statement. No one has any use for it, though; no one will take the matter any further. Because then they'll start checking up; the FSB intelligence service will show up to investigate how the bag with the cartridges wound up in the possession of two idiot soldiers, someone will get busted in rank or locked up in jail. Who needs all that? It's far easier just to beat them up back in the barracks. Timokha and Boxer will give them another working over and that will be an end of the matter. A smashed-up face is a whole lot better than twelve years' hard labor in a camp.

I pass by the lit windows of the Butterfly. Smiler's face is badly busted up, blood is seeping from his lips and dripping onto the statement he's writing, and he wipes it off with his sleeve. Chuk stands in the corner. I notice all of this fleetingly as I pass and go to my army car. I'll sleep here tonight.

The next evening the recon guys manage to sell the launchers and one bag of stuff. They get back from Mozdok late at night with a bag full of food and drink, not to mention a whole packet of heroin, and they start their party in the storeroom.

I am called in there and, as an accomplice to the whole ruse, they pour me a glass of vodka.

'Good lad, you did well, get this down you,' says Timokha.

He's already done a hit and his eyes gradually glaze over so he can barely see me. A candle burns in the storeroom, a blackened spoon lays on the table. Boxer is sitting with his arm tied tight by a tourniquet, the end of which he holds in his teeth, while Sanya injects the dose.

I drink. It's that revolting local vodka they've bought in the boiler house, and apart from everything else it's warm. They give me a piece of bread with some sardines, and then pay no more attention to me. After shuffling around for a while I leave the room.

Loop, Zyuzik and Osipov are already in bed, covered in blankets. Murky and Pincha are puttering around somewhere, and Khariton is on orderly duty.

'So what are they up to in there?' Loop asks.

'Getting hammered. They even poured me a drink,' I answer.

'Oh shit!' says short-sighted Zyuzik and squints. 'That means they'll beat us again tonight.'

'Maybe we should get out of here,' Loop suggests. 'Let's get out of here.'

That would be the best thing for us to do, of course, but we would have to go out into the corridor, and then we'd run into the recon there.

We doze until midnight, half listening to the conversation in the storeroom and waking every time we hear shouts coming from there. Later the drunken, wasted recon tumble into the corridor.

'Radiomen!' Boxer yells, glassy-eyed and teetering as he walks into our billet. 'Radiomen, get up!'

He tips Zyuzik out of bed and starts to hit him, then Osipov. The beating continues.

Loop and I lie in the dark, covered from the head down by blankets, watching the strip of light from the corridor.

Someone is shooting right under our window; two tracer rounds fly into the sky and we hear loud swearing. There are weapons lying on the beds, grenades, and webbing waistcoats, their pockets stuffed with magazines. We try not to move.

Boxer hits Andy over the head with a stool; he groans and falls to the floor, foam bubbling from his mouth.

'What are you moaning for, as if a shell's blown you to pieces?' Boxer shouts. 'Have you ever even heard a shell explode? Get up!' he screams and kicks Andy in the stomach with his boot. Andy doesn't react and it seems like Boxer will beat him to death. He's capable of it. They all are. They have already tasted killing and they are stronger in spirit than we are. Our lives are worth nothing to them; they have seen many others like us lying dead in the dirt, ripped pants hanging in threads from blue legs, mouths gaping, and they don't doubt the same will happen to us. What does it matter where we die, here or there?

Someone whips me between the shoulder blades with a belt, and the unexpected blow sends me flying onto the floor. Loop lands on top of me.

'Get up!' someone yells above us.

I rocket to my feet and immediately get a heavy, booted kick in the stomach. I feel a heaving inside but no pain. The blow was hard but slow, dulled, and just scooped me up and sent me flying a couple of feet like a kitten.

'Take him to the sick bay,' Boxer says, motioning to Osipov.

There's no one around in the regiment now, the square is empty and there are no lights on in the barracks. The sick bay is closed. Andy comes to and seems to have a concussion.

'It turns out we were in heaven back there in training,' Loop says finally.

Only toward dawn do we return to the barracks.

We are on muster. We stand there being dressed down by the regimental commander as he tells us about bullying. Beside him, eyes turned to the ground, stands a new recruit, a 'spirit,' with huge bruises under his eyes. He feels like a snitch; they somehow manage to beat us here in such a way that we even feel guilty. And the recruit is now in terror of the night to come—he knows that he's done for.

'You are supposed to be soldiers,' the commander says. 'All of you are soldiers, why do you beat each other up? All of you deserve to have monuments erected to you for what you are doing there in Chechnya! Every one of you is a hero, and I bow before you. But it's a curious thing, you're heroes over there and here all we have are drunks and shitheels! I warn you now, stop beating the young ones! I don't want to have you jailed, but so help me God, this had better be the last beating! Next time I'll press charges, I swear on my honor as an officer. I'll start locking people up, regardless of the medals they may have. You'll get the full treatment from me: ten years behind bars.'

Behind our backs we hear the crash of broken glass and the splitting of wood and we turn around. A young recruit flies out of a ground-floor window and hits the ground with a grunt, covering his face with his arm as bits of glass and wood scatter around him. He lies there without moving for a few seconds, then jumps to his feet and runs out of sight. A drunken face looms at the window and shouts after him:

'I'll kill you, you little shit!'

The regimental commander watches the scene in silence and dismisses us with a wave of his arm.

Today the company officers appear for the first time. Apparently we do have some; they were just in Chechnya and we didn't know about them. The commander of the company, Major Minayev, and the sergeant-major, Warrant Officer Savchenko, had brought back a burned-out armored carrier from there. Now right outside our window stand two wrecked BMPs, two armored cars drilled full of holes and a burned-out carrier. Who died in them we don't know.

Minayev and the sergeant-major spend half the day boozing in the storeroom and then summon us. On the table stand a half-empty bottle of vodka, bread, tinned food and onions. The major is draped over a pile of jackets in the corner, and Savchenko is sitting on the windowsill, surveying him impassively.

'See,' he says, rapping himself on the leg with a metal rod and nodding to the drunken major. 'Never drink with Major Minayev. You can drink with me, or Warrant Officer Rybakov, if he calls for you, or with Lieutenant Bondar, but never drink with the company commander.'

You can tell that the sergeant-major is a regular soldier. He is about thirty-five, not too tall, and his features are slightly elongated, bony—a tough-looking face. His camouflage uniform fits him perfectly. The most striking thing about his dress is the cap with a huge brim that towers on his head, his pride and joy.

He gets off the windowsill and plops down in the major's chair, throwing his legs up on the table.

'So,' he says, looking up at us from under the brim. 'First of all, I want to congratulate you on joining the 429th, holder of the awards of Bogdan Khmelnitsky, Kutuzov and some other guy, the Kuban Cossacks' motor-frigging-rifle regiment. Or, to put it simply, Mozdok-7. I am the sergeant-major of the radio company, Warrant Officer Savchenko, and you will now serve directly under me. Well, and under Major Minayev, of course,' he adds, nodding toward the pile of rags. 'There are about fifteen more people in the company, ten of whom are on government assignment, restoring constitutional law in the republic of Chechnya. The major and I have just come back from there and, God willing, you'll go there as well. Five more soldiers of this fine radio company are wandering around somewhere. I haven't seen them for a while, maybe they went AWOL, who knows. So let's just say this regiment is not exactly exemplary, and God knows, your company sure is shitty. See your major sleeping there!' He raps the metal rod on the table, almost breaking the bottle. 'So if there are any problems in the barracks with our neighbors, the recon company, tell me and I'll tear them all a second one. Well, I imagine you've already got the idea. Judging from your face, you certainly did!' he says, motioning to Osipov's purple cheeks. 'Don't just piss your pants, give them some back, OK?'

'Yes sir,' we answer feebly.

'That's good. Now, who's got good handwriting?'

I step forward.

'What's your name?'

'Babchenko.'

'What's your name, I asked?'

'Babchenko,' I say louder. Is he shell-shocked too, or what?

'Have you got a first name?'

A first name? No one ever calls us by our first names here. Everyone is known by his surname or his nickname, it's just easier. There aren't enough first names in Russian for that many soldiers.

'Arkady,' I answer.

'Raikin?' he jokes, referring to the famous comedian. I've heard this too many times before but I smile all the same.

'No sir, Arkady Arkadyevich Babchenko,' I say, adding my patronimic name.

'How about that, you're Arkadyevich too? With that name you'll never need a nickname. You're going to have a rough ride here, Arkady Arkadyevich from Moscow. Sit down. We're going to write a report. The rest of you can go.'

I sit behind the table and the sergeant-major starts to dictate:

'On 7 June armored carrier BTP-60pb was destroyed as a result of a direct hit from an enemy rocket launcher on a company observation point. The carrier's crew was not harmed. The enemy was dispersed by return fire from our tank and machine gun. As a result of the fire, the following equipment was destroyed . . . '

He pulls a list out of his pocket, takes a deep breath and rattles off: 'Thirty-two pairs of felt boots, seven wool blankets, eighteen sets of winter underwear, twenty-two jackets, two P-141 radio sets, spare batteries . . . '

There are twenty-seven different types of items in all. Everything that has been ruined, stolen or just mislaid in the company during the entire war is written off as lost in this carrier fire. It turns out that every vehicle that has been burned was stuffed full of junk; every dead soldier was wearing three pairs of boots and eight sets of equipment. It's a simple way of doing business every time someone is killed.

As it happens, the carrier wasn't knocked out by the enemy; one of our guys set fire to it while drunk. A student who was just about to be demobilized from our company fell asleep with a cigarette in his hand. He barely managed to escape with his life. The sergeant-major and the student tried to get away with it by towing the carrier into the undergrowth and firing a rocket at it, but the story still reached the commander's ears. Now the student owes the state money. A whole lot of money. Even after everything was written off as lost or worn out, the sum was still four hundred million rubles. If you take into account his soldier's pay of 18,500 rubles a month, his demobilization is going to be postponed for quite some time. He has already done an extra three months but his active service still hasn't earned much, not even the price of one tire.

'Right, what else?' he asks me when we finish the list.

'Don't know, Sergeant-Major.'

'What do you mean you don't know? Are you telling me nothing was stolen during this time? A fine bunch of soldiers you are, Arkady Arkadyevich. So you didn't pinch anything from the armored car?'

'Not a thing.'

'You don't say. Well, let's go and have a look.'

We go to the vehicle and it turns out that it has no generator, no carburetor, battery or pumps, and other bits and pieces are missing too. To put it more simply, apart from its frame, all that's left is the engine, the steering column and its four wheels. We come back to the storeroom and I include the missing items in the report. The sergeant-major has a drink and takes a few sardines from the jar with his fingers. He pushes it over to me.

'Want some?'

I can't refuse. This is payment for my work. I eat the sardines, and shoot a few glances at the vodka, but he seems to have no intention of giving me a drink.

'Finished, Sergeant-Major,' I say eventually.

He reads it through.

'Good,' he says approvingly. 'Only take out that bit about the tank—it comes across too literary.'

We hardly see Major Minayev in the company. Sometimes he spends a few days sprawled drunk in the storeroom, urinating right where he lies, and then he vanishes for days on end. We take our orders from the sergeant-major. He's a good guy and an excellent commander. Sometimes he spends the night in the barracks, and on those days no one beats us. With him around a more or less normal life descends on our company.

The first thing he does is submit a report to the regimental commander who is amazed to hear he has a communications company, and he immediately assigns us to a duty detail.

'Hell,' wails Loop when he hears this. 'We should have got out of here before they knew about us. Now they're going to kill us with duty details.'

He's right. The day we arrived they put us on our allowances and then just forgot about us. We didn't go to the sentry musters and our company just dropped out of the regiment's life. No one had any interest in the eight soldiers who got beaten up on the second floor of the redbrick barracks at Mozdok-7. It would have been the easiest thing to go AWOL and no one would have come after us. They could kill us in this regiment, drag us off to Chechnya at night or just butcher us in the barracks—that had happened before—and no one would look for us or care where the radio company had gotten to, and they wouldn't inform our families of our disappearance.

I'm on orderly duty almost all the time now. The recon don't want to relieve us on duty details so we relieve ourselves for the second week running, and we are on every other day.

So here I am doing sentry duty and watching Zyuzik washing the floor. When he reaches the post with the dent it will be the exact middle of the corridor and we'll swap places. He'll stand as sentry and I'll wash the floor.

The recon are drinking in their billet. Before, when I was on orderly duty and I couldn't get away from the barracks, I tried to stay in the latrines, away from the drunken recon guys. I would sit on the narrow windowsill and watch the runway for hours. Occasionally they would call me into their billet and beat me, and then I would go back into the latrines and sit on the sill. I might sit there all night long. Whenever I heard footsteps in the corridor I hid in a cubicle, thinking they wouldn't find me. Sometimes they didn't, but when they did they'd beat me right there on the crapper. Once I decided not to open the door, then Boxer brought a rifle, loaded it with a blank round, stuffed a cleaning rod into the barrel and fired it straight through the cubicle door above my head. Almost half of the rod sank into the wall, and after they'd beaten me I had to pull it out.

Now I don't bother to hide in the latrines. I am long since used to the blows and I know that if they want to beat me up they'll do it wherever I am, in the toilet or in the next bed.

'Orderly!' comes the shout from the billet. I jump up and run to them.

The next morning Chuk shows up in the barracks. He's the regimental duty officer today—talk about a stroke of luck . . .

When I leave the armory Chuk is holding Zyuzik by the shoulders and methodically smacking his back against the wall, to and fro like a pendulum. Zyuzik looks devotedly into Chuk's eyes, his head swinging around like a doll's.

'Why is there such a mess in your billet, orderly?' he asks me. 'Why is the orderly asleep on sentry duty? I can't hear you!'

Zyuzik is always falling asleep, slumped on the sentry's platform. The rest of us, Loop, Andy and I, have developed some kind of sixth sense and we manage to open our eyes in time. No sooner does the officer set foot on the staircase than we bark in his face: 'Nothing to report in your absence, sir!' Zyuzik has no such instinct and wakes up only when he is hit.

Chuk wakes him with a jab under his rib and, as the half-crazed Zyuzik struggles to work out what's going on, kicks him in the groin. And so it goes—day in, day out.

'What does he have to go and kick me in the balls for, the son of a bitch!' Zyuzik wails afterward. His face is red from pain, he can't breathe and he gasps for air like a fish. 'I'll go and hang myself and write a note that it's his fault! Bastard! When is this going to stop?'

None of us gets enough sleep; we grab short snoozes in the armored car at night while on duty, or under the staircase if we can sneak in there without being seen and the recon don't find us. Zyuzik has it worse than the rest of us; he was not cut out to serve in the army, so small and weedy and defenseless. Lack of sleep is wrecking him and now he nods off while he's on sentry duty. Chuk kicks him in the groin every time, and it has already become a kind of ritual.

'Orderly, come with me,' says Chuk, and he goes into the latrines. I'm confident they are clean enough to pass muster; Zyuzik and I scrubbed those crappers all night so I have nothing to fear now. Sure enough, Chuk is satisfied with his inspection. He'll go now, I think, but he suddenly turns into the utility room. On the ironing board someone from recon has left a tiny cassette radio and a Tetris game, which is very popular in the regiment.

'What the hell is this?' Chuk screams. His already bulging eyes fill with fury. 'I'm asking you, orderly!' He knocks the player onto the floor with his enormous hand and then breaks the Tetris over my head.

He rages for another twenty minutes and then he finally leaves. I pick up the pieces of the broken game. Shit! Now recon will make me conjure up a new Tetris. It won't bother anyone that Chuk whacked me with it like a stick—it broke on my head, which means it's my problem.

When the recon come back to the barracks after lunch I tell them about Chuk's visit.

'Did he break anything?' Timokha asks me.

'Yes, Timokha, he broke the cassette player and the game . . .' I start to mumble. 'I didn't know they were lying there, someone left them at night, I didn't see who, I . . .'

'Fucker!' interrupts Timokha. 'What a fucker that guy is. Shame Sanya didn't knock him down yesterday!'

Timokha takes the news surprisingly well. I get away with it, thank God. Where would I get a Tetris here anyway?

Zyuzik is in the latrines, crying by the window. He is leaning with his head against the wall, his hands pressed between his knees, red-faced.

'Bastard,' he says with a muffled moan. 'Why does he always go for my balls . . . bastard, bastard, bastard.'

Strictly speaking, there is no *dedovshchina* bullying in our regiment. *Dedovshchina* is a set of unofficial rules, a kind of a code of laws, which, if violated, incur corporal punishment.

For example, your walk. Your walk is determined by the amount of time you have served. The 'spirits,' those who have just been called up, are not supposed to walk at all, they are supposed to 'flit' or 'rustle.' Those in their second six months—the 'skulls' or 'bishops'—are entitled to a more relaxed mode of walking but their gait is nonetheless supposed to reflect humility. Only the 'lords,' who are about to be demobilized, can walk with a special swagger that is allowed only to the older recruits: a leisurely pace, their heels scraping the floor. If I had even thought about walking like that in training I'd immediately have been showered with punches. 'Up for demob now, are you?' they'd have asked, and then they'd have given me hell. If I stuck my hands in my pockets I'd also get a thump on the head: that is the privilege of the older soldiers. A spirit should forget about his pockets entirely. Otherwise they fill them with sand and sew them up. The sand chafes the groin and two days later you have weeping sores.

You can get a beating for anything at all. If a spirit doesn't show respect in his conversation with an older soldier, a 'granddad,' he'll get beaten up. If he talks too loudly or goes about the barracks clattering his heels, he'll get beaten up. If he lies on his bed in the day, he'll get beaten up. If the people back home send him good rubber slippers and he decides to wear them to the shower, he'll get beaten up and lose his slippers.

And if a spirit even thinks of turning down the tops of his boots or walking around with his top button undone, or if his cap is tipped back on his head or to one side, or he doesn't do his belt up tightly enough, they'll thrash him so hard he'll forget his name. He is a spirit, the lowest dregs, and it's his job to slave until the older soldiers have been discharged.

But at the same time the older soldiers jealously guard their rights over their spirits. Every self-respecting granddad has his own spirit, a personal slave, and only he is allowed to beat and punish him. If someone else starts to harass this spirit then he'll go straight to the granddad and then there are conflicts: 'You're bugging him so you're bugging me . . .'

It's also good for a spirit to have his personal granddad. First of all, only one person beats you. Then you can always complain to him if someone else makes claims on you, and he'll go and sort it out. If a skull, a soldier in his second six months, thumps a spirit's head or takes money from him, then he'll get a good sound beating—only granddads are allowed to rob the young ones. A spirit is obliged to rustle up money, cigarettes and food only for his own granddad, and he can ignore anyone else's demands. The only exception is a granddad who's stronger than yours.

But there is none of this in our regiment. All of that stuff—the unbuttoned tunics, the belt and the walk—is just child's play. It's the big league here. I can walk how I like and wear what I like and it doesn't bother anyone. They beat us for completely different reasons. Our older conscripts have already killed people and buried their comrades and they don't believe they'll survive this war themselves. So beatings here are just the norm. Everyone is going to die anyway, both those doing the beating and their victims. So what's the big deal? There's the runway, two steps away from here, and they keep bringing back bodies by the dozen. We'll all die there.

Everybody beats everyone. The *dembels*, with three months' service to go, the officers, the warrant officers. They get stinking drunk and then hammer the ones below them. Even the colonels beat the majors, the majors beat the lieutenants, and they all beat the privates; and granddads beat new recruits. No one talks to each other like human beings, they just smack each other in the mouth. Because it's easier that way, quicker and simpler to understand. Because 'you're all going to bite it anyway, you bitches.' Because there are unfed children back home, because the officer corps is addled with impoverishment and hopelessness, because a *dembel* has three months left, because every second man is shell-shocked. Because our Motherland makes us kill people, our own people, who speak Russian, and we have to shoot them in the head and send their brains flying up the walls, crush them with tanks and tear them to pieces. Because these people want to kill you, because your soldiers arrived yesterday straight from training and today they are already lying on the airstrip as lumps of charred flesh, and flies lay eggs in their open eyes, and because in a day the company is reduced to less than a third, and God willing you'll stay among that third. Because the one thing that everyone knows is how to get drunk and kill, kill and kill some more. Because a soldier is a stinking wretch, and a spirit doesn't have any right to live at all, and to beat him is to actually do him a favor. 'I'll teach you what war is about, you pricks! You can all have a smack in the mouth so you don't think life is too rosy, and thank your mother that she didn't have you six months earlier or you'd all be dead now!'

Everyone hates everyone else in this regiment—the hatred and madness hang over the square like a foul black cloud, and this cloud saturates the young boys with fear, just like pieces of barbecue meat being marinated in lemon juice, only they get stewed in fear and hatred before they get sent off to the meat grinder. It will be easier for us to die there.

I stand on sentry duty as Timokha walks past. He swings around and kicks me in the chest so hard I fly off my feet and hit the wall, knocking down the wooden sign with the timetable of the company's activities: 'The company is engaged in fulfilling a government assignment.' They call this war a government assignment. In death notices sent to families they could just as well write: 'Decapitated while on government assignment.' The sign falls and its corner hits me hard on the back. I crumple up with pain. Timokha keeps walking.

A construction company shuffles barefoot across the stones to the canteen. The construction battalion lives separately in a different barracks, and they show their faces in the regiment only to go and eat. What goes on in their section no one knows, but the rumors give you goose bumps. The bullying there is like a well-oiled machine. The *dembels* hit the young conscripts with spades, beat them so hard that some hang themselves. They carry out bodies from there with frightening regularity. And yet we'd never heard of even one criminal case being opened in the construction battalion.

The builders stand at attention, silently, without moving. No one looks around or down at his feet. The older ones had taught them that to stand at attention means just that. If anyone makes the slightest movement, he'll get a beating. This column of walking dead cares nothing about anything: the war, Chechnya, the heaps of bodies at the airstrip. They are worried only about tonight, when the officers leave the barracks after the evening muster and they will get beaten again with shovels.

In the morning the officers will come back, the thick-headed morons, and beat them for having shovel marks on their faces.

They stand silently in front of the canteen. It's like terror itself is standing here, after shuffling its way barefoot across the stones to feed, seeing nothing, paying attention to nothing, just waiting.

'Now that's a shitty place they're in,' whispers Loop, looking at the builders. 'God forbid we end up serving there. It's already bad enough here, but there it's real hell.'

Loop knows what he's talking about. Timokha once sent him to see the Greek, and he got the barracks mixed up and ended up in the construction battalion. They beat him so hard that he had to smash a window and jump from the first floor to escape.

We get a holiday period: almost the entire recon company goes to Chechnya. Only Smiler and Maloi are left, but they don't touch us. Every morning they go to the park and muck around there doing something to the wrecked BMP and come back only toward evening. Yelin ordered them to reassemble the engine and gave them two weeks to do it. The fuel pump got wrecked by shrapnel, and now they are racking their brains to work out where they can steal a replacement. They have eight days left to do it.

Timokha went on leave. As a farewell gesture he beat up Zyuzik and me and smacked Osipov across the face with his elbows. Now Andy's cheeks look like a pair of eggplants: they have a nice purple sheen, are slightly swollen and quiver like jelly every time he speaks. It's pretty funny, as it happens, and every time I tell him he gets annoyed.

'How would you like a beating like that?'

'Take it easy, I've had my fair share,' I answer.

We sleep like human beings for three days, waking to the sound of a drum roll that tells us it's already nine in the morning and time for muster. We stretch blissfully in our beds and take our time getting up. The sergeant-major doesn't come for another half an hour at least. We skip breakfast, loath to swap our precious sleep for food, especially as we don't get that hungry in such heat, and the last night's supper easily sees us through to lunchtime. If not, we go to the pilots' canteen and scrounge some bread there.

We rise at our leisure and go and wash when the parade passes the regimental commander to the accompaniment of a ceremonial march. Then the sergeant-major takes us to the park or we tidy the billet, or just do sweet nothing and laze on the grass.

It's a happy time—we belong to ourselves and no one beats us.

And here we are, lying in the orchard by the pilots' quarters, smoking and chewing on ripe, juicy apricots. At lunchtime we filled our bellies with rice and chicken bones, and we have an hour and a half before the evening muster. You could say that we are pretty happy with life.

We come over to the pilots' quarters every day after lunch. It's nice here; their barracks are surrounded by a shady orchard where we can hide without anyone finding us. It's my favorite place, better than the most comfortable hotel in the world with all of its luxury—I just feel good here.

At the edge of the orchard stands a great, thick oak tree, surrounded by moss that's like a down pillow to sleep on, uncovered, in the summer's warmth. All around there are free apricots and mulberry trees, the birds are singing and the sun tickles our cheeks through the leaves. It's heaven on earth.

On the way here we shook down a load of apricots and now we bask in the pleasure of life as we eat them, feeling almost like real people.

We are discussing Lena, with her hoarse smoker's voice, small black eyes and shapely figure. Lena's a little over thirty, swears like a trooper, raps cheeky soldiers over the knuckles with her ladle and dishes out generous portions, more than the ration.

Loop falls in love with her on the spot, insisting that it's nothing to do with food. Strangely enough, I believe him. When Lena doles out the food Loop doesn't even look at his plate, and with him this is indeed a telling sign. He can't tear his eyes away from the object of his adoration, especially not from her firm bust, which is visible beneath her white coat.

'Lenochka,' he moans while sitting at the table, shifting on the bench, 'Oh Lenochka, how I'd love to . . .' Loop doesn't elaborate on his dream.

I don't find her attractive myself, but she gives us double portions and I'm grateful to her for that.

And who are we to even talk about being in love with her or not, or whether she's really a looker? Once, back in training, we all had to be checked for venereal diseases. They lined us all up on the parade ground and ordered us to drop our pants. We stood there naked and a female doctor, a very beautiful Asian woman, made her way down the rows, examining us. Each one of us had to display his goods to her for a close-up.

None of us had ever stood waiting for a date with his heart missing a beat, or kissed a girl in a doorway, or declared his love for anyone or performed any feat or foolhardy deed for a girl. And here we were, standing naked in front of a beautiful grown-up woman, among hundreds of other stinking, dirty soldiers being examined like cattle. We were obliged to have a medical examination, and that's what we did, as quickly and as practically as possible. What we all felt at that moment was of no interest to anyone. What love or romance could there be here, for God's sake? It wasn't the place for all that.

'Loop, have you ever been with a girl?' Osipov asks.

'Of course I have,' mumbles Loop, offended. 'Natasha, who I was at school with.'

I don't really believe Loop; it seems he is making it up. Mind you, he did receive some letters from someone but he never read them out loud.

'What about you?' Andy asks me.

'I dunno.'

'How come?'

'It was at a party, I was drunk out of my mind and I don't remember anything. Maybe that counts?'

'Sure that counts,' says Osipov. He is the only one of us who had been with a woman properly, and his authority in such matters is unshakable.

'What about you, Zyuzik, have you been with a girl?'

'Yes,' he answers, digging at the ground with a twig.

Osipov looks at him closely.

'Like hell you did, liar,' he says eventually.

'So what if I didn't, what about it then?' Zyuzik retorts. 'That's all ahead of me, get it? Why are you bothering us with your stupid questions! Maybe I don't want to do it like Loop, with some cook. I want a real love, understand?'

'What if you never have time?' Andy asks him.

'Fuck off!' Zyuzik replies and falls silent.

'All right, all right, I'm joking, take it easy. It's all still to come for you.'

'Spit for luck then, idiot,' I remind him.

Andy spits over his shoulder three times and knocks on wood. We light up another cigarette each and say nothing for a while.

'Shit, I wish we'd just go to Chechnya. What is this anyway? It's not the army, but some kind of never-ending humiliation,' Loop lisps through his swollen lips.

'What, do you reckon there's no recon in Chechnya?' objects Osipov.

'Yes, but they won't beat us there.'

'Why won't they?'

'Why does a cow have udders between her legs?' snaps Loop. 'What don't you understand? No bastard will hit me if I've got a rifle in my hands.'

'Sure, Loop,' I say. 'But they'll have weapons too, and unlike you they know how to use them.'

'You can say that again,' Osipov backs me up. 'When I heard they were taking us to Chechnya I thought that at least they'd teach us to shoot properly. But no one teaches us anything here, they just knock us around.'

'How are we supposed to fight, guys?' Zyuzik asks.

It's a rhetorical question and no one is about to answer.

We don't know how to dig trenches, or take cover from machine-gun fire, and we don't know how to set a trip-wired grenade without it blowing up in our hands. No one teaches us any of this stuff. We don't even know how to shoot; the guys in our company have handled weapons only twice. If we landed in a combat situation right now, after we come out from under this apricot tree, we would be lucky to last a few hours.

'We've got to get out of here,' says Zyuzik.

'You reckon? And just how do you intend to do that?' asks Osipov. 'Have you got money? Clothes?'

'We've got car stereos we can sell. We'd probably get enough to travel.'

'And what about a passport? No one will sell you a ticket without a passport,' Osipov continues.

'They can send you a passport in the mail. You just have to write to your parents,' I say.

'Right!' exclaims Zyuzik, taken with the idea. Now he really does think he is ready to go AWOL. He has initiated this sort of discussion pretty often in recent days.

'Well, boys? Let's write home and get them to send us passports and we'll get the hell out of here.'

It turns out that he left his passport with the military draft board, and Osipov too.

'We won't have enough money for everyone,' says Loop. 'And what's the point of getting out now anyway, there's no recon here at the moment. When they get back, that's when we should go.'

'I hope they all get killed there,' says Andy.

'No, not all of them, Vitalik's all right.'

'Vitalik yes, but the rest can go to hell.'

'What do you have to do to get into the hospital?' says Zyuzik, resuming his favorite tune. He can't shake off the idea of deserting the regiment.

It seems nothing could be simpler. The camp isn't guarded, you just leave and go wherever you want. The great shame of it all is that there is nowhere to go. Run off home? All that awaits us there is prison, since we'll be branded deserters. And we'd still have to get home. Plenty of soldiers have been murdered or kidnapped on the way, getting whisked off to slavery from the station. And there are patrols everywhere. So it's safest of all in the regiment.

'You can mess up your kidneys,' says Andy. 'Dissolve half a cup of salt in water, drink it and jump off the windowsill. That's a sure demobilization. Or you can inhale broken glass. Then you're guaranteed to cough up blood and spend at least half a year in the hospital. Or if you're lucky they'll decommission you.'

'You can also cut your veins,' I say. 'One guy at our training camp cut himself. You just stretch the skin on your arm and slash it a few times with a razor blade. Very effective, blood everywhere, and most importantly it's absolutely safe.'

'You're best off asking Timokha—he'll smash your jaw and *bingo!*' says Loop. 'You don't even have to ask him, he'll do it some day anyway.'

'Yeah, your jaw, that's not bad,' says Zyuzik, warming to the theme. 'That's at least two months in the sick bay. Or smash the jaw out of joint altogether, that's even better. Then it'll start to come right out, all you have to do is open your mouth wide. That's a demob for sure. You just have to find someone who will knock it right out for you without breaking it. There's bound to be someone who can do that in the hospital. Aw, I'd love to get into the hospital.'

'Right, and if grandma had a you-know-what she'd be a grandpa,' Loop says.

'Listen, you're from Moscow, you know everything. So tell us, who started this war?' Osipov asks me.

For some reason he seems to think that Muscovites know everything there is to know.

'I haven't the foggiest idea, ask me something easier.'

'No, come on, why do you think?' he says, not letting go.

'Well, the president, I suppose.'

'What, him personally?'

'No, he consulted me first.'

I don't feel like talking. My belly is full, my lunch is turning over lazily in my guts and I feel like a nap. We laze around in the shade; no one is beating us and our lungs are warmed with tobacco smoke. What more could we ask for?

'What I want to know is whether the defense minister can start a war on his own without consulting with the president.'

'No he can't,' says Zyuzik. 'Our president is the supreme

commander of the armed forces and he is the only one who can start a war.'

'So how did this one start?' asks Osipov, trying to think it through. 'Why do wars happen at all?'

And we all wonder.

'Because of power,' says Zyuzik, in one of his occasional moments of incisiveness. 'Why else would they happen?'

'So what's it all about, having power? How can you kill so many people because of it? Yeltsin was already president—what more power could he need? Or was the Chechen president Dudayev trying to overthrow him?' Osipov asks.

'God knows who wanted to overthrow who. Maybe someone didn't share the pickings evenly. What does it matter to you now anyway?' I say.

'It doesn't, I just wondered. Look at you all, lying under the tree having had a good beating all night, and with more in store today. And if you don't get smacked in the head ten times a day, then you regard it as a day wasted. And then they'll stick you on a carrier and take you to Chechnya. That's of course if you haven't managed to get your jaw broken by then. Have you guys not thought that some of us are bound to get killed in this war?' Osipov asks, propping up his head on his elbow. 'How many boys have they got killed already and how many more are to die? I don't want to die, I've only got four months left till demob. Someone should answer for all of this. Do you reckon the president knows?'

'About what?'

'About all of this,' says Osipov, waving his hand toward the regiment. 'How they kill us like flies here, how they beat us, about this whole lawless mess.'

'I doubt it, how could he? The regimental commander is one of us, and not even he knows.'

'No way, he knows all right,' says Loop. 'You think he's blind or something? It's enough to look at your face to know what's going on. He knows full well, he just can't do anything about it. You can't put the entire recon against the wall and you can't demobilize all the older conscripts before their time. Soldiers always got beaten in the past and they always will get beaten.'

'So that means the president knows too. Then I say he is the biggest criminal of the bunch,' Osipov concludes, looking at us triumphantly, as if he has uncovered the greatest truth of all.

I couldn't agree with him more. I think this entire band of bureaucrats and officials exists solely for the purpose of breaking us down in these barracks, taking us to the airstrip and putting us in helicopters to be finished off on the other side of the ridge. Somehow they are making money from this, and although I can't fathom how they can turn a buck from my smashed-out teeth, they have worked out a way. Apart from this, they are of no use whatsoever. The war has been going for more than a year and there appears to be no end in sight.

'Listen, are the Chechens our enemies or not?' Osipov presses on with his questions. With his curiosity he should work in army intelligence.

'No, we aren't fighting the Chechens but rather the so-called illegal armed formations,' Zyuzik answers.

'But what are they then, Chechens or not?'

'Chechens.'

'So we're fighting the Chechens,' Andy concludes. 'And what do they want?'

'Independence.'

'So why can't we give them independence?'

'Because it says in the Constitution that no one can just go and break away from Russia just for the asking,' all-knowing Zyuzik explains.

'What I don't get is this: are Chechens citizens of Russia or enemies of Russia? If they are enemies then we should stop messing around and just kill all of them. But if they are citizens, then how can we fight against them?'

He gives us another triumphant look and no one challenges him. This sort of conversation is typical for the army. No one, from the regimental commander to the rank-and-file soldier, understands why he is here. No one sees any sense in this war; all they see is that this war has been bought off from start to finish. It has been waged incompetently from the very beginning, and all those mistakes by the general staff, the defense minister and the supreme command have to be paid for with the lives of soldiers. For what purpose are these lives being laid down? The 'restoration of constitutional order,' the 'counterterrorist operation' are nothing but meaningless words that are cited to justify the murder of thousands of people.

'Zyuzik, are you prepared to kill children for the constitution of your country?'

'Go fuck yourself.'

'If the war isn't going to end, then what are we fighting for? Why kill so that there is even more killing? Who can explain that to me?' Osipov demands.

'Amen,' says Loop.

'No one can explain the whys and wherefores to you,' Zyuzik tells Osipov, 'so I'll tell you what, why don't you fuck off with your questions.'

'What I want to know is whether Yeltsin knocks our defense minister around?' Loop asks. 'He outranks him after all, just like Chuk knocks the warrant officers about. Imagine, General Grachyov briefs him incorrectly and *wham*, he gets a smack in the mouth. Well?'

'It would be really cool if they led Yeltsin and Dudayev out onto the landing strip and let them get stuck into each other. The one who cripples the other wins. What do you reckon? Who would get the other down, Yeltsin or Dudayev?' says Zyuzik.

'My money's on Dudayev. He's short, nimble, and looks like he'd have a pretty good uppercut.'

'Yeltsin's got longer arms,' points out Osipov. 'And he's much taller and stronger.'

'So what? He's also lumbering and not too agile. No, my money's on Dudayev,' I say.

'Mine too,' agrees Loop.

'I'll go with Yeltsin any day,' says Zyuzik. 'And may they smack the crap out of each other for as long as possible until they both get what's coming to them.'

We burst out laughing. I picture this scene in my mind, two presidents beating the pulp out of each other on the runway like two sergeant-majors. The sleeves on their expensive suits rip and their elegant tailored pants split open. We stand around and cheer them on: we cheer our guy and the Chechens cheer theirs. And no war, no corpses.

'All right, that'll do,' says Osipov, still quaking. 'No one is going to have a fistfight with anyone. Why would they bother when they've got us?'

'That's right, it's down to us to do the fighting. Let's go.'

We get up and return to the barracks. It's already deserted by the canteen and we line up in single file, with Osipov commanding our little group.

'Left right, left right, left!' he yells as if there is at least a reinforced army corps standing in front of him.

'Company!' he shouts, and we take three paces forward. 'Quick march!'

I stamp my heels on the asphalt with all my might as we punch out the steps, and Loop and Zyuzik keep up with me. We hammer the parade ground so hard that the presidential guard could learn a thing or two from us.

'Lift those feet, tighten up the pace!' Osipov orders with a smile.

Zyuzik, Zhikh and I march along in quickstep in the middle of the empty square, laughing like maniacs.

They send some young recruits to join our company. Three country boys who all got called up from around here somewhere. After we hear this we lose interest in them; what they do is their own business and vice versa. So they keep sending us new faces, what of it? They'll desert anyway. Everyone who lives around here runs away. We are the ones who have nowhere to run to. I live closest to Mozdok and my home is a thousand miles away.

That night the recon get them up and set them sparring.

'OK radiomen, let's see what sort of young'uns you've been sent,' says Boxer.

We lay in our beds as if in theater stalls and watch. They won't beat us today; it's not our turn.

The recon form a circle and shove one of the new recruits into the middle, a strong, sturdy guy with round shoulders. One of the recon emerges from the other side of the ring.

They start to dance around each other and exchange a couple of body blows. The conscript is doing OK and even manages to connect a good one to the recon's liver and then dodges two powerful jabs. Then the recon hits the young kid in the nose. His head snaps back and blood flows down his chin. He presses his palms to his face and tries to leave the ring but gets shoved back.

'No, that's not what we agreed,' he says naively. 'If you're going for the face I won't fight.'

They start kicking him and make him fight. He goes into the ring again and the recon knocks him to the ground with two punches.

The fight is over.

We fall asleep.

The next morning there is no sign of the boys—all three have deserted. Once again we are the first in line for beatings.

We are sitting in the storeroom, sorting out the company's junk: jackets, body armor, helmets, all heaped in a big pile in the corner, and the sergeant has decided to sort it all out.

The flak jackets are in terrible shape, unbelievably filthy, covered in oil and gasoline, with pounds of dirt in the pockets, missing half of the armored plates, and some with bloodstains. But we're still able to use two or three of them to piece together a whole one.

Loop shows us a breast plate with a bullet hole drilled through it. It has a big stain on the inside.

'Private Ignatov, radio company, blood group A (II) Rhesus positive,' he reads from the collar.

We continue the work in silence.

Holed and dented helmets, shredded flak jackets, holed uniform jackets, name plates with pieces of shrapnel lodged in them, brown stains of dried blood that we try not to touch. These signs of people's deaths are just lying around on the storeroom floor. Our soldiers died in these things, soldiers of the radio company of the 429th regiment. They went off to Chechnya in January 1995 and then later some sergeant-major brought the flak jackets taken from their cold bodies and threw them in the corner of the storeroom. And then he went on a drinking binge for a few months. And then he got killed,

someone told us later. Now we are sitting here piecing together flak jackets for ourselves from this pile of bloody rags.
Savchenko will take us to war just the same way and will come
back a few months later with a pile of bloody flak jackets,
throw them in the corner and go on a bender for a few months.
Then they will send more new recruits from training, probably
from the same camp as us, Elan. They will also sit here on the
floor waiting to be sent to Chechnya, reading our names on
the flak jackets, showing each other bullet-holed plates and
helmets, and then another officer will take them to war and
come back half crazy.

The recon get back from another mission and assign us to a
new detail. From now on we do telephone duty at the communications exchange. The exchange is called Accoroid, but no
one knows what the word is supposed to mean. We have the
simple task of connecting callers. For example, the phone
rings, I pick up and say 'Accoroid.' 'Accoroid?' they ask. 'Put me
through to the regiment commander.' And I do, and that's all
there is to it.

Every day information passes through Accoroid saying that
the Chechens are about to take Mozdok by storm. Every day we
receive warnings from HQ to step up patrols and post armed
guards by the barracks. The precautions are not in vain—there
were cases when whole barracks full of soldiers were slaughtered in their sleep.

And today they are also telling the regimental commander
that Chechen rebel leader Shamil Basayev seized two Grad missile systems and is advancing on Mozdok. On previous occasions
when I got these sorts of messages I wanted to run somewhere
and do something, get ready for battle, take up defensive positions or something. It's unbearable to sit at the switchboard just

waiting for Basayev to ride onto the parade ground with two Grads. Now I'm used to it, but that doesn't mean for a moment that I'm not afraid. For us the war is concentrated in this little box that constantly emits messages about death, shot-down helicopters and destroyed convoys. Somewhere the Chechens are attacking, somewhere else a regiment is under fire, or a unit has been butchered in Grozny. Somehow there doesn't seem to be any news about our successes and we are starting to get the impression that we are losing on all fronts. We believe the Chechens are strong—we can't afford not to believe it. There's the runway outside the window with helicopters landing on it nonstop. We will all die in this war.

I am sitting in the armory, counting the weapons and comparing the tally with the entry in the book. It's evening now, and everyone is out and about somewhere. Loop went off to the runway this morning; now he goes there every day and asks to be taken on one of the flights. He doesn't care where to, as long as it's far away from here. But no one takes him. Zyuzik is skulking around somewhere. The last time he appeared was when the sergeant-major booted him out of the closet under the stairs, where he had spent almost two days sleeping. Osipov has gone to get some grub from the pilots' canteen, and Savchenko and Minayev are nowhere to be seen. The recon are almost all in Mozdok, where they have some kind of business going with the locals and often stay in town overnight. So I am left to my own devices.

To my surprise I don't want to sleep and I lock myself into the armory. The only key is with me, so I am in no danger if the recon reappear in the barracks in a filthy mood. Of course, if they wanted to they could smoke me out of here with flares or thunder flashes, but that's only in the extreme.

It's night and the barracks are empty and silent. You can't even hear any fighter bombers. I have no fear now as I hunch over a newspaper and write. I imagine that I am a writer working in my own study while my children are playing on the other side of the wall, my wife is drinking tea and the dog is playing with a toy, and all I have to do is come out of the armory and I will find myself in a fairy tale.

A loud bang interrupts my daydream, and right after it the howl of a descending mortar round. I throw myself to one side with the book, sweeping rifle bolts and grenades from the table, and freeze between some shell crates, screwed up like a fetus.

The mortar round screams and whistles like the devil as it heads straight toward me. My back seems to swell to a huge size as if to present a target that cannot be missed.

The Chechens are in Mozdok, I manage to think to myself.

The round flies for an eternity, probably all of half a second, but there is no explosion. But then everything is lit up outside the window with a poisonous chemical light. A pleasant tremble of relaxation passes through my legs and my whole body breaks out in sweat. It's only a signal flare. Sometimes they are fitted with a siren that, when activated, shrieks with a whistling sound like a falling mortar round.

The flares howl down one after the other, red, white and green, illuminating the armory through the window with an uneven flickering light. I lay between the crates, clutching the book in my hands, my body aching as if from hard physical toil, and I am loath to move my arms or legs, as if I have been hauling stones all night. Fear is very exhausting.

Said returns from the hospital. He got shot through the shin during the storming of Bamut and spent two months in the sick bay, and then had a long period of leave that he had awarded himself. Now he has arrived to quit.

His eyes are misty, his hair uncut and dirty, and he is wearing some sort of ragged Afghan cap and army boots with greasy trailing laces. But he has authority here. Said is a thief; he has several burglaries to his name and people do what he says.

He hated me from the moment he met me. I don't know about love but hate at first sight definitely exists. He doesn't extort money from me. I have money after selling those stolen car stereos, about half a million rubles stashed away in the closet under the stairs. I'm a resourceful soldier after all, and if Said wants money I can hand it right over and he won't beat me. But that's not what he's after. He wants me to bring him bananas. He knows I won't be able to get any right now, during the night, so he gives me two hours to come up with some.

I have no intention of even leaving the barracks. I return to our quarters and go to bed. I've got two hours at least. In two hours on the dot I am woken—out of some kind of thief's honor he has stuck to his word.

'Get up, you're wanted,' says Smiler.

I go to the storeroom. Said is sitting with his injured leg on the table, and one of the recon is massaging his injured shin.

'You called for me, Said?' I ask.

'To some people I'm Said, to others I'm Oleg Alexandrovich,' he answers.

'You called for me, Oleg?' I say again.

'Say Oleg Alexandrovich.'

I say nothing and look at the floor. He can kill me right here, but there's no way I'm going to do him the honor of calling him Oleg Alexandrovich.

'Well, what have you got to say?'

'You called for me, Oleg?' I said.

He smirks.

'Did you get any?'

'No,' I reply.

The usual foreplay begins.

We could skip this bit really, but Said is enjoying his power and I don't get hit in the face.

'Why?' Said says with surprising calm.

'I don't know where to get bananas, Oleg.'

'What?'

'I don't know . . .'

'What?' he says, finally letting rip. 'What, you don't want to look for what I told you to find? Useless prick! You'll go and look, got it?'

He starts to hit me viciously. If the others beat me because that's the way it is, Said beats me out of sheer hatred. He enjoys it, gets a real pleasure from it. A stinking nobody in the outside world, he is top dog and master of souls here.

Said is weak, and his punches are not as hard as Boxer's or Timokha's, but he's stubborn and vicious and he hits me a long time, for several hours. He does it in bouts; he batters me, then sits down and rests while forcing me to do push-ups. As I do, he kicks me in the back of the head with his heel and sometimes smacks my teeth from below with his boot. He doesn't do this so often, evidently the hole in his shin hasn't fully healed over and is bothering him, but he lays into the back of my head with vigor in an effort to bust up my face on the floorboards. Eventually he manages, and I fall and lie there on the filthy boards, blood running from my split lips.

Said lifts me up and starts to hit me again, using his palm on my broken lips, aiming all the time for the same place, because he knows that will be more painful. I jolt heavily from every blow and moan. I am tiring now as I press myself up and shield myself with my arms, tensing my muscles so that the kicks don't go deep into my body. I have lost count of the blows and it seems Said has been beating me from the moment I was born, and this was all I have ever known. For heaven's sake, I'll get you your lousy bananas! But Said no longer cares about bananas. He is joined by a few more of the recon and they surround me and smash me in the back with their elbows. I stand doubled up, shielding my stomach with my arms, but they don't let me fall over so they can also kick me from below with their knees.

They shove me into the latrines, where a stocky Tartar named Ilyas hops and kicks me in the chest. I fly backward and smash the window with my shoulders, sending shards of glass cascading over me, over my head and stomach. I manage to grab the frame and stop myself from falling right through. I didn't even cut myself. Once again they knock me from my feet and I crash to the floor. This time I don't get up, I just lie there among the broken glass and all I can do is try to cover my kidneys and groin. Finally the recon take a breather and have a smoke.

Said flicks his ash straight onto me, trying to get me in the face with the burning tobacco grains.

'Listen boys, let's take him down a few more pegs—let's screw him,' he suggests. Beside my face there is a large, jagged piece of glass. I grab it through my sleeve and it sits snugly in my palm like a knife, a long fat blade, tapering at the end.

I get up from the floor, clutching the shard. Shame I don't have the keys to the armory . . .

Blood drips onto the shard from my split lip. I stare right at Said, Ilyas and the rest of them. I stand in front of them holding a blood-smeared piece of glass, watching them smoke. Said doesn't flick any ash on me now.

'OK,' says one of the recon, 'leave him, let's go. We haven't got any antiseptic anyway . . .'

They leave. The cicadas trill in the expanses of the steppe outside the broken window. Fighter bombers take off from the runway and head for Chechnya. A single lamp shines on the empty parade ground. There isn't a soul around, not a single officer or soldier.

The swarthy major was right. I am alone in this regiment.

That night they rough me up even worse, wreaking vengeance for that flash of resistance in the latrine, and the whole recon company piles on top of me to administer the beating, not even letting me get out of bed. This isn't even a beating—they are grinding me down to nothingness, like scum, and I am supposed to act accordingly, not try to wriggle out of it. They throw a blanket over me and force me from the bed, drag me into the corridor and beat me there. It carries on in the storeroom, where they lift me up by the arms and pin me to the wall so I don't fall. I start to lose consciousness. Someone delivers a fearsome punch to my right side and something bursts, piercing my very core with a burning pain. I gasp hoarsely and fall to my knees, and they carrying on kicking me. I pass out.

The recon has gone. I am lying in the corner of the storeroom on a pile of jackets and the walls and the ceiling are spattered with my blood. There's a tooth on the floor. I pick it up and try to push it back into the gum. In the end I throw it out of the window. I lie motionless for a while.

The pain is so bad I can't breathe; every muscle feels mangled and my chest and sides have become one huge bruise.

After a while I manage to pull myself up and along the wall to the door. I lock it and collapse again on the pile of jackets where I remain until almost morning.

When dawn breaks I take a razor and start to scrape the

blood off the walls. I can hardly breathe and I can't bend over. Something in my right side has swollen up and is pulsating. But I have to clean the blood off and I scratch away with the razor on the wallpaper. It takes me a long time to scrape away the brown drops, and I'm not too careful as I work, tearing away the wallpaper. 'Radiomen!' yell the drunken recon, their feet pounding on the floor. If they remember that I'm in the storeroom they will smash down the door, drag me out and finish me off.

I start to sort out the jackets and hang them in the cupboard. The sergeant-major is coming soon and everything has to be in order.

I find a letter in the pocket of one of them. It's to a guy named Komar, written by a girl. I unfold it and read.

My darling Vanya, sunshine, my beloved sweetheart, just be sure to come back, come back alive, I beg you, survive this war. I will have you however you come back, even if you lose your arms or legs. I can look after you, you know that, I'm strong, just please survive! I love you so much Vanya, it's so hard without you. Vanya, Vanya, my darling, my sunshine, just don't die. Stay alive, Vanya, please survive.

I fold up the letter and start to bawl. The dawn light is shining through the window, and I sit on the pile of jackets and howl from my battered lungs. Blood seeps from my ravaged lips. I'm in pain and I rock backward and forward, the letter clenched in my hand, bawling my head off.

That morning Sergeant-Major Savchenko takes one look at my swollen face and without saying a word goes into the storeroom to the recon. Said is sitting in the armchair, his leg up on the table like before. The sergeant-major pins him to the arm-chair with his knee and beats him with his fist from top to bottom, smashing his head back into the seat with all his fury, and now it's Said's blood spattering onto the walls.

Savchenko beats him long and hard, and Said whines with pain. Then he throws him onto the floor and starts kicking him. Said crawls out of the storeroom on all fours with the sergeant-major kicking him from behind as he goes, before he finally throws him down the stairs.

I listen to the sounds of the beating in the storeroom without even raising my head. I'm glad that Savchenko is beating Said, or rather I'm overjoyed. My liver, jaw, teeth, every part of me rejoices as I hear how this piece of shit squirms and begs Savchenko, 'Please, Sergeant-Major, don't, please, I am already injured.' And the sergeant-major hits him and hisses through his teeth: 'I'm not just "Sergeant-Major" but a senior warrant officer, you fucker, understand? A senior warrant officer.'

I am elated but at the same time I know that I am fucked. When the sergeant-major leaves, Said will come back and put a bullet in me.

Savchenko also realizes this and he spends the night here. He takes the armory keys from the duty officer and sleeps in the barracks. We carry two beds out of the storeroom and put them side by side at the entrance, behind the wall, so no one can come and fire a burst through the door, and then we fall asleep. For the first time I sleep soundly the whole night without waking. I don't dream anything and open my eyes only when the sergeant-major touches my shoulder.

'Get up, Babchenko,' he says. 'Muster.'

Good for him. If I had a tail I would definitely be wagging it now.

*

It is August 1996, and in Grozny it's hell on earth. The Chechens entered the city from all sides and captured it in a few hours. Fierce fighting is under way and our forces are cut off in isolated pockets of resistance. Those that get surrounded are mercilessly wiped out. Our guys have no food, no ammunition, and death roams this sultry city.

Several burial detachments are formed in our regiment and they stick our company in one of them.

The bodies keep on coming, a steady stream of them, and it seems it will never end. There are no more of the pretty silver bags. Bodies torn to pieces, charred and swollen, are brought to us in any state, in heaps. Some bodies are more than half burned— we refer to these among ourselves as 'smoked goods,' to the zinc coffins as 'cans,' and to morgues as 'canning factories.' There is no mocking or black humor in these words, and we say them without smiling. These dead soldiers are still our comrades, our brothers. That's just what we call them, there's nothing more to it than that. We heal ourselves with cynicism, preserve our sanity this way so as not to go completely out of our minds.

So we unload bodies, again and again. Our senses are already dulled, and we don't feel pity or compassion for the dead. We are so used to mutilated bodies by now that we don't even bother washing our hands before we have a smoke, rolling the tobacco in the Prima cigarettes with our thumbs. We don't have anywhere to wash them anyway; there's no water around and it's a long way to run to the fountain every time.

One day there is a girl on the helicopter, a Chechen of no more than fifteen. Her face is serene as if she is asleep, no torn-off jaws or rolled-up dead eyes. There's a hole the size of a fist in the side of her head where a stone hit her, driving her brain out of her skull like a piston.

I can't tear my eyes away from that round, dry hole in her

head. It seems that if you were to tap on the inside of her skull it would make a dull sound, like plastic, as if you were tapping on half of a globe.

Zyuzik is standing in the hatchway. He looks at me and then asks:

'What's wrong with you?'

'Nothing.'

We lift her out and put her on the ground.

'Fucking war,' says Zyuzik. 'What had the girl done to deserve this, that's what I'd like to know? What?'

There are dead soldiers, dead women, dead children. Everyone's dead.

Shorn-headed boys, sometimes morose, sometimes laughing, beaten up in our barracks, with broken jaws and ruptured lungs, we were herded into this war and killed by the hundred. We didn't even know how to shoot; we couldn't kill anyone, we didn't know how. All that we were capable of was crying and dying. And die we did. We called the rebels 'uncle,' and when our boys' throats were cut they'd beg the rebels, 'Please, uncle, don't kill me, what did I ever do to you?' We so wanted to live. Get that into your heads, you fat, smug generals who sent us off to this slaughter. We hadn't yet seen life or even tasted its scent, but we had already seen death. We knew the smell of congealed blood on the floor of a helicopter in a hundred-degree heat, knew that the flesh of a torn-off leg turns black, and that a person can burn up entirely in lit gasoline, leaving just the bones. We knew that bodies swell up in the heat and we listened every night to the crazed dogs howling in the ruins. Then we started to howl ourselves, because to die at the age of eighteen is a terrifying prospect.

We were betrayed by everyone and we died in a manner befitting real cannon fodder—silently and unfairly.

By night they kick the living crap out of us, by day we unload corpses.

We start to spend more and more nights on the runway and even sleep in the tent where the two soldiers chop up the bodies. They were called up at the same time as us and so they let us spend the night there out of solidarity. I have no dreams in this tent, and no charred bodies chase me at night. I just plunge into a dark pit where there is nothing, not even war, and I open my eyes when it gets light.

Sometimes there are cigarettes in the pockets of the dead, or money or something else. We never search them deliberately, but if we find cigarettes we keep them simply because the guy is dead and no longer needs anything.

A person changes very quickly in war. He may be scared by a dead body on the first day, but a week later he can be eating from a can while leaning on human remains to be more comfortable. The bodies that lie with us in the tent are just dead people, that's all. But there is still a line between necessity and cynicism, and it can never be crossed. I still don't have any dreams, nor does Zyuzik—I asked him.

In Mozdok, mothers start to descend on us in droves. They are looking for their lost sons, and before setting off on foot to Chechnya with their photos they have to look through a mountain of corpses in the refrigerators at the station and in the tents. Constant shrieks and moans can be heard from there and the women have aged ten years when they are led out. Many of them are unable to speak for some time.

I watched an inspection like that once. A relatively young, cultured-looking woman, a bit like a teacher in a gray cape, with a black scarf around her head, stood near the tent and they carried bodies out to her. I remember how they brought one of them, burned to death in a tank, nothing left but bones and a left leg still in a boot. The medic took off the boot in case the woman could identify the body from the toes, and a brown foot slithered out.

You won't find any smart, handsome boys in these tents. They were gotten out of the war by their rich daddies, leaving it to us ordinary folk to die in Grozny, the ones who didn't have the money to pay our way out. Heaped in these tents are the sons of laborers, teachers, peasants and blue-collar workers, basically all those who were made penniless by the government's thieving reforms and then left to waste away. These tents contain the ones who didn't know how to give a bribe to the right person, or who thought that army service was the duty of every man.

Truth and nobility of heart are no longer virtues in our world—those who believe in them are the first to die.

They take Zyuzik to the hospital after Boxer broke his finger by beating him with a stool. They say a fair bit of bullying goes on at the hospital too, but at least Timokha and Boxer are not there. And if that's the case, I imagine the bullying should be tolerable enough.

Zyuzik shows up again in the regiment four days later. He finds me during dinner near the canteen, whistles from the gate to the pilots' quarters and waves.

I go over.

'I've come for you,' he says. He has put on some weight in the past few days and his taut dry face has taken on some round-ness; he's even grown some cheeks. 'Let's go to the hospital—it's fantastic there!' he suggests. 'All normal guys and no one hits you. Let's go right now, how about it?'

'What about dinner?' I ask.

'Forget about dinner. You haven't seen dinner yet. Come on. We'll feed you.'

I am slightly put out by the 'we.' In the past, when they beat us on the floor of the corridor, 'we' was he and I. Now it's 'we'll feed you.' But of course I agree.

We stride along on the dusty grass as Zyuzik tells me about the white pillows, about sleeping on clean sheets, more grub than you can eat and daily hot showers with no time restric-tions—it seems he is leading me into a fairy tale.

I'm excited at the prospect of a new stage in my life where everything will be all right. What if I manage to hang about a little longer in the hospital, or even stay there altogether?

The hospital is located at the edge of Mozdok. We take the fa-miliar route through the steppe, cross the highway avoiding the guardhouse and arrive at two isolation units. The first thing Zyuzik does is to send me for a shower. I wash with inde-scribable pleasure; I have almost forgotten that there is such a joy as hot water. Meanwhile, Zyuzik brings food: meat cutlets with potatoes and a handful of dried fruit.

There are a few people sitting around me, and they ask me what it's like back at the regiment. I tell them about the airstrip, about the bodies and the recon.

Next to me sits a large swarthy lad, and Zyuzik introduces us. It's Komar. He lost his heel after they shot up his carrier with a heavy machine gun. Now the bullet wound to his right heel is permanently infected. The doctors have cut his foot open and fitted a drain tube to remove the pus, and Komar leaves a thin, whitish trace wherever he goes.

He offers around his cigarettes and we light up.

'I was sorting out jackets in the storeroom and, well, I found this letter to you,' I tell him.

'Aha! Did you read it?' he asks, emitting a stream of smoke.

'Yes.'

'Great girl, isn't she? Everyone cries when I read her letters here.'

'Is she your wife?'

'Sort of. I'll probably marry her when I get back.'

In the evening the patients gather around the television. There's a film on but I don't watch it. I'm fine just being left in peace, among clean sheets and near a shower. I bask in the pleasure of it all.

'Do you reckon other hospitals are like this?' I ask.

'No,' says a boy with a bandaged arm. 'Only here. When I was in the hospital in Vladikavkaz they used to beat the hell out of us, total lawlessness like in the regiment. But it's good here, I've had two months of it.'

These people seem almost godlike to me. Two months without being bullied! I look at them with envy. I long to become one of them and live in this Garden of Eden. Jesus, I would do anything, wash the dishes, carry firewood and clean the toilet, if I could just stay here a month.

I'm not allowed to stay in the hospital, not even spend the night. At ten on the dot a young nurse takes me to the gate and closes it behind me. I stand on the street and watch her put the lock on. I am definitely not going back to the regiment tonight.

I go to a building site separated from the hospital by a fence, find a little room without windows and lie down to sleep.

Someone has brought a bench in, and I'm clearly not the first poor bastard to spend the night here. The bench is narrow and uncomfortable but I can sleep on it.

I live on the building site for a few days. In the evenings I go on forays for food and during the day I sleep. As it goes, it's not a bad existence and I even think about moving here permanently. What's the big deal? All I need to do is bring a mattress and a blanket and I can live here until autumn. I'll scrounge food at the hospital—as long as Zyuzik is there I won't starve.

One night a litter of kittens appears in my room. They climb up on the bench and cling to me from all sides, meowing as they burrow into my armpits. Once they have warmed themselves they fall asleep.

I don't chase them out; the nights have gotten cold and they give off a fair bit of warmth. Their mother was probably killed, or at least I never saw her in the days I spent on the site.

In our company I am the only one left. Ginger and Yakunin deserted and Osipov is in Chechnya—he went for a day as a radioman with the commander of an infantry company and stayed there. Zyuzik is in the hospital, and Loop's mother came and took him home for ten days' leave. I know he won't return. You'd have to be a complete cretin to come back here. I don't know what happened to Murky and Pincha, nor does anyone else. Maybe they are already at home or maybe they had their heads cut off long ago.

I don't run away. I have already gotten settled in here, used to this regiment, and this airstrip is my fate. That's just the way things turned out and I no longer have the strength to change anything. In fact, running away would be the easiest thing right now: no one needs me here, no one knows about me apart from the commander, but he's in Chechnya.

I don't go to the airstrip any more. They have some team of new recruits working there now, maybe infantry or some special unit. I live in the army car, sleep under a blanket I stole from the company, and in the mornings after breakfast I go into the steppe or into town. The recon catch me in the canteen and send me to the barracks to wash the floors, but I let it ride. Sometimes they manage to force open the door to the car and drag me outside for a beating; other times I lock myself in securely, and after hammering on the outside awhile they leave empty-handed. On those days I go into the steppe without having breakfast.

All I have is loneliness. I am completely alone, left to my own devices. I don't figure in any lists any more—our company roll book met its end in the latrines a long time ago and they never entered me in the regimental roll book; no one bothered. I could just simply run away from here, but I don't.

I go into town more and more often and just wander around the streets, observing civilian life. It's chilly, and people hurry to work. There are cars at the railroad crossing, townsfolk waiting at the bus stop. It's strange seeing people leading a normal life in this town so close to the front line, strange seeing them go about their business. It had seemed to me that the world turned upside down at the start of this war, that everyone had gone crazy, and that all that was left now was death, corpses, brutal beatings and fear. Apparently the world is the same as it ever was.

As they go to work people pass mangled personnel carriers standing at the cargo platforms. Our men burned to death in them. Fighter bombers loaded with more death fly overhead, and these awful refrigerator cars stand at the station with the charred remains of soldiers. A hundred yards away, on the square in front of the station, men drink beer and taxi drivers haggle over fares with their passengers.

It's a peculiar town. Life and death exist side by side here— routine work by day, robberies and shootings by night. After nightfall you can't set foot outside because of the risk of being abducted into slavery or gunned down. Being killed here is as natural as being late for work. But still people leave their homes every morning and go about their business, as if the worst that can happen to them is that they miss the bus.

No one pays any attention to me. They've already seen thousands like me, young soldiers with stupefied eyes wandering in crowds through this town, perhaps filling their lungs with life for the last time this dreadful summer before being killed. They wandered the streets and hoped for a miracle that would spare them from having to fly over the ridge and die; they would look people in the eye and silently cry: 'Help, they want to kill us! Hide us, we are so scared, help!'

Now those soldiers are all dead.

I walk through the town in the morning, looking at the people enjoying the scent of the steppe and of this southern town. Ripe mulberries scatter onto the asphalt. I pick up a handful of berries. This is my breakfast, and my lunch.

I wander around until dark and then return to the barracks on the regimental bus.

The bus goes three times a day, at eight a.m. and at three and seven p.m. It is now five to one. I have gotten myself nice and comfy on a bench and I am dozing, my cap pulled over my eyes, occasionally glancing at the stop. Our postman is sitting there with a pile of newspapers and letters. I'm interested to see if there are letters for our company, but I can't be bothered to get up.

An elderly woman comes out of a house.

'Where are you from, soldier?' she asks.

I answer.

'What are you doing sitting out here? Come on, I'll make you tea.'

I decline. Then she brings me a bottle of tea and a few buns on a plate. Delicious. I haven't eaten homemade buns for ages.

When she comes back down for the plate she asks me in once again. This time I accept—it's still half an hour until the bus goes and it's hot on the street.

I live at her home for five days.

Her name is Aunt Lusya.

There were many soldiers who lived with the Chechens and Ossetians, who found temporary shelter in their homes from the horrors of war. There were plenty of good people among the Chechens. Auntie Lusya is Russian. She used to live in Grozny, but when they started to slaughter the Russians she moved to Mozdok to stay with her daughter-in-law. If it weren't for this house she probably would have gotten killed, just like they killed her youngest son—Chechens broke into her house and stabbed him to death right in front of her, then they cut off his head and dumped it in the dustbin.

Her eldest son died in an air raid when he was taking his mother out of town in the winter of 1995. All Aunt Lusya has left of him is the bundle of bloody clothes they had given her at the morgue. She shows it to me a few times, an ordinary sheet stamped with a number, and wrapped inside it a shirt, a jacket, a pair of track suit bottoms, a T-shirt and underpants. All covered in dried blood, big brown stains. She fishes through the things her son died in and shows me the entry and exit holes made by the piece of shrapnel, first through the jacket, then the shirt followed by the T-shirt. And she tells the story, almost oblivious to my presence, each time reliving his death: the shard pierced him from top downward, entering his chest and exiting at the base of his spine. Then she bundles up his clothes and puts them back in the wardrobe, where she keeps them together with her own things. The bundle lies on a pile of neatly folded clean sheets.

'I survived the Second World War. I was five,' says Aunt Lusya. 'A German gave me a loaf of bread. And a Russian killed my son.'

I leave her on a Sunday. Before I left regimental headquarters I heard a column was supposed to leave for Chechnya on the Monday, and I want to go with it.

Aunt Lusya gives me two bags full of food to take with me. At first I refuse, but she is very insistent.

When I get back I discover the column left two days earlier. I hide one bag of food in the car with all the items that will keep longest in the heat: dry soups, tinned food, some sweets. I'll take this bag with me to Chechnya for the lads. I put all the perishable stuff in another bag and take it to the recon. They eat my sausage and cheese, tell me I'm not such a waste of space after all, and they don't beat me for two days. I sleep in peace in my bed for two nights, then I leave the barracks again.

I don't go to the hospital or to Mozdok but out into the steppe.

During the day I live at the airstrip. I don't even rig up a shelter or awning, I just lie in the shade of the bushes and that's all I do. Usually I lie on my side, prop up my head on my arm and watch the vehicles passing on the road. After breakfast a column of two or three Ural trucks rumbles past toward the arsenal, the Mozdok-12 munitions depot, and in the evening they roll back to the regiment in the lamplight, filled to bursting with ammo.

I have nowhere to wash myself or brush my teeth so I stop bothering. I start to stink; my puttees are now black with grime but I have nowhere to change them for new ones.

It's cold at night and I go back to the car where I sleep until breakfast, woken by the sound of marching companies audible through the ventilation window. Then I get up and go to the canteen.

I just tag onto the tail of any company and go in with them. Sometimes the duty soldiers catch me—'he's not one of ours'— so I tag onto the back of another company. If I don't manage to get into the canteen I go begging for bread at the pilots' quarters, then pick apricots and mulberries and eat them with the scrounged bread. It's not a bad meal, as it goes.

Then I go out into the steppe again, away from the regiment, and lie down on the ground.

Three weeks pass like this. I have fifteen months and twenty-four days left until I am demobilized.

Hi Mom! I'm fine, everything's OK. Today is the sixty-seventh day I have served in Mozdok. I don't want to stay here any more. I need to get out of here, I've had it with the bullying. Just don't faint, it's not all that bad. You have to send me a summons. Give someone money or get Dad admitted to the hospital. Then send a telegram to the regimental commander, saying, 'I request that you grant Junior Sergeant Babchenko compassionate leave because of his father's serious illness.' That's the only way I'll get out of here.

Mom, I can't write you any more letters. I thought hard about it and in the end decided to tell you that we will soon be sent to Chechnya. The fighting has started again there and they need replacements—we're all going. Just don't worry, we're in the middle of nowhere here—people don't even know there's a war on, and the radiomen are always close to headquarters in the rear somewhere. Really. So don't worry, I won't get killed. It's almost like I'm going to a sanatorium to breathe fresh air—the air here is just amazing. Say hi to everyone for me. I love you both.

On the envelope I draw a banner and write on it 'Greetings to Civilians!!' And underneath, 'Get a move on, mailman.' Then I decorate it with various military stars and insignia and take it to headquarters.

On the way back I duck into the pilots' canteen. It's already eleven p.m. and it is shut, but I know one little window I can knock at. A fat cook appears in the darkness and looks questioningly at me. I ask her for bread; I tell her I am going on leave and that my commanding officer is drinking vodka and told me to fetch him a snack. If I don't bring him food he won't let me go home. The cook sighs and goes to the kitchen.

She brings me a loaf, a few eggs and two cold cutlets. She knows perfectly what it's all about; all she has to do is look at my busted face to realize that a guy like me is not going on leave any-where. She gives me the food and closes the window without a word. There are hundreds of us like this; every night we knock on the window and ask for bread. And every night she gives us some.

Somewhere there is music playing, and dogs bark in Mozdok.

I go to the barracks and up to my floor and stand awhile at the door listening to what's going on inside. All is quiet, so I carefully pull on the door. It isn't locked. I open it sharply and quickly go through to the storeroom, clutching the bread to my chest and fearing that I'll drop the cutlets. I slouch my head down to my shoulders, imagining that this way the recon won't notice me and stop me.

I lock myself into the storeroom and have my supper on the pile of jackets.

The cutlets are pork. Delicious.

They keep on sending columns to Chechnya. They leave every week. Combat operations have resumed and now there are far more bodies than when it was 'truce.'

They are no longer placed in a line along the runway but immediately loaded into Ural trucks and taken to the station.

There's hardly anyone left now. Our guys got hemmed in near Achkhoi-Martan and the regiment took a lot of casualties. Now they are urgently forming columns here and sending them off over the ridge. Before long the commander doles out dog tags. I get the number 629600, Zyuzik has 599 for his last three digits and Osipov 601.

The tags are made of aluminum. If you roast in a carrier they'll just melt and no one will be able to identify you.

The soldiers go to Mozdok and buy their own dog tags made of galvanized metal. You can buy them all over the place—selling dog tags in a frontline area is a profitable business.

At the engravers you can get all the necessary information put on the tags: your surname, date of birth, address and blood group. The main thing is your home address. No one wants to lie around as a lump of unidentified meat in one of the refrigerators at the station.

Those who have no money make their own tags. They break up

ladles and teaspoons and use a nail or pin to inscribe their name and blood group. The canteen is permanently short of spoons as a result, and soon they'll get replaced with aluminum ones.

The whole regiment gets ready to move out; everyone writes letters, makes dog tags and tattoos his blood type with a needle and ink onto his chest.

'I wonder, do you think my number—629601—is in sequence?' says Osipov, examining his tag.

'Hardly,' doubts Zyuzik. 'That would mean they've already sent more than half a million people to Chechnya.'

'So what? The war's been going on for two years.'

'No, that's still too many,' I say. 'This probably includes all the conflicts in the past few years: Abkhazia, Nagorno-Karabakh, Transdnestria, maybe even Afghanistan.'

'Hell,' exclaims Zyuzik. 'If we've sent more than half a million soldiers off to these wars, then how many of them died?'

13/ The Summer of 1996

'**Your orders are to cover the route** Mozdok–Malgobek–Karabulak and the combat area by Achkhoi-Martan. The engineer company will keep watch to the left and ahead, the communications company to the right and behind. To your vehicles!' commands Colonel Kotenochkin, jumping up onto his carrier.

The gravel road we are driving along was built by German prisoners after the Second World War. A road from an old war built for a new one. People like killing one another.

Our column is made up of two armored carriers and three Ural trucks. We are carrying humanitarian aid.

I sit on the armor and look in the direction I have been instructed. On the other side sits Zyuzik, looking behind and to the left. Osipov sits at the front.

There are a few boxes with aid supplies between us; we chew sweets and wash them down with lemonade. The wind catches the blue wrappers and carries them off behind us. Sometimes they snag in the radiator of the Ural that follows us. The truck has steering trouble and the driver can't make the curve at first try, so I prod Kotenochkin in the back with my rifle barrel and say: 'Comrade Colonel, the trucks are lagging behind.'

We stop and wait, watching the driver spinning the steering wheel, and then we set off again slowly.

Low hills hide the road. I don't know if this is already Chechnya or not yet, and I am scared. I sit on top of the carrier eating sweets and when the Ural gets stuck again I poke Kotenochkin in the back once more.

'Comrade Colonel, the trucks are lagging behind.'

The column stops.

We don't speak. Only once does Zyuzik silently nudge me with his rifle and motion toward a jutting cliff edge. Written there in big letters are the words ALL LIFE IS CROWNED WITH DEATH.

'Goddamn philosophers,' Zyuzik mumbles to himself.

Our column is stopped at a checkpoint near Karabulak. It's manned by police. We leave them a crate of grenades and two Fly launchers—they have been sent to fight with practically no weapons and are grateful for the contribution.

A sergeant with a pockmarked face lifts the barrier and we cross the border into Chechnya. He eyes us from top to bottom, looking each one in the face as if he wants to remember us, all the boys he lets pass. Like Cerberus guarding the gates to Hades, he stays on this bank and the people go past him on their way to the underworld from where there is no return. He just stands there and watches us go.

The road to war is not at all like the winding road from Mozdok. No one has driven on it for a long time and it is covered in cut branches and clumps of dirt from explosions.

The drivers follow each other's tracks and the trail loops along the asphalt between the craters and haphazardly dumped concrete blocks. On both sides of the road all the trees have been felled and the tree stumps gleam white. Not a single living soul or moving vehicle, a dead road on dead ground.

From time to time we pass burned-out vehicles at the road-side, decapitated armored cars without turrets, shot-up and scorched antiaircraft guns with their barrels turned up life-lessly to the sky. People have driven on this same road that we are now driving on and were killed in this very place. The asphalt still bears the stains of burned oil and the surface is broken up. Tanks plowed the mangled carriers and guns off to the side of the road. The wind raises little whirls of ash. Maybe it's ash from human bodies.

'Look!' Zyuzik points to a smashed bunker. Thick beams have been thrown skyward and the ground is scattered with rags, papers and other debris. Nearby stands a carrier, apparently in one piece but scorched black. On the other side of the bunker stands a tank, also black. A whole platoon must have died here.

We are silent. There is no need to say anything. We are all gripped by the same feeling that affects any living creature in the presence of death.

We have suddenly become different—Zyuzik, Andy, the commander, all of us—as if our places have been taken by mannequins, while our souls remain on the other side of that barrier at the checkpoint. It's as if we have aged a thousand years.

In an instant the day becomes black too—no sun, no sky, no life, just a dead road, craters and burned-out vehicles. That barrier has separated us from the world that existed before as if with an invisible borderline.

The road winds through some hills. On one of the bends the Ural gets stuck again. I prod Kotenochkin with my rifle, the column halts and I look at the Ural. The driver looks in his mirrors and reverses, lifts his head and for some reason stares me right in the eye. Still looking at me, he shifts the gear stick into first. At this moment a blast throws the hood upward and the cab door is blown open as a plume of flame engulfs the vehicle.

Between the fiery tongues I see the driver slide onto the ground from the open door. He falls into a pool of burning gasoline, makes a movement with his arm and freezes. Tracer rounds smack into his body.

I watch a person burning on the road and then shift my gaze up to the hillside. The tracer rounds are coming from up there, racing at the road in long, thin strings and then speeding up as they pass between Zyuzik and me. A few bullets strike the armor.

'Chechens!' someone screams fearfully.

'Dismount!' shouts the colonel. 'Defensive positions!'

We all jump down and scatter. Everything that's happening seems like some kind of rehearsal or a game I hadn't been warned about, and in which I have become an unwitting participant.

Kotenochkin starts firing upward and is joined by the sergeant-major, Zyuzik and Andy. What are they firing at? I don't see anything, the sun is shining straight in my eyes and the top of the hill is just a blur.

I pull Andy by the sleeve. 'Who's up there, where are you firing?'

He doesn't answer, jerks his arm free and pulls the trigger again, his face set in concentration.

I start firing too, loosing short bursts upward and searching with my eyes to see if there is anyone to shoot at properly.

Bullets sing over my head, surprisingly melodically. A few hit the ground near my right foot, sending dust and stones flying into my face. I get scared and crouch down, raise my rifle above my head and blindly let off a few bursts.

My hearing comes back as if the sound has been switched on, and the roar of the shooting batters my ears. Time seems to slow down and regain normal dimensions.

The sound of heavy machine guns now drowns out everything

else and it seems my eardrums are about to burst. It's the carriers firing, aiming their turrets toward the hills, and the cannons have started up. Meanwhile, the carriers are maneuvering back and forth, ten yards forward and ten backward, but they can't escape the fire. The second truck is stuck on the bend and the driver is frantically spinning the wheel as he tries to turn around. I catch sight of his crazed eyes and his white lips, which are pursed in a grimace. Bullets strike the sides of the vehicle and blue candy wrappers flutter overhead.

The shooting dies down. Kotenochkin jumps up and runs up the hill. We run after him.

It turns out we were firing at a kind of barn at the top. The dirt floor is covered in cartridge cases and there is a used Fly launcher. The Chechens have only just left, the bushes are still moving and it seems I can hear twigs crackling underfoot. But we don't pursue them. Kotenochkin orders us to head back down.

The blown-up Ural truck stands still at the roadside. The dead driver lies near the wheel, his back all burned, charred ribs showing.

The driver of the second truck managed to reverse and he survived. They put the dead driver under our carrier's turret. As we drive he keeps slipping down onto me. At first I am afraid to touch him, but later I put my hand on his knee and press him to the armor. His knee is warm.

The sun is now shining brightly and the heat is unbearable. The clouds are dazzling white above. I want a drink and a smoke.

We bring two dead to the regiment and tow in the burned-out Ural.

'We're here,' says the sergeant-major as he jumps down. 'Welcome to the ass end of nowhere.'

It's hellishly hot. Tanks and carriers are dug into the ground, surrounded by tents and trenches.

Half-naked people wander between the tents with rifles slung around their necks. These are soldiers. There is not one Russian soldier in Chechnya who wears full uniform. White long johns cut off like shorts, slippers or sneakers on bare feet—that's what our entire army looks like. Grease-soaked tank crews change tracks, and someone squints at us from under his palm.

'Look!' Zyuzik says, touching my arm and pointing toward the command tent. Sitting nearby in just his underwear is Smiler, fiddling around with an engine part that he is holding to the ground with his bare feet. Bowlegged Sanya stands above him.

Smiler tears himself away from his work and looks at us.

'So, Tall Boy,' he says instead of a greeting and repeats the sergeant-major's words, 'welcome to the ass end of nowhere.'

The plains of Chechnya are surrounded by mountains and we are literally at the bottom of a giant, scorched bowl. The air is scorched, and the armored vehicles, rifles, ammo boxes, tents, everything smells scorched. If you leave your boots out in the morning you can't pick them up until the sun goes down in the evening and they cool off. Then again, nobody wears boots; you can easily cripple your feet in them.

'You have to look after three things here,' explains Berezhnoi. 'Your feet, your teeth and your head. Make sure you brush your teeth twice a day—I'll break the jaw of anyone who doesn't. Throw your boots away and go barefoot, or your feet will rot and never heal. And keep your head down. If there's any shooting get back to your tent; they'll take care of it without you.'

I like Berezhnoi. He treats us well, doesn't beat us and teaches us everything he can. We follow his advice and go barefoot. Andy even cuts off his long johns to the knee, revealing his white calves like a seaside vacationer. I don't go that far, I don't feel I have served long enough.

Thirst torments us in the sweltering heat and we are always stealing water from the kitchen. Our company has two ten-gallon tubs of water made out of ten empty howitzer shell cases and a plastic child's bath. One of our duties is to fill these to the top every day, which isn't as easy as it sounds. The company gets allocated four gallons of water (not enough for everyone to even drink their fill), and it's up to us to find the rest. The kitchen is run by a contract soldier named Sergei, who now knows us by sight and gives us a thrashing if he catches us. So we try to sneak up to the water truck unobserved.

The driver of the water truck is from Moscow like me, and this solves a lot of problems. Every morning he sets off for Achkhoi-Martan with an armored escort, and every morning we try to intercept him on the way back. An observer is perched like a hawk on an ammo box in front of the tent. When a cloud of dust rises over Achkhoi-Martan we grab our containers and race to intercept the truck. If we make it, Zhenya is happy to fill us up. It's the tastiest water, still so icy cold that it makes your teeth tingle, and it has no chlorine.

Today we overslept and missed the water run. Pan bursts into our dugout and drags us out by the feet, and we dash with the bathtub to the kitchen, hoping that there is some left there.

Abandoning all caution and happy to find a taut flow of water we catch it with our lips. It's cold and tart-smelling—the medics have already dumped two cups of chlorine into it. We scoop it up in our palms without spilling a drop—we're aware of its value. Then Sergei appears. You can smell the stale alcohol a mile off; he's evidently on a bender lasting more than a day.

'Hell, you fuckers again,' he mumbles and kicks Pan with all his might, catching him in the coccyx. Pan cries out and falls doubled up onto his back. He lies moaning in the puddle of drinking water that has formed at the wheels of the truck and is unable to get up. Sergei seems to have hit some nerve end.

'What the fuck are you moaning for, dickhead, you think you're injured or something? Get up! Stand at attention! One of these days I'll shoot all of you, you assholes,' he shouts as we line up in front of him with the containers. 'I'm sick to death of you, and I'm going to hand you to my eagles who will tear you to shreds! Won't you, eagles?' he asks his cooks, who are cleaning pans on a table next to the water truck.

The cooks all have an unbelievably haggard look about them. They are even more wretched than we are. Sergei continually batters them about in punishment for something, or just for the hell of it, and makes them sweat away for twenty hours a day. The cooks are caked from head to toe in a layer of stinking fat that doesn't wash off, and the skinniest one has a string of spaghetti hanging from his ear.

'Yes, we'll rip them apart,' they answer.

The skinny one brushes his ear with the back of his hand.

'They'll rip you apart, you just remember that,' warns Sergei. 'If I catch you again I'll have your hides. Dismissed.'

We go to our tent, not forgetting to take our containers with us. We didn't even manage to fill the bathtub, which Pan carries along, limping and rubbing the base of his spine.

'Bastard, almost broke my ass,' he says with a moan.

We sit in the perimeter trench, heads drawn into our shoulders, listening into the darkness. The darkness of the southern nights is impenetrable. If you peer a long time into the dark you tire quickly, so we sit with our eyes closed. It even seems I can hear the lice moving in Pan's armpits. He too is sitting motionlessly, but I know he's not asleep.

Just over the top of the trench there's a minefield so we don't worry too much—if someone comes this way we are sure to hear. But the rebels can still remove the trip wires and we have to watch out for this.

A carrier towers over us like a mountain. We hear voices from inside and chinks of light show from the loosely closed hatches. That's bad—any light is visible through night sights from a long way off, making the carrier a prime target.

Pan and I have crawled to the far end of the trench so we don't get hit if the rebels decide to loose a couple of Fly rockets at its side.

Sanya occasionally opens the hatch and bothers Pan and me about something, either to bring him candy or to go and scour for smokes or whatever. I feel a mix of love and hate for the guys in the carrier. They're assholes, but if the shit goes down then these two recon guys with their carrier will be the most important people on earth for me. All I have is a rifle and four magazines.

There's marijuana growing on the minefield. A whole field of weed that reaches as far as the mountains. I suggest to Pan that we pick a couple of bushes.

'You can't even spit there,' he says. 'There are trip wires just beyond the trench and then land mines.'

I give up the idea.

The hatch on the carrier swings open once again and Sanya appears.

'Radiomen! You, Tall Boy!' he says in my direction. 'Got any candy left?'

'Yes, Sanya, in the tent.'

'Go and get them then.'

I get up and see Pan looking at me.

'Don't go,' he says.

'Why not?'

'Why are you running errands for them? They've got their own greenhorns, let their guys run errands for them.'

'What are you piping up for? I'll smash your head in with a rifle butt, you piece of crap!'

'Sanya, you know Fixa doesn't let them run errands like that for you,' Pan says in justification.

Fixa is a serious argument. To me he is the most important guy in the regiment. He wants to get the communications team standing on its own feet and tells us not to do the recon's bidding. He is my senior and his every word is gospel. We just have to listen to him and do what he says.

'I couldn't give a damn about your Fixa, that dumb *dembel*. I'll go and smash his head in right now. So, Tall Boy, get moving.'

I get up and go for the candy in silence.

'Climb on,' Sanya says when I return with a handful of caramels and a bottle of lemonade.

He is wearing his webbing over his bare torso, sunglasses (even though it's pitch black), bullet belts around his neck and a Kalashnikov on his knee. Rambo. He sets off the whole picture with a beret and the recon badge of a bat with its wings spread against a globe.

I climb up and sit next to him, my back resting against the barrel of the machine gun. Sanya offers me a couple of my own candies: 'Help yourself,' he says. I take some and we chew.

'Where are you from, Tall Boy?'

'Moscow.'

'Ah. Have you seen Red Square?'

I nod.

'Me too. I've been to Moscow twice, not bad. But where I'm from is better.'

'Where's that then, Sanya?'

'Nizhny Novgorod.'

The hatch opens and Boxer climbs out holding a gun magazine in his hand. He looks at me for a second and hurls it at me. A loaded magazine is pretty heavy and it gives me a hard crack on the head.

'What the hell are you sitting in front of the barrel for, dickhead!' he yells. 'Get the hell out of the way, I nearly shot you, you idiot.'

I move over.

'Pick up the magazine,' he orders and goes back inside the hatch.

He swings the turret around and lets off a long burst of fire at the mountains. The shells disappear with a rustle toward the peaks and the gorge lights up when they explode. When the noise dies down, Sanya calls me again. It's a running dispute between him and Boxer: who's the boss and which one I will obey, just like a dog. If I climb up on top again, Boxer will give me a thick ear; if I don't, then Sanya will.

I decide that Sanya is better and climb up again next to him.

'Hey, you got any weed?' he asks.

'No,' I answer. I don't like this conversation as I realize where it's heading.

'How about you go and get some?'

I shake my head.

He clambers over and lowers his head toward me. 'Do you

hear me? Go and rip up some weed. Well? Are you going or not?'

'Sanya, don't, he'll get blown up,' Pan says from the trench.

'No, he won't. So are you going?'

'No,' I say hoarsely, my throat drying up in anticipation of the blows. 'No, Sanya, I'm not going.'

'Is that so? We'll see about that. Now fuck off.'

I jump down from the carrier and return to the trench.

A mortar bombardment is a strange thing. It seems nothing is happening: the village stands unaltered a half mile away, the metal roofs are still shining and the only visible movement is the plane trees swaying in the wind. But the mortar shells are coming from there and explode among us. You can't see them flying or who is firing them. Death just appears as if from nowhere. No shot, no flash, it materializes from thin air and lands with a sharp whistling sound among the soldiers clinging to the ground.

I sit in the trench, my cheek pressed against the dirt, clutching my rifle as I watch soil crumble from the walls in the blasts. Behind me, having just as much fun, are Andy, Zyuzik and Pan. Our whole battalion is now sitting in trenches, pressed into the earth, waiting.

Time has long since lost its meaning. I don't know how long we sit here like this, a month, a century, longer? But it's only a few hours.

We open fire on the village, aiming at the source of the mortar shells. Our bullets disappear into the yards of houses, and once again everything is just the same, the roofs shine and the trees sway, and death and emptiness. It's just nonsense, some idiotic dream.

The shells finally stop falling. We wait awhile and then climb out of the trench. The ground is a mass of craters as if the earth has suffered from chickenpox. A few shells have landed in the pond and turned it inside out. Mud and slime float on the surface and the water has turned black.

We have one dead guy, a tank crewman, killed by the very first shell. He is still lying there covered in his ground cloth. Another guy had a leg torn off.

It turns out there is nothing out of the ordinary about war. It's still just ordinary life, only taking place in very tough conditions with the constant knowledge that people are trying to kill you.

Nothing changes when someone dies. We still steal water at the kitchen, eat foul-tasting milk soup and get smacked in the eye. We live the same life that people lived in the steppe a thousand and even ten thousand years ago, and death here is just another natural phenomenon like hunger, thirst or a beating.

Sometimes the bombardments are pretty intensive and then turn into firefights. Occasionally underbarrel grenade launchers join in and we shoot in the dark at the red flashes. The carrier cannon opens up, and then everything goes quiet again. Sometimes one of our guys gets killed or wounded, sometimes not.

After the bombardment we sit in the trenches until morning with our rifles pressed to our cheeks. One of us keeps watch, the others listen, no one sleeps. At night the diesel generator chugs away but the noise doesn't bother us; it merged long ago with the other night noises and we don't notice it any more.

In the morning life begins anew. The water truck arrives and we take containers and go and steal water, and in the kitchen we get our ears boxed. And that's all there is to it.

We get sent to the Severny airport in Grozny. The city is in ruins—nothing is left here, not a single house, not a single tree, not a single person. The streets, sewn with craters, are heaped with bricks and branches, with the odd body still lying unretrieved in the mess.

This is our first visit to Grozny and our heads turn in all directions as we take in the dead city.

There is shooting on all sides, uninterrupted for even a second. But there is no one to be seen, and it's not clear who is shooting at whom. Fighting rages in the courtyards that we race past without stopping.

'It's like Stalingrad,' shouts Zyuzik, trying to outshout the roar of the head wind. No one answers.

I always used to think that war was black and white. But it's in color.

It's not true what the song says, that birds don't sing and trees don't grow in war. In fact, people get killed in the midst of such vivid color, among the green foliage of the trees, under the clear blue sky. And life hums on all around. The birds brim with song, the grass blooms with brightly colored flowers. Dead people lie in the grass, and they are not a bit scary in appearance as part of this multicolored world. You can laugh and chat alongside them—humanity doesn't freeze and go crazy at the sight of a body. It's only frightening when people shoot at you.

And it's very frightening that the war is in color.

*

On the way back from the airport our column comes under fire. We hurtle along a wide street and they take potshots at us from the windows of houses. There are so many of them it seems like bullets are coming from every window.

Two vehicles are knocked out but the column doesn't stop to pick up the wounded. Survivors try to jump onto the moving vehicles, jumping and scrabbling at the handles. One grabs hold and he is pulled aboard.

I am lying on my back and firing at the windows. We are all firing at the windows. The carrier shakes along and the bursts of fire fan out, sending spouts of dust from the walls.

Above me is the bright blue sky. You can't kill people with such beauty around.

A burst of fire sweeps a soldier off the carrier in front of us. Our driver doesn't manage to swerve around him and he flies under our wheels. The carrier jumps and I hear the crunching of bone.

We emerge from the field of fire. We have come to the end of the street. I don't understand why I am alive.

I really want to know what the street is called, and it seems so important to me that I go and ask the sergeant.

He is standing near the tent and drinking water straight from a hose. Water runs down his chin, washing the dust from his skin.

'Who cares,' he says hoarsely. 'I don't know. Maybe it's Lenin Street, maybe not.'

We brought seventy-three new conscripts to the regiment. Two vehicles were burned out, thirteen men were killed, eight more are missing in action.

*

Fighting rages on in Grozny. No one collects the bodies any more and they lay on the asphalt and on the pavement, between the smashed trees, as if they are part of the city.

Carriers rumble over them at speed, and they get tossed around by explosions. Blackened bones are scattered around charred vehicles.

When it gets dark, strange silhouettes in skirts appear on the streets, lots of them, wandering from curb to curb, stopping at the corpses. They turn them over onto their backs and study their faces for a long time.

We can't figure out who they are, and meanwhile the silhouettes steadily approach us.

'Maybe it's some kind of mountain tribe. Maybe the highlanders here wear skirts like the Scots,' ventures Osipov.

No one replies.

The moon shines over the dead on the street and ghosts in skirts wander between the bloated corpses.

Someone's nerves don't hold out and he opens fire, joined by two or three others. They fire a few bursts and even drop one of the silhouettes before cries are heard from over there.

Women's voices shout in Russian and we finally realize that these are the mothers of soldiers; they have come here to find their missing sons and are searching for them among these mangled bodies.

'Hold your fire!' shouts Loop. 'They're mothers, our mothers!'

Some of the women run over to the one who fell. She is wounded and they pick her up and carry her into one of the courtyards.

The mothers have it worst of all in this war. They don't belong to either side, they get the brushoff from the Russian generals in Khankala or Severny, our soldiers shoot them. And as one priest we freed from captivity told me, the Chechens take them off into the mountains and rape them, kill them and feed their innards to their dogs. They have been betrayed by everyone, these Russian women, they die by the dozen, yet still they wander around Chechnya with their photos, searching for their sons.

At dawn there are even more of them. They move from one body to another, study the mangled faces for a long time, holding a handkerchief over their mouths. They don't cry—in the heat it's hard to breathe near the bodies.

One woman manages to find her son. The commanders give her a vehicle and she takes the body to Khankala.

No one collects the other bodies.

'Hey, Russians,' the Chechens shout from one of the houses. 'Take your guys away! We won't fire, pick them up!'

The next night our side brings up a bulldozer and pushes all the bodies into a crater. No one bothers them and they bury them all during one night.

Then the Chechens start killing our guys they took prisoner. They shout from the end of the street to get our attention and show a few soldiers, badly beaten and with their hands tied behind their backs. The Chechens laugh and shout something at us in their language and then quickly put one of the prisoners on his side on the asphalt, pin his head with a foot and stab him twice in the throat with a knife. The boy jerks his tied hands and whimpers, and a black trickle spreads from his slashed throat onto the road.

The Chechens go back around the corner, leaving him to die on the asphalt.

He lies a long time on his side without moving, and then he starts to twitch. He jerks his bound hands and tries to turn over as if he is uncomfortable, then he falls quiet again. It is painful for him to move and he obediently lies on his side, with a gaping throat that keeps pumping a black trickle. When we think he is already dead he starts to twitch again and tries to crawl, then goes still again. This goes on a long time. Blood pours from his throat and smears across his face. His jacket has slipped down to his elbows, and when he jerks his arms blood spurts from an artery onto his bare shoulder.

'Bastards!' says Murky, unable to bear it any longer. He jumps up and shouts over the buildings, 'Just kill him you fuckers! Shoot him you bastards. Bastards!'

He unslings his rifle but Osipov and Loop manage to grab the barrel. They grip his arms and press him to the ground.

Murky squats, holding his head in his hands and moaning.

'Bastards, bastards, bastards,' he whispers.

The boy soon starts to choke; he can't breathe and blood sprays from his mouth as he coughs. Sometimes he loses consciousness for a while and lies motionless, then he comes to and once again tries to crawl.

When he stops moving altogether the Chechens shoot him in the back with tracer rounds. The bullets pass through his body and ricochet into the sky.

They also kill the rest of the prisoners. This time they don't appear from around the corner; all we hear are screams. Before they cut each boy's throat, they shout *Allahu akbar*. We hear this several times, and an hour later they throw the bodies out onto the street.

Pan gets wounded. A bullet goes through his cheek, knocking out his front teeth and exiting on the other side.

'Pretty good, Pan, a nice flesh wound that'll heal in time for your wedding, you'll see,' Andy says.

'Teeth are no big deal,' agrees Zyuzik. 'They can make such

great dentures now that you can't tell them from the real thing, isn't that right?'

'Oh yes,' I say, backing him up.

We are standing in front of the helicopter pad, smoking and looking at Pan as he lies on a stretcher, looking up at us.

'You're lucky, Pan,' says Andy. 'You're going home.'

He doesn't answer. Without thinking Andy had stuck three shots of promedol into him, and Pan is under so deep that he seems not to take in what's happening to him.

His wound really isn't serious, considering the damage a bullet in the face could do: rip your jaw out or take off the whole lower part of your head. Pan just got holes in his cheeks and front teeth knocked out. A helicopter will come for him and off he'll go to the hospital.

We don't say anything to each other but I know what my pals are thinking: every one of us would like to be in Pan's place. Every time they take a wounded guy to the hospital—even the most serious cases that have lost legs or arms—we all want to be in his place.

Authors of lousy war books say that it's better to be dead than a legless cripple, but that's bullshit, of course. We know that the main thing is to live, and we are willing to live in whatever form that may be, even as a bluish trunk with no arms or legs on a beggar's trolley. We just want to live. To live, not die. That's all there is to it.

We give Pan water and he gulps a few times, leaking water from the holes in his cheeks. He finds this funny and deliberately squirts us. Clots of blood plug up the holes, and he pokes them free with his dirty fingers and sprays the grass. We swear at him; there isn't much water to go around and we gave him our last.

At last the chopper arrives. The blades whip up clouds of

dust from the ground and we crouch down, shielding our faces with our hands. The medics cover Pan's head with a blanket, and without waiting for the rotors to stop they run him over to the aircraft.

'Pan! Pan!' shouts Andy, but Pan doesn't hear.

The helicopter flies off. We sit on the grass and light up. Andy spits and throws a long cigarette butt onto the ground. He's stressed out. I pick the end up and finish it. Nerves or no nerves, it's a crime to throw away such a big dog end. I take a few more puffs until the cinders start to singe my fingers and I stamp it out.

The battalion is seized by TNT fever. Everybody is busy searching for shells, trading cigarettes for them, getting them from friends, begging or stealing them. Then they melt the TNT from them. No one knows what it's for. They say you can get a good price for it in Grozny's central market, but this seems doubtful to me. Why would the Chechens need to buy explosives when Grozny is already overflowing with unexploded shells that are littering the streets waiting to be collected? Once I even saw an unexploded five-tonner, an enormous bomb like a hot air balloon. It lay in the middle of a crater like a fat pig in a puddle of mud, its tail dug into the ground. You could get five tons of TNT in one go from that, so why waste time on small-fry shells. And even if they are buying explosives at the market, we can't get there.

This doesn't deter anyone and the soldiers keep on melting the stuff out. It's very simple to do. You just have to unscrew the detonator and put the shell into a fire, and that's all. A while later the stuff leaks out in the form of liquid plasticine. The heat doesn't trigger it and it only blows from a fuse or an electronic impulse, so it's perfectly safe.

Loop extracted enough to fill a whole backpack and now

carries it with him as if it contains the currency reserves of a superpower.

In the day he keeps his knapsack in the commander's carrier, right under Major Bondar's seat. If anyone else had tried to stash a sack full of explosives under a commander's seat they'd have found it immediately. Just imagine what would have ensued if the company commander had found out that one of his own soldiers had stuck fifty pounds of TNT under his backside! But Loop always gets away with it.

We smelt explosives until a shell goes off in someone's hands. How this happened, no one knows. The blast throws him a few dozen yards, straight over headquarters and onto the battalion commander's carrier. The poor guy had his chest blown out, leaving a big gaping hole in the middle of his body.

But Loop doesn't empty his backpack and continues to use it as a pillow.

'It doesn't hurt to have some stock,' he says, plumping it with his fist before settling down for the night.

He's right. The explosives are already extracted, so there's no sense in throwing them out.

It won't help the dead guy, will it?

'So why did we learn this stupid Morse code then?' grumbles Loop, rinsing the bathtub before he goes on the next water run to the kitchen. 'What's the point of it? No one uses it in the army any more. All we do is steal water and get knocked around, and that's about the sum total of our military learning. They'd do better to give me the money they spent on my training. I'd find a use for it all right.'

He's right. Morse has been redundant for twenty years and no one has any use for it here. I can't imagine a radio operator in combat will start tapping out dots and dashes and send a coded message. At moments like that you shout and swear down the line, forgetting all about codes and call signs, and just blurt everything straight out.

'That's right,' says Andy. 'It would make more sense to teach us how to shoot.'

'Fuckers, all of them,' says Loop. 'I'm telling you, we're nothing but cannon fodder. Replaceable cannon fodder, and cheap with it, just 18,500 rubles a month for 165 pounds live weight.'

'Private Zhikh! You are panic-mongering! Or do you regard the constitutional order of our Motherland as just so many words? For such faintheartedness you deserve to go into the first wave of the attack without body armor,' I say, dressing him down so convincingly that I have him fooled.

Loop crumples like he just took a blow in the gills, and his eyes are suddenly fearful.

'No, no, not that,' he whispers. 'Let me at least wear a helmet.'

'Stand at attention Private when a senior rank is talking to you,' I say menacingly. 'Remember I'm a sergeant.'

Andy and I are indeed already sergeants while Loop is still a corporal. I got the rank for nothing after Savchenko stole a stamp from headquarters and used it to bump me up in my service book, almost up to lieutenant. Andy got his third stripe back in training for exemplary service. But none of it means anything: we still get beaten up the same as the privates, or maybe worse. To be higher in rank having served less time is an unforgivable transgression. 'So you're a sergeant are you?' the *dembels* say before they give you a couple of extra smacks. That's why I never wear the stripes. No one does. All that counts is how long you have served.

'Now, tell me pronto,' says Andy, joining in the game, 'what is task number 41 for using special equipment? In doing so you will render the Motherland a great service.'

'Comrade Sergeants! Fuck yourselves!' comes Loop's clipped reply as he stands at attention. His eyes are ablaze with zeal to sacrifice his insignificant life for the good of Russia's constitutional order.

'Bad, Corporal Zhikh, very bad,' says Andy, imitating the commander of our training company, Major Remez. 'Perhaps you don't know the tactical and technical characteristics of the P-111 radio unit? Let's hear them!'

Loop rattles off the characteristics from the manual by heart. Andy and I stand there gawping at him. I've pretty much forgotten all of it but now it stirs in my memory. It's hard to forget the Morse code if you have it beaten into your head with a heavy army stool every day for six months. We would learn it parrot-like, lying on our fronts. A blow in the kidneys is the best way to stimulate a thirst for knowledge.

'God, we spent six months learning this shit!' Andy says with astonishment.

'Who needs it anyway?'

'Yes, indeed,' I say. 'We learned all this shit as if our lives depended on it. But no one explained to us how to stanch blood, or pinpoint a sniper in night fighting, or steal water from the kitchen.'

'Fuckers,' says Andy. 'All of them, one big group of fuckers.'

You could say a soldier is the simplest creature in the universe. When we are terrified we are afraid, when we are sad we mope, when something's funny we laugh. No, we never forget; each day of war weighs down heavily on our souls, and someday we'll be left to face our memories. But today this is the furthest thing from our thoughts. We are alive, what else do we need? After all, we are still just boys, with imaginations to match.

'If I were in government, I'd propose setting up a special

firing range to be set up where countries would send troops to sort out their differences,' says Oleg. 'Like here, in Chechnya. No really, where Russia could lease out Grozny. If, say, Israel and Palestine wanted to go a few rounds with each other, they could send their armies here and go for it. Whoever wins gets to run the show in Jerusalem. And the money from the leasing could be given to our wounded who've lost arms and legs. Then at least they wouldn't beg in the underground.'

'Even better, let the foreign intelligence services in here. Let them learn how to fight terrorism in real-life conditions.'

'Not a damn thing would come of that,' says Murky. 'You'd have to put the Chechens on allowances and pay them a wage. They wouldn't last long anyway: the Germans or even the Israelis would make short work of the rebels. They'd drive them into the mountains and blow them to bits with self-propelled guns. What kind of war is this anyway? First we fight, then we don't, then we advance, then we pull back!'

Meanwhile, stories of horrors elsewhere in Chechnya kept filtering back to us. A friend of mine told me how his battalion entered some village or other. It didn't get shelled much and was almost intact, but around the main square were large crosses upon which Russian soldiers had been crucified. They'd been nailed up by their hands and each had a few bullet holes in his chest. They had all been castrated.

The commander ordered them to do a sweep through the village. All the men who could be found were herded into the square. They were thrown down in piles and then our soldiers started to hack them up. One guy pinned a Chechen to the ground with his foot while another pulled off his pants and with two or three hefty slashes severed his scrotum. The serrated blade of the knife snagged the skin and pulled the blood vessels from his body.

In half a day the whole village was castrated, then the battalion moved out. Our dead men remained on the crosses—special units removed them later.

One day we get sent to the command center in Kurchaloi, this time accompanying an engineer reconnaissance group. Every morning while it is still dark we set off with the engineers along the same route, down Dzhokhar Dudayev Street to the crossroads, then right into the private residential sector and then a few miles down the road. We pass two signs over the gates: 'Soldier, don't touch anything—it's dangerous!' and 'Soldier, careless talk costs lives!' They put up the second sign after a wizened old man went up to one of our boys and asked him the way to headquarters. As the boy turned away the old guy pulled out a pistol and shot him in the back of the head.

We exit through the gate and split up into groups. Ahead goes an engineer with a mine detector—today it's Pashka—and behind him two guys with metal prodders, Slav and Tom. Two more move along the roadside and check the undergrowth and the milestones. One is called Vasily, the other I don't know, some small, fair-headed kid, easygoing and with a ready laugh. More often than not these are the ones who get the 'Christmas presents' left by the rebels.

Loop, Andy and I and a few others follow behind the engineers, and behind us crawls our covering carrier like a lazy brontosaurus. We have to go about six miles and then turn back. We know this road back to front by now, down to the last dent and stone. The engineers remove about three or four land mines a month here. Generally they are simple things, made from a length of pipe or an artillery shell, but sometimes there are some nasty surprises. Once we found a football containing a light-sensitive trigger. Another time, in Grozny, the Chechens slaughtered a whole barracks, laid them in a row on the road and cut their throats. We didn't see this ourselves, though. When we got there, there was no one in the bunker, just a can of condensed milk in the middle of the road, and underneath it what we call a 'petal,' a mean little mine that doesn't kill but only cripples you, tearing off half your foot or your toes. Pincha threw a loop of wire around it, jumped in the ditch and tipped the can over. After the blast, we scooped the sticky-sweet stuff with our dirty fingers right there at the barracks where they killed our boys.

It wasn't sacrilege; they were already dead and beyond caring. Every one of us could have been in their place. And if they had still been alive, we would have done all we could to get them out. But they were dead.

We walk slowly. Pashka sweeps from side to side with the detector; Slav and Tom dig at the ground with their prodders. I keep an eye on the roadsides. Finally the fair-headed engineer raises his hand: Caution! We crouch down and the carrier stops behind us. The boy goes to the edge of the road, kneels down and gingerly parts the grass with his hands. This is the most dangerous moment. If a land mine has been planted there, then there can be a bearded bastard lurking nearby ready to detonate it. The rebel will kill the boy and then nail us all from the undergrowth with bursts of rifle fire.

I lie down on the ground and press my cheek to the dust. Loop does the same on the other side of the road. Through the parted grass I see a long object. The boy reaches out and touches the shell. Then he picks it up.

'It's just an empty case,' he says.

The next time our find is a piece of pipe from a drilling rig that they use to bore into the ground when they look for water. Next to it there is a coil of wire and a box of nails hidden in the grass. We put the drill onto the carrier, intending to blow it up later, in case the Chechens are still tempted to pack it with TNT and nails, and we proceed.

We stop where Igor was killed. He got blown up two weeks ago. The plaster on the sides of the houses still bears the marks of the shrapnel that killed him. The mine was attached to a tree at the height of a person and there wasn't even a crater to remind us of him.

'Well, come on,' says Pashka.

We remove from the carrier a homemade cross that Pashka has fashioned from some water pipes. There is a plaque on it that says 'Igor Ivanchenko 1977–1996.' We dig it into the ground and stand there silently for a while. We haven't got any vodka and we pay our respects just as we are. I hardly remember him; he died the day after we arrived and all I recall is that he was tall and stocky.

There's another cross on the next street. That's Hamster. He got blown up three days after Igor. We'll stop there next.

'Come on,' says Pashka, taking a last puff on a cigarette end and picking up the mine detector.

'Watch out!' Slav says on the bend, raising his hand.

We crouch down.

There are no rear positions here, nowhere to withdraw to for a rest, but we still get some days of peace. On these days we stop being soldiers and become normal boys; we may have a laugh or we're just tired, and more often than not we're pissed off and irritated, but we're boys all the same. On those days we throw off our uniforms and the war with them. We stop talking about death and killing, we shed any thoughts of all the terrible things that happened to us the day before and we simply live. And for this reason every minute seems sharp and fresh.

We strut around in our cut-off long johns and play, having been short-changed in play when it was peacetime. The urge to fool around is still very strong in us. We catch tarantulas and put them in glass jars, or gorge on candy, washing them down with condensed milk, or we fire off bullets. Not even heavy bombardments could kill our boyish fascination with weapons, and when it's quiet we shoot tracer rounds into the sky or fire at jars.

We are strange boys—we have grown-up eyes and grown-up conversations; many of us already have gray hair and our eyes no longer light up with glee, even when we smile. Yet we are still boys.

But as soon as the fighting starts the mischief vanishes in an instant and all that remains is the need to survive. We cease being human and become killing machines. Boys? We have the same arms and muscles as adults, and although we are weaker than fully grown men, we are just as good at placing the crosshairs on a moving figure and pulling the trigger. Pincha and Murky aren't even nineteen but they have already killed people. We don't have an age any more. We have no hobbies or interests. We are turning into animals, honing our hearing like a cat's while our eyes detect the slightest movement. We know when to freeze and lie still, when to run across open ground, we can find our bearings at night and gauge the distance to a machine gun from the sound of it firing. Each of us can drop to the ground a split second before a shell explodes and there's no way of explaining how we know. All we can do is survive: you may be sitting by a fire or running across a yard, and before you know it you are lying facedown on the ground with bits of soil showering onto your back and head, and you realize that a bombardment has started. You didn't even hear the whistle of the shell or the report of the gun but you feel the projectile as it flies through the air, sense it with every cell in your body, which suddenly crumbles into a billion molecules and becomes as big as the universe. And you feel every cell inside you crying out to live—just live! And an unbelievable fear consumes your entire body and there you are, lying on the ground, with pieces of shrapnel flying over your head and not one of them even touches you. If we were to rely on our sense and judgment we'd have been dead long ago. Instinct works faster.

This is life itself talking inside us, making us fall and look for a deep enough hollow in the ground while it turns over inside us like a slippery cold worm. It's the only thing that saves us.

We sometimes surpass adults in our cruelty, simply because we are young. Children are cruel by nature, and this cruelty is the only bit of our true age that remains. And it helps us to live and to kill others.

In war a person is basically not himself at all but some other kind of creature. We don't have just five senses; there is a sixth, seventh, tenth even, growing from our bodies like tentacles and grafting themselves onto the war. And through them we feel the war. You can't talk about war with someone who has never been there, not because they are stupid or dim-witted but because they don't have the senses to feel it with.

A heavy red sun descends on the horizon. We are dying together with the sun. We have no age—our life is but one day. We are born as babies at dawn, reach maturity by midday and die in the evening. We hustle and bustle as we live out our lives. Now we are already old men. We are twenty-two hours and fifteen minutes old.

The next regiment lost fifteen men at once. They were driving in an armored Ural when a Fly rocket tore into them. The truck had windows, so they didn't all die. The survivors got out clutching their heads, vomiting, blood running from their noses and ears. They crouched down and lit cigarettes, their hands trembling, while other soldiers looked at them and thought: *The lucky fuckers survived a rocket hit on a Ural and now they'll be loaded into helicopters and flown to a hospital.* Yes, they're in bad shape; they're vomiting, they probably have ruptured kidneys and lungs, they can't hear a thing and might not be able to speak for a while, but they survived and that's all that matters.

All these people did die in the end. The impact was so powerful that they succumbed to the aftereffects within a day, and nobody survived the explosion inside the truck.

They call another cease-fire. This time the truce is for a month and we are under strict orders not to rise to provocation. Those who disobey are given to the Chechens for investigation, and a worse fate you couldn't think of. No one returns from that kind of investigation.

'For Christ's sake, what's going on at headquarters? Have they got straw for brains or something?' grumbles Loop.

'Fucking war,' says Osipov. 'Everything's been sold off, bought up by the highest bidder, I'm telling you.'

In Grozny they set up joint commandant's offices. Now the Chechen checkpoint stands next to ours and to pass along a road you have to stop twice, like at customs.

'How can there be a joint commandant's office?' Murky wonders. 'Are we all friends now or something? What about January '95? What did we fight for? This is treason! Listen, what's happening now is treason through and through, there's no two ways about it. So all those deaths were for nothing?'

So the Chechens set up their checkpoint next to ours. Their commander is a young guy, a rocket man. There are seven notches on the shaft of his RPG launcher, which he tells us means he's knocked out seven of our vehicles and killed at least twenty-one guys. He laughs, talks loudly and is perfectly good-humored.

We are not allowed into town. Soldiers get killed there at the drop of a hat; youths will immediately surround a lone soldier, drag him into a corner and slit his throat.

We pull out of Grozny, surrender the city, and the Chechens are jubilant; they openly drive through the streets in cars, waving their green flags and carrying weapons. We can do nothing, our orders are explicit: Do not open fire. The rebels are now declared Chechen freedom fighters rather than bandits, and we are to treat them with respect.

We leave through streets that we took in combat only yesterday and try not to look to the side. The Chechens laugh behind us and make throat-slitting motions.

The war has hardly touched the village of Achkhoi-Martan and only a few houses have bullet holes in their gates as we wind our way through the streets. Hate-filled eyes watch us from behind the gates, windows and courtyards. No young men are visible, only old ones, women and children who stop and watch us driving past. God forbid that we break down here.

We sit there, the barrels of our weapons bristling. One movement and we will open fire; a single stone or bottle thrown at us and we'll tear this village to shreds.

Chechen kids are playing on the streets. When they see our column they raise a fist and shout 'Allahu akbar!' The older ones also draw a finger across their throats.

In Achkhoi-Martan we pass a checkpoint manned by Chechen militia officers who had fought on our side. As usual there is a site hut, but this one has been so riddled with bullets that not a single bit of it is unscathed. It's impossible to live inside, but that's their home now.

Two officers stand in front of the checkpoint, one of them wounded, his arm hanging in a dirty bandage. They watch our column in silence. Their entire arsenal amounts to two rifles. We know that they will probably be killed this very night, and they know it too. We have betrayed them.

'Don't leave us behind,' one of them says finally.

We turn away.

The column drives past and the dust settles on their hair and eyelashes.

I see them before my eyes for a long time after, these ghosts on the roadside at Achkhoi-Martan.

Forgive us, boys.

We stop before the bridge. The Chechens have set up their checkpoint here and don't let us go any farther. One with a green band around his head is unhappy about something and an argument starts between him and Kotenochkin.

'Shoot the bastard, what are you talking to him for?' says Osipov indignantly. 'Are they out of their minds, not letting the column through?'

I sit up top and watch to the right. Our column stands on the central square. Today is Saturday, market day, and it's busy. The Chechens have laid out pastries, canned food and water by the window of a destroyed department store and a brisk trade is under way.

A young Chechen is sitting on a folding chair right in front of me, selling cigarettes. He looks me in the eye, then says something to his neighbor and looks at me again. They laugh.

'What are you looking at?' he mouths at me, drawing his finger across his throat.

His wares are arrayed on a big table covered with a plastic sheet; he could easily have a rifle underneath it. All of the men on this square are armed, we know this, and we feel their superiority over us as we sit stuck here in this trap. One move from us and tracers will fly into the column—there are eyes and barrels at every window.

The Chechen is still looking at me and laughing. He's laughing as if he's killed me and I'm his trophy. He doesn't see me as a living person, all he sees is my severed head. I raise my rifle and aim it at his head. He also feels fear but the smile doesn't leave his face. Why doesn't he turn away? Why is he looking at me? I slip off the safety and put my finger on the trigger. He doesn't turn away, and his eyes are full of fear and defiance.

The column sets off and we pass over the bridge. There is a box of grenades at the feet of one of the Chechens standing on it: the bribe we gave to be let across.

If we had stood there for a few more seconds, I would have killed that Chechen. Then they would have blown up our column.

'Greater love hath no man than this, that a man lay down his life for his friends.'—John 15:13

We don't know what we are fighting for. We have no goal, no morals or internal justification for what we do. We are sent off to kill and to meet our deaths but why we don't know. We just drew the short straw, happened to be born eighteen years ago and grow up just in time for this war. And there our blame ends.

The only thing we have is hope, the hope that we will survive and preserve our sense of self, and be able to remain human beings.

We feel the injustice of it all so acutely with our eighteen years. Each one of us that survives this war will truly believe that such evil should never happen again.

We weren't fighting the Chechens; our real enemies were the lies and treachery that created this monstrous conflict. And every shell that was fired at us was fired at all the young men of this world who might so easily meet the same fate.

Every shell that hit us tore apart both the flesh and the soul. Our whole outlook on life crumbled and collapsed beneath this demonic fire, and there was nothing to fill the emptiness it left. The only thing we have left is ourselves and our brothers in arms. 'All we know of life is death,' as the song has it, all that we love is our past, a phantom mirage in this turbulent world. We were left with just one virtue—the will to look after those who stood beside us in combat. If anyone ever asks me, 'What were you fighting for?' I will reply, 'For those who clung to the ground next to me.' We fought only for each other. Our entire generation may have died in Chechnya, a whole generation of Russians. Even those of us who stayed alive—can they really be those same eighteen-year-old laughing boys who once got seen off to the army by their loved ones? No, we died. We all died in that war.

14/ Special Cargo

This is what happens to soldiers who die in Chechnya. *First they get hit by a bullet or shrapnel and then they fall and die. A day or two later someone might manage to slip a belt around the leg of the stiffened bodies and drag them out at a crawl under sniper fire. They wrap them up in the special silvery bags, load them onto a helicopter and take them to Rostov. In Rostov they are identified, welded into zinc coffins and shipped to Moscow.*

In Moscow they are met by soldiers at the airport or railway station, loaded into trucks and taken to another station or airport. Then they are loaded into plane holds or railroad cars and the boys go home.

The soldiers get back into the truck and return to the barracks at the first command regiment in Lefortovo. It's the same one that mounts the ceremonial guard at the airports to welcome visiting presidents of other countries. A show unit.

But in this ceremonial regiment there is one barracks, over to the right from the gatehouse. This is the 'diesel stop,' as they call it, where they gather deserters, those waiting to be sent to disciplinary battalions, soldiers who left their units for whatever reason, who got sidelined with a wound, or those who didn't return from leave on time or just went AWOL when they couldn't stand the bullying any more. Nearly all of them come here from Chechnya.

*They live for a while at the diesel stop, waiting to see if they'll be
sentenced or have their case closed and be sent to finish their service in
a normal unit. They are the ones who go for the 'special cargo,' carting
the zinc coffins around. Some smart commander with sadistic inclina-
tions decided that the diesel boys were fit to deal with the special cargo.
Probably so that they see their dead comrades and realize how wrong
they had been to flee from Chechnya and stay alive.*

The coffin was very heavy. Covered in rough, yellow planks, it
was almost seven feet long and three feet wide and tall. The
plaque nailed onto the head end was covered in snow. Wiping
it clean with his hand, Dachsie read it. 'A colonel. From Chechnya,' he said. 'Fuck, he's a heavy one. They must have eaten
their fill of government grub down there. Come on.'

Puffing, we grabbed the handles nailed along the side,
braced ourselves and shoved the coffin up into the truck.

Our boots slipped on the smoothly trampled crust of snow as
we tugged and pushed it, an inch at a time, into the back. With
a grunt we finally shoved it into place, nearly crushing the foot
of a porter who was helping. 'Well, let's go then.'

The commander of the group, a swarthy major with mean
eyes and bushy eyebrows, stood alongside the vehicle, stamping
his feet to keep warm. The frosty morning had chilled him to
the bone and he was irritated at how long we'd taken with the
coffin. Not that it occurred to the major to help—it was written
all over his arrogant face that to work side by side with his
subordinates was beneath his dignity as an officer.

'Where to now, Comrade Major?'

'Domodedovo airport. Come on, move it!' he barked, jumping
into the warm cab.

It was unbelievably cold. The wind whipped through the
tattered canopy as the truck raced around the Moscow beltway.

The sharp winter air mixed with prickly ice-cold grit that rushed in past the flap and went under our hats, froze on our eyelashes and blocked our nostrils.

I wasn't thinking about anything as I huddled on the bench seat. I was intensely cold and overcome by total apathy. Since the morning we had hauled our way through traffic jams for two hours to collect the colonel's body from the customs terminal at Vnukovo airport and then hung around there with the load, only to have to take it to Domodedovo now.

'Four more hours at least,' I calculated. 'We have to get there, then the major needs time to sort things out, unload and drive back . . . yes, four hours . . . I may lose my toes like this.'

Two pairs of wool socks and newspapers wrapped around my feet didn't help; my perpetually sodden boots were cold as hell and didn't retain any warmth. I had stopped feeling my toes long ago.

I tried to push my feet under the coffin to shield them from the wind. Sitting on the bench opposite me, Dachsie asked: 'Cold?'

'You can say that again.'

He moved over and sat on the coffin, bracing himself with one foot on the tailgate, got out a cigarette and handed it to me.

'It'll warm you up.'

Banging his foot on the side of the coffin, Dachsie said, 'I can't believe how fucking heavy this colonel is. And big too—look at the size of this coffin.'

He took a drag on his cigarette and exhaled the smoke thoughtfully. 'Maybe there's no colonel in there. Maybe they filled it with dirt for the weight, and then here you are, relatives, go ahead and bury him. You can't open the zinc up anyway. Yesterday we moved a kid from Tambov and the coffin was as light as anything—Whale and I lifted it on our own. The guys from his company who were coming home with him said there was just a leg inside. But it definitely belonged to him, so they said.'

I looked at Dachsie, who had been so nicknamed because of his lively character and long nose that he tends to stick in everything going on around him, like a dachshund digging at a burrow. A crude, simple villager's face but cunning nonetheless. And although he was only nineteen like the rest of us, his fast-receding hairline and the terminal weariness in his eyes indicated that he had had his share of tough times in his short life. As luck would have it Dachsie, like me, managed to wind up in the last draft that got sent to Chechnya and he got his taste of the war.

We were friends all right, but now, looking at his impudent face, I suddenly felt a sharp disdain for him, almost disgust. As he smoked, Dachsie had spread out on top of the coffin and lay there dangling his leg in the air. I looked at the plaque. Yes, just as I thought, we'd loaded the coffin bottom end and feet first, an unlucky portent with the dead, although I had never paid much attention to such superstitions. Feet or head first, so what, it didn't matter much to the colonel either way. But now the coffin lay there bottom-end first, and it occurred to me that Dachsie was sitting with his backside right over the colonel's face, that is, if the colonel still had a face. And it wasn't a nice thought.

'Get off the coffin.'

'What?' Dachsie asked, not hearing properly and leaning casually over to me.

'Get off the coffin, you prick!' I yelled. My disdain instantly turned to rage and I thought that if he started his usual monkey business I'd throw him out of the truck. He evidently sensed this too.

'Dickhead,' he replied, and without a trace of hurt he moved back onto the bench.

I looked at him as he gazed indifferently at the road. The rage disappeared as suddenly as it had surfaced, and I couldn't work out what had come over me.

We always sat on the coffins, providing there was no escort, and it had never bothered us. Coffins were much more comfortable than the low, frozen benches, and we were used to being in close proximity to death. Feigning mournful faces as we carted coffins around airports and stations five times a day was just stupid. It wasn't disrespect for the dead; it was just that these people had died and didn't give a damn where the kids moving them sat.

It could have been us that died; each of us had had plenty of chances to lie there rattling around in a truck behind the lines, lurching around frozen solid in our metal coffins. But we had been lucky and now we were moving those who had been less so.

We're all cynics, I thought every time I looked at the boys. We're only nineteen but we're already dead. How are we supposed to live now? How are we to sleep with girls after these coffins, or drink beer, and rejoice in life? We are worse than senile, hundred-year-old men. At least they are afraid of death; we're not afraid of anything, and we don't want anything. We are already old, since what is old age anyway if it's not living with memories of a past life? And all we have left is our past. The war was the main thing we had to do in our life and we did it. The brightest, best thing in my life was the war and there won't be anything better. And the blackest, lousiest thing in my life was also the war, and there won't be anything worse. So my life has been lived.

*

It grew dark. Nocturnal Moscow lit up its streetlamps and in the watery light of the bulbs the heavy, falling snowflakes seemed deceptively warm.

I was now frozen through. For six hours we'd bumped around in the utterly freezing, wind-blasted back of the truck and the cold had driven me to a state of exhaustion.

There was more space in the back of the truck after we handed over the colonel in Domodedovo, so now we stamped our feet on the floor and huddled together in an attempt to get warm, constantly rubbing our noses and cheeks, which were covered with white spots of frostbite. When the truck stopped at traffic lights pedestrians turned in puzzlement toward the source of the groans and swearing inside the truck.

I took off one boot and frenziedly rubbed my frozen foot. I stuffed the sock into my armpit to warm it up while I rubbed and rubbed my glassy toes, restoring the circulation.

A voluptuous blonde in a mink fur sitting behind the wheel of a red Nissan stared at me, her lips pursed in disgust. We were standing at the traffic lights by the Balchug hotel and I felt that my bare foot looked stupid in the center of Moscow. And here by the Balchug, among the expensive cars, casinos, dance halls, beer bars, girls, fun and general carefree air, I also felt run-down in my old, stained jacket and coarse boots, having endured four months of death, undercooked dog meat, corpses, lice, despair and fear.

'Stupid cow! What the hell are you staring at! I'd like to get you and your curls in the back of this truck, you fancy bitch!' I angrily looked into the blonde's eyes and then suddenly and to my own surprise I spat on the shiny red hood of the car.

The truck passed the gatehouse, turned onto the parade ground and stopped near the barracks. I heard the cab door slam and a second later the major's head appeared over the tailgate.

'Wait here. I'll report back to headquarters. Then I'll take you to supper.'

We stirred, tearing our frozen pants from the bench, and jumped down from the truck.

I was the last to approach the tailgate. I was afraid that my frozen legs would shatter into a thousand tiny pieces like cut glass from the impact of the asphalt, so I let everyone else out first, delaying the moment I had to jump.

Finally I climbed out over the tailgate, stood for a second and, looking down at the black frozen square and inhaling a little deeper, I leaped. A sharp pain hit my feet and pierced my whole body and it felt like a white-hot nail had been driven into the crown of my head. I groaned.

Stamping his feet, Dachsie came over and handed me a cigarette.

'Like hell I'm going to wait for him. As if I won't get any supper without his help! He'll spend half an hour in there talking while we freeze out here.'

He stood up straight and looked over at headquarters.

'Speak of the devil, there he is.'

The major was heading hurriedly toward us. Even before he reached us, he shouted: 'Where's the truck?'

I got a nasty ache in the pit of my stomach and looked at Dachsie, who looked back.

'Yeah, great supper we had.'

Dachsie stared with hatred at the major, spat and shouted back: 'Gone to the motor pool, Comrade Major, what happened?'

Panting, the major said, 'Someone go and get it, we have to make another run. To Kursk station and then to Kazan station. A mother and her son. Come on, look alive, they've already called several times. Now I'm going to catch hell from the regiment commander.'

Dachsie silently handed me a cigarette and we lit up. I sat back as comfortably as I could, stretching out with my foot resting on the zinc coffin's wooden covering. Then I remembered and drew it back quickly, glancing toward the back of the truck, where squeezed into a dark corner sat a little woman in a gray coat, taking a coffin containing her son back home. She sat quietly, hemmed in on all sides by soldiers, her vacant eyes staring blankly in front of her.

The woman's presence disturbed us. She had appeared just after we had jumped down from the back of the truck, swearing as usual, and grabbed hold of the coffin handles. She came up quietly and looked at the coffin, then leaned down and removed an ice-cream wrapper that had stuck to the underside. She did it like she was taking care of her son, as if he preferred to lie in a clean coffin. And she stood beside us watching as we loaded it into the truck.

We immediately bit our tongues and worked in silence after that, without looking at her, trying to be as careful as we could with the coffin, as if it were made of expensive crystal.

Her presence broke down the defensive shield that we threw up around ourselves with our swearing, spitting and profane joking. We felt guilty in front of her, the guilt any living person feels before the mother of a dead person. And although we had all been through the same experiences as her son, and every one of us had the same chances of being killed, and it wasn't our fault that we had stayed alive, still . . . We, the living, were now carrying her dead son back home, and not one of us could look into her empty eyes.

*

'Fall in!' the major ordered as soon as the truck stopped at the Kazan station goods yard.

What does he mean, 'fall in'? I thought as I jumped out of the truck, flapping my arms to try and warm up. Let's just unload as quickly as possible and go back. It must be five below and we haven't had a thing to eat since early morning.

The major came over, his officers' boots squeaking on the snow.

'I said fall in. Right here, in one line.'

Resentfully we did as ordered, giving the major surly looks and trying to figure out what he was up to.

The major strode around in front of us, his hands clasped behind his back. He smelled of the warm cab he'd been riding in. Finally he spoke.

'You committed a crime in wartime. You deserted the Motherland in her hour of need, cast your weapons aside and fled like cowards. Before you sits the mother of a soldier who did his duty to the end. You should be ashamed to stand in her presence . . .'

I didn't immediately understand what he meant. When it dawned on me I had a hot flash, frozen as I was. My palms became moist and I heard a roaring in my head. Son of a bitch, rear-lines scumbag who warmed his backside in the supplies regiment and now stands here telling us off. Now I'll tell you what's what, I'll tell you who should be ashamed!

Hardly aware of what I was doing I walked forward, fists clenched, and at that point my gaze met the mother's eyes.

She was sitting in the same pose in the back of the truck, quite still, watching us in silence with her empty eyes. She was completely engulfed by her grief and her gaze didn't fix on us but rather looked right through us to a place where her son was still alive.

The heat in me suddenly abated. I couldn't say anything in my defense, could offer no words of justification beneath this mother's gaze. Indeed I suddenly felt very ashamed. Ashamed of the major and his pat phrases, ashamed of how the major couldn't see the mendacity of his words, and how ridiculous his staged little show appeared. Ashamed for the army that had killed her son and had now put on this display in front of her, and ashamed of myself as a component of that army.

I wanted to sit down with her and tell her it wasn't true, this label of 'deserter' that the major had slapped on us; that it wasn't true I hadn't done my duty; that each of us had also died a hundred times; that I had come here to bury my own father, straight from the trenches, starving and lice-ridden. I wanted to tell her how I had intended to go back after the funeral but my body hadn't held out and I'd succumbed immediately to dysentery and pneumonia, and while I lay in the hospital my ten-day leave had run out. And about how, when I finally appeared at headquarters to be registered, they took away my belt and shoelaces on the spot, despite my protestations, and then threw me in a cell and opened a criminal case against me. And that most of the others were in the same boat.

I swore at myself, pulled out cigarettes and gave one to Dachsie and we lit up.

The pain in my frozen feet gradually abated and relief spilled through my body with a hot rush, relaxing my muscles. The half-lit barracks was filled with warmth and lulled me gently. I was drifting off when Dachsie turned over in the next bed and asked: 'You asleep?'

'Yes.'

'Hey, the sergeant-major says we've got two trips lined up already for tomorrow. Back to Kursk station and then somewhere else. Shame we didn't get supper today after all. It's a fucking dog's life.'

'Uh-huh.' I curled up, pulled the blanket around my chin, enjoying its warmth against my skin and the languor of sleep. I had no wish to think about driving anywhere tomorrow and being shaken around all day in the freezing cold, loading and unloading coffins. I wanted to sleep. Tomorrow . . . who cared about tomorrow? What counted was that today was over. Thoughts turned over heavily and lazily in my head. I remembered the coffin and the soldier's mother sitting in the depths of the truck, her vacant eyes and her thin coat. Then I remembered the major. 'I'd have told you all right, you goat-faced fool,' I said out loud. 'I'd have told you.'

15 / New Year's Eve

New Year's Eve of 2000 was to have been the most exotic of my life. What plans I'd had! What great celebrations I'd imagined to greet the millennium! Paris, Milan and London opened up before me, inviting me to welcome the twenty-first century in their embrace. Such a date happens only once in a thousand years! I was going to save money and head for Europe to have a time to remember for the rest of my life.

I remember it, all right . . . As they say, Man proposes and God disposes. And that's just what he did. Instead of Paris I got a slush-covered field in Chechnya; instead of a five-star hotel, a smoky dugout; and instead of a celebration, an antiterrorist operation.

We didn't manage to get any vodka. The fifteen gallons of diesel that Kuks tried to sell to the Chechens in Urus-Martan went to their 'free assistance fund,' that is, they cheated us. Pity. Three canisters of diesel—that's a fortune here.

We are sitting around our festive shell box, stirring the lukewarm tea in our cups. The dismal winter covers the field right up to Goity. Somewhere behind the fog a lone self-propelled gun is firing, and occasionally the infantry shoot from the perimeter trenches. It's cold and damp.

Still, we are content with life. Yesterday Pincha traded some cigarettes with the artillery for two shell crates, and we also have some firewood. He is an indispensable soldier to us; now he's cutting the boards with his bayonet and throwing the chips onto the fire. He's a city boy, but you can't tell. In his crumpled, holey boots, singed jacket and ripped pants he is the scruffiest member of our platoon. He spends every spare second sleeping, and he can't even be bothered to wash. The lice make the most of this and crawl over him in columns, having laid their paths to the most succulent places, his belly and armpits. But then Pincha knows how to make a fire in a puddle of water, light a cigarette in driving rain or sleep like a baby during mortaring.

Best of all, he has an incredible instinct for food and cigarettes. As well as finding firewood he's also managed to pawn to the cooks a case of rifle rounds with a displaced center of gravity, so they spin. We don't need them and the cooks use them to dice cabbage. It's an easy trick: you cover the cabbage with a helmet and fire one of these spinning rounds into it, the bullet goes *ratatatat* inside, and your cabbage is instantly diced. All you have to do is hold the helmet down with your foot so it doesn't spin off.

Red flecks dance on Pincha's face and heat radiates through the dugout. We feel good. We don't have warmth very often, even more rarely than food and tobacco, and because we now have two whole shell crates to burn, our spirits are soaring. The warmth instills in us the expectation of some miracle—something must happen, something good. Maybe there will be peace, maybe we'll get demobbed, and maybe—the things that come to mind, right?—the supply officer will in a fit of generosity give us a double portion of pearl barley today instead of oats. It *is* New Year's Eve, after all.

Our table of goodies is resplendent to the point of disbelief.

Between the twelve of us we have two cans of beans, two cans of stewed meat, five cans of fish and, best of all, three cans of condensed milk! One can between four of us. We haven't had such abundance for a long time.

We've also got humanitarian aid biscuits to go with the milk, thirty each, courtesy of President Boris Yeltsin. It's good that ours is the smallest platoon in the battalion—it makes it easier to divide up the aid packages. They also contain New Year's cards:

'Dear Russian soldier,' writes the president. 'In this difficult and trying hour for our Motherland, when dark forces . . . We shall not yield an inch . . . We will strike back . . . But don't forget that your duty is not only to defend constitutional order, but also to cast your vote in the coming elections. I hope that you will make the right choice on that day.'

'And ashes to ashes, dust to dust,' adds Oleg. 'May you rest in peace.'

'Amen,' says Pincha.

In the end we didn't get to make any choice. The election campaign agitators decided not to go to the combat zone with their mobile ballot stations.

'What time is it, Oleg?' I ask.

'Five to twelve,' he answers. He is the only one in our platoon with a watch; he picked it up in Grozny and has guarded it like the apple of his eye ever since.

'So, gentlemen, what do you say we get down to it?'

We clink cups of tea, drink, and set upon the condensed milk, scooping it out with biscuits. The war taught us to eat properly, and we scoop out a little at a time and chew it thoroughly. If you eat in small measures then you can fool a hungry stomach and create the illusion of plenty.

Condensed milk! My oh my! Back home I couldn't stand the stuff, but here a can of it is my ultimate dream.

After we've eaten our fill we all collapse back from the crate and contentedly stroke our sated bellies. We light up. Life's pretty good right now after our feast with condensed milk, and even the president had spared us a thought.

'Oleg, what time is it?'

'Ten past twelve.'

'Shall we go and shoot?'

'Come on.'

We take magazines that we filled earlier with tracer rounds, throw back the dugout flap and go out into the black southern night.

The dark is impenetrable; you can't even see the hand in front of your face. It seems there is no sky, no ground, no life, no light, no joy, no love, and no heroism. Just night and death. Because night is the time of death. Every time the sun goes down life dies. We don't know if we will live to see the next day, and all we can do is freeze motionless in our trenches, press ourselves into the ground and wait for sunrise as we listen into the darkness. Our eyesight is useless but our hearing is razor sharp.

At night the wounded die. At night soldiers go out of their minds. Back on that wretched mountain, trapped within fifty feet of the enemy trenches, we heard their shouts, heard the screams of the prisoners as the rebels cut off their fingers and then burst out laughing.

At night we are alone. Now I am sitting with Oleg, two little glimmers of life under a heavy black sky. Each of us is on his own.

'Fuck, it's a bit unnerving, this silence,' says Oleg.

'Screw all of them! It's New Year's after all. A new century! A new millennium! It's our given right, come on,' I say.

We point the barrels at the sky and pull the trigger. The rifles kick and thunder in our hands, shattering the silence. Two lonely streams of tracer rounds shoot over our heads, enter the low clouds and vanish in the frosty murk.

And suddenly, as if receiving an order, the whole battalion joins in. Everyone is firing ceaselessly, letting off magazines in one burst as if in protest of the wretched life of the soldier. Tracers fan out and divide the sky, fly into the mountains and into the field. To the right of us the recon fire from a machine gun, to the left the drivers use their underbarrel grenade launchers. In front of us medics throw smoke flares and behind us antiaircraft gunners pound away. The shells crackle into the clouds and explode and illuminate the positions of our battalion in misty, watery flashes.

It's a fantastic sight. Green, red and white tracers, illumination flares, orange smoke. War would be very beautiful if it weren't so frightening. The HQ commander comes out of the command tent in his slippers and runs over to us. He punches me in the jaw. Oleg manages to dodge.

'Are you out of your minds or what, you idiots!' He is afraid that in the noise someone will deliberately shoot at him or the battalion commander.

We go back to the dugout. The infantry keep hammering away for half the night. They are far away and the chief of staff doesn't run over to them in his slippers.

I suddenly feel pissed off. Just my luck! I'm the only one from the whole battalion to get a smack in the mouth tonight. No, it's time to go and join the infantry. We may be better off for biscuits but, as they say, the farther from the commander and closer to the kitchen you are, the more intact you'll remain.

I stow my boots away and crawl into my sleeping bag, stretch out and wiggle my toes. The sleeping bag's pleasant synthetic liner gives the illusory effect of a clean sheet.

'So, Happy New Year, Arkady Arkadyevich!' I congratulate myself.

'Happy New Year,' I answer, and contented I fall asleep.

I dream about Paris.

16/ Alkhan-Yurt

A vile drizzle had been falling since first light. The sky was full of heavy black clouds, low and cold, and we crawled out of our dugouts with disgust that morning.

I sat in front of the little army stove with my jacket slung over my shoulders, idly poking at the fire with a cleaning rod. The damp boards wouldn't catch and acrid smoke snaked through the tent, settling in a grimy layer in my lungs. The wet, miserable morning smothered my thoughts like cotton wool and left me feeling listless. Lazily I poured some diesel into the stove in the hope that the wood would catch. Otherwise I'd have to grope around in the half-light for the ax, which had been trodden into the mud somewhere, and go and split some slippery woodchips.

We had been wading in slush for a week now. The cold, the damp, the dank mist and constant mud killed our spirits and our platoon was gradually falling into apathy. We'd let ourselves go and didn't worry about our appearance any more.

The mud was everywhere. Greasy Chechen clay churned up by tanks stuck to our boots in great lumps and immediately got tracked through the tents. The clay lay in clods on the bunks and blankets, found its way under our jackets and ate into our skin. It got caked onto the headphones of the radio set, clogged up our rifle barrels and was practically impossible to clean off. No sooner had we washed our hands than they were dirty again; all we had to do was touch something. Numbed and covered in a layer of clay, we tried to move around as little as possible, and life ground slowly to a halt, frozen together with nature, concentrated only inside the jackets that we piled onto ourselves to try to keep warm. None of us had the strength any more to crawl out of our tiny worlds to have a wash.

The wood began to burn. Red flickers gave way to a steady white heat, the iron stove crackled and shot out sparks, and its effect radiated in waves through the tent.

I held my blue, cracked hands to the stove, which was now glowing red at the sides. I basked in the warmth, clenching and unclenching my fingers as I watched the dancing flames.

Someone threw back the tent flap and it gave a squelching wet sound. I shuddered as a wave of cold air hit my feet. A soldier stopped at the entrance, without closing the flap after him, and started to clean the clay off his boots with an engineer's shovel. I barked at him angrily:

'Think you're in a streetcar? Shut the door.'

The flap slapped back again and the platoon commander came into the tent.

He was about twenty-five, maybe a couple of years older than me, but I felt more grown up than this boyish, gleeful commander with his large protruding ears. He'd reached the front line only a month earlier and he hadn't yet had his share of knocks.

There were two peculiar things about him. First, no matter what he did, nothing seemed to work out for him, or it worked out the wrong way. For this he was regularly hauled over the coals when we were on parade, and he was known in the regiment simply as Villain. The chief of staff joked that Villain

alone brought us more losses than all the Chechens put together.

The other thing about him was that every time he came back
from a meeting he had to give us something to do. Chirping happily in his child's voice as if he had just been given a lollipop, Villain would rattle off jobs for us, his growling malcontent
subordinates, and then kick us outside, sending us along the
line to look for a break or off to bury cables or whatever.

He glanced at me, went over to his bed, threw himself down
onto it and lit a cigarette. A greasy clod of clay slowly separated
from his boot, like an iceberg breaking off from a shelf, dangling briefly from a blade of grass before dropping into someone else's boot that was drying by the stove.

Exhaling a stream of smoke, Villain stared at the ceiling.

Here we go, I thought to myself as I watched the platoon
commander. He looked like a kid who knows a secret and can't
keep it to himself any longer; any moment he'll tell me, even if
I don't want to know. He always has to have something to
bother us with, the dick, and every time he has to make a big
song and dance out of it.

Villain took a couple more puffs, looked over as if seeing me
for the first time and said happily:

'Get ready. You're going with the staff commander to
Alkhan-Yurt. The Chechens broke out of Grozny, six hundred of
them, and the interior ministry troops have them surrounded
in Alkhan-Yurt.'

'If the interior ministry have them surrounded then let
them finish the job,' I said without looking up. I continued to
poke away in the stove. 'Mopping-up operations are their business. What's that got to do with us?'

'They're using us to close a gap,' Villain answered cheerfully.
'In a swamp. The 15th are already there and they'll be to the

right, the interior troops are on the left, but in the middle there's no one, so that's where they're sticking us.' Then he looked serious as a thought came into his head. 'Take the radio and two spare batteries. Make sure you wear your body armor, battalion commander's orders. If you need to, you can take it off there.'

'Is this something serious?' I asked.

'I don't know.'

'Are we going for long?'

'I don't know. The Kombat said until sometime this evening, then you'll be relieved.'

Three carriers stood ready in front of the command tent. Glum infantry sat like humps on the top of two of them, shielding their heads from the rain with their ground cloths.

The staff commander, Captain Sitnikov, sat on the lead vehicle with one leg dangling into the command hatch; he was shouting something and waving his arms. Amid the bustle of headquarters, I detected nervousness. The closer I got to the command tent, the faster I walked, succumbing to the general rhythm of activity. Taking the radio off my back I went up to the first vehicle and reached out for the handle, about to climb on.

'So, are we ready to start then, Comrade Captain?'

'In a minute—we're just waiting for Ivenkov.'

I was glad that Sitnikov's orderly hadn't yet arrived.

I stayed on the ground; I was in no hurry to climb up onto the wet armor. As we waited for Ivenkov I banged the mud from my boots against the wheel, delaying the moment when I'd have to take off my gloves, grab the wet handle and clamber up the slippery carrier—it even *looked* cold.

I banged my rifle butt on the armored side a couple of times: 'Hey, driver!'

'What?' A grubby driver-mechanic I didn't know stuck his head out of the hatch and looked down at me with unfriendly eyes.

'Give me something to stick under my ass—the armor's wet.'

The driver disappeared back inside and rummaged around. A minute later a filthy cushion flew out of the hatch, tumbled down the side of the vehicle and landed in a small puddle right at my feet. Swearing, I picked up the cushion with two fingers and tried to wipe it on the side of the carrier. Clay smeared itself across the fabric. I swore again and threw it back on top of the vehicle.

Ivenkov raced out of his tent and ran over to us, wide-eyed. He was hugging a Bee incendiary rocket launcher and a Fly missile to his body with both arms, and the weapons banged against his legs as he ran. I quickly climbed up onto the carrier, took the weapons and radio from Ivenkov and held out my hand to him. We plunked ourselves down back to back on the filthy cushion.

'Move out!' shouted Sitnikov, and with a jolt the driver set the vehicle rolling in the direction of Alkhan-Yurt.

The rain grew heavier. With its engine groaning, the carrier crawled along a narrow path flattened down by vehicles. Great clods fountained into the air from beneath the wheels, thumping down on the armor and sending small lumps into our faces and down our necks.

But most of it landed on the 9th platoon's vehicle, which was driving right behind ours; I smiled as I watched the infantry swearing at the idiot behind the wheel. Then someone tapped the driver on the head and he let the carrier fall farther behind ours.

A helmet was spinning around on top of the carrier and it

struck me on the hip. I caught it, drank the rain that had collected inside and put it on. At least my hat would stay clean now.

Ivenkov jabbed me in the back with his elbow.

'Hey, Arkady!'

'What?'

'Got any smokes?'

'Yeah.'

I reached inside the breast pocket of my flak jacket and felt around a long time for cigarettes and matches among the stale biscuits, cartridges and God knows what else, and finally I produced a crumpled pack of Primas. I took out two cigarettes and passed one to Ivenkov. Turning toward him, I shielded the flame with my palms and we lit up.

The cigarette quickly grew damp in my wet hands. Spitting out bits of tobacco that had stuck to my lips, I pulled the helmet lower and huddled deeper into my jacket. I wrapped the rifle sling around my arm and pinned the radio to the carrier with my leg. I put one earpiece onto my left ear to monitor the airwaves and moved the other one around to the back of my head. There was nothing on the air. I called 'Pioneer' a couple of times and then 'Armor,' but no one answered, so I switched off the radio to save the battery.

Gray Chechen fields flowed slowly past, covered by storm clouds and fog, with no beginning or end, breeding melancholy in our ranks. A fine drizzle ran down our helmets and faces and under our collars, while mud from the wheels spattered us from below.

I was already wet through and filthy. My damp gloves didn't retain any warmth and stuck unpleasantly to my hands, and the stiff collar of my jacket smeared more dirt on my cheeks. Behind me, the armor plating cut into my back.

This is all nonsense, just some idiotic dream, I thought to myself. What am I doing here? What am I, a Muscovite, a twenty-three-year-old Russian kid with a degree in law, doing in this strange field thousands of miles from home, practically in a foreign land, in a foreign climate and in this foreign rain? How did I get here and why? Why do I need this rifle, this radio, this war, this greasy Chechen clay muck instead of a clean warm bed, neat and tidy Moscow and the white snow of our beautiful winter?

No, I'm not here, by all normal and logical laws I shouldn't be here, in this alien place where I have no business to be. What does Chechnya have to do with me for God's sake, and where is it anyway? This is definitely a dream—what shit!

Or is Moscow the dream? Maybe I've spent my whole life since birth rattling around on this armored carrier, steadying myself against a handle with my foot, with a rifle sling wrapped around my arm?

I got out another cigarette.

It was amazing how quickly I'd gotten used to riding on the carrier. At first I used to grab at all the handles and protrusions I could get my hands on, and still I got thrown all over the place like a sock in a washing machine. But in just a week my body had found its own optimal position and now I could sit on any part of the moving vehicle, even the gun barrel, hardly holding on to anything and never falling.

The carrier was leaping around from side to side through potholes and puddles, while Ivenkov and I smoked in a comfortable, half-reclining pose, idly dangling one of our legs off the side, no sweat. The only thing that bothered us was the damn rain and mud.

I called out to Ivenkov, who turned around with an inquiring look. I had to shout in his ear.

'Hey, Ventus, where are we going? You hang around at the command post all the time. You know what's going on.'

'Somewhere near Alkhan-Yurt.'

'I know that, but what's going on there? What does Sitnikov say?'

'There are Chechens there. Basayev. They got out of Grozny along a branch of the river, six hundred of them, and ran into the interior ministry troops at Alkhan-Yurt. They've got them hemmed in there.'

'Oh for . . . ! Yes, I know that! What I want to know is, what do we have to do? Take Alkhan-Yurt?'

'God knows. Doesn't seem like that. Right now we're going to set up an ambush. The interior troops will engage and pressure them from that side and they'll come out toward us, and then we'll chop them to pieces.'

'What, with one platoon?'

'We have a mortar crew following and then our infantry's already in place there, the 9th or the 7th company, I don't remember.'

'Well, that's quite a plan. Seems like it's going to get pretty hot there.'

'Seems so.'

Finally we came to the end of the field. After the last winding bend, our path brought us out onto the highway.

The carrier coughed and jerked and began to gather speed, its engine whining. The tires spewed off great lumps of clay that had caked onto them, and then hummed on the asphalt. The mud fountain petered out.

I got out a rusk, broke it in half and gave a piece to Ventus. We chewed.

Beneath our wheels rolled the Caucasus Federal Highway,

the same one I used to hear about all the time back in civilian life. Its very name, the Caucasus Federal Highway, used to fascinate me; it sounded good to the ear. It had an imperious ring to it, like the 'Emperor of all Russia.' Not just Tsar, but Emperor. And not just a road but a Federal Highway.

Now here I was driving on it and I saw that there was nothing federal or imperious about it at all; it was just a normal, provincial three-lane road that had not been cleaned or repaired for a long time. Pocked with craters and covered with branches, it looked pathetic, like everything else here in Chechnya.

To the left I could see the wrecked houses of Alkhan-Yurt. On one half-destroyed white building with minarets on each corner, someone had written in huge green letters RUSSIANS ARE PIGS. Underneath, in equally large letters, someone had written in coal, KHATTAB IS SCUM. I jabbed Ventus in the side and pointed at the inscriptions. We grinned.

The carrier slowed down and turned into a path, crossed a huge puddle and stopped by the side of the water next to a trailer that was surrounded on all sides with sandbags. A homely trail of smoke drifted lazily from a chimney pipe that stuck out through a piece of plywood covering the window. Soldiers thronged around a kitchen.

Sitnikov asked for the company commander. Some of the soldiers pointed at the trailer. He told us to stay put and jumped down.

I stood up, stretched and looked for familiar faces among the group by the kitchen. I didn't recognize anyone, so I went up to the trailer to have a smoke and get the latest news.

Near a hand basin I spotted an old friend named Vasya looking downcast. He had a towel thrown over his shoulder, his white body was shining and he was kicking around empty water bottles that lay in the mud

I went up to him and we greeted each other and hugged.

'So, Vasya, how's life with you?'

'Crappy. Some son of a bitch sniper set up somewhere in the forest and started shooting at us. Half an hour ago they hit us with mortars as I was coming back from the kitchen. I'd just dived into a ditch when a shell landed slap-bang in a puddle five feet away. They covered me with mud, the bastards.' Vasya wiped his head with his palms and showed me his clay stained fingers. 'See? You could plant a potato on my head. Bastards! And there's no water.'

Vasya went off toward the kitchen to look for someone, kicking an empty bottle as he went. 'Where the hell is Petrusha. He's slow as a snail, he is . . .'

I smiled. Vasya looked really funny: he was white and half-naked but with a dark, weathered face, and his hands were so covered in mud they looked like gloves. I followed him.

'OK, take it easy. So are you in the infantry now, Vasya?'

'Nope. They gave us to the 7th as reinforcement—we're over there,' he said, nodding toward a large, unfinished house about fifty yards from the company's positions. The barrels of the antitank company protruded from its brick-filled windows.

'Got yourselves set up nicely, I see. Is Misha with you?'

'Yeah, right, nicely set up. There's no roof, no floor, just bare walls. We put up a tent inside and blocked the windows but it's still cold, the chill comes straight off the bricks. And we're already sick of getting shelled. We're the nearest to the forest and we get hit more than anyone. No, Misha isn't here. His transmitter broke down so he's at the repair company. So what are you doing here, I thought you were in comms?'

'I am. I'm here with Sitnikov,' I said, nodding at the carriers.

'So why are you here?'

'To loot. I hear the looting here's great. Elegant houses, leather couches, apricot jam . . .'

'Really? The officers are pigs. They don't let us loot, they just help themselves to the leather couches. Bastards. The Kombat caught two guys carrying a mirror and, boy, did he give them a seeing to. Just for a mirror! How else are we supposed to shave?'

'Were they your guys?'

'No, some moron infantry. I mean, what did they get? A mirror, a couple of chairs and a blanket. There's not much left here to take anyway, it all went ages ago. There's not even any food.'

'Where do you go then?'

'That way, left down the highway. That's where the interior troops are. Now *they* have a nice life! Their houses only got hit recently and aren't as trashed; there's still stuff in them to take. What are you after?'

'I wouldn't mind a couple of blankets. And some pants to put on under my camouflage.'

'I've got some. Come on, I'll give you a pair.'

'No, I can't come now. We're going to the marsh as your reinforcements.'

'What for?'

'Haven't you heard? You infantry make me laugh! All around you the war has kicked off big time, there are six hundred Chechens in Alkhan-Yurt and you don't even know it! Basayev got out of Grozny and now they're surrounding him, the 15th and the interior ministry troops, and they're going to force them out toward us. We're plugging the gap in the marsh.'

'What, seriously?'

'No, I'm joking. Actually we're just out for a stroll!'

Sitnikov came out of the trailer with Korobok, the commander of the 7th company. They shook hands and Sitnikov went back to our vehicles. I headed back there too.

'OK, Vasya, I'm off. Don't give anyone else the blankets and definitely keep the pants for me. I'll drop by for them if I can.'

The infantry vehicles got stuck in a ditch and lagged behind. We didn't bother waiting for them and went on ahead.

Our carrier drove into a clearing. On three sides—behind us, on the left and on the right—the clearing was surrounded by damp, gloomy woods that began sixty or seventy yards away from us. Deep inside the woods some constructions towered over the treetops, either grain silos or an oil refinery, enormous surreal beasts sketched onto the cloudy sky. The wind whipped around their metal innards with a deep howl, low and full of dread like the dogs of Grozny as they scavenged meat from the dead. On the fourth side the clearing was bordered by a marsh thickly overgrown with rushes.

The carrier crawled up a small hill near the edge of the swamp and bounced to a halt. 'We're here,' Sitnikov muttered, sounding more like 'We're done for.' He jumped down from the top of the carrier and ran along the edge of the marsh to the nearest clump of hawthorn bushes, which grew everywhere here. I grabbed the radio and dismounted by the wheel to cover him. Ventus jumped down on the other side, crawled under the back end of the carrier and covered our rear.

When he reached the bushes, Sitnikov turned to us and waved. I adjusted the radio on my back and looked at Ventus to say: 'I'm going, cover me.' I ducked down and ran over to the staff commander and threw myself down with a thump on the wet moss. We lay quietly, side by side, listening and looking around.

Just beyond the bushes, the swampy river plain stretched

about a half mile to the edge of Alkhan-Kala, the upper part of Alkhan-Yurt, situated opposite us on a high precipice. To our left, about three hundred yards away, I could see the edge of Alkhan-Yurt, and, in front of it, flood lands on a loop of the river. We didn't need to worry about the left flank; it was clear and we had a good field of view. To our right and in front of us were tall clumps of rushes the height of a man that stretched two or three hundred yards into the marsh. Behind us, reaching as far as the mountains, there was another floodplain about a mile or two in length.

And ... silence. There was none of the fighting we had expected, nothing and no one. It was quiet as the grave.

What a lousy place, I thought to myself. Rushes in front and to the right, behind us woods, and, in Alkhan-Yurt, Chechens. They're probably in the lowlands too, and in those silos in the woods. They could hide all six hundred of them there, easy as anything, and we'd never see them. And they'd make short work of us and our three vehicles, for sure.

Behind my back, as if to confirm my thoughts, came the droning of an engine. I tried not to make a sound as I unslung my rifle. Sitnikov didn't move, he just kept on looking at the marsh through his binoculars.

The engine noise ebbed and then picked up again as the vehicle climbed slopes. Its distance from us seemed to vary with the surge and fall of its engine; first it was close, then far away. I waited, glancing at the staff commander as he motionlessly studied the marsh.

Was he posing for my benefit? Was he just trying to show how brave he was, or was he really the nutcase they say he is in the battalion, indifferent to everything: his life, mine, Ventus's. In war there is a breed of people who, like bears that have tasted human flesh for the first time, will keep killing to the end. They look normal enough, but when it comes down to it all they can think about is plunging themselves into yet another slaughter. They care little about anything, they wait for nobody and they see nothing but battle. They make great soldiers but lousy commanders. Like the rest of them, Sitnikov will get right into the thick of it and drag us all in behind him, failing to measure his experience against that of his men. Dangerous people. They survive but they lose their men. And later these are the people they write about in the papers: the hero, the only one to survive in his regiment.

Then the infantry carriers appeared in the forest, crawled into the hollow and turned onto the hillock. I relaxed and lowered my weapon.

'Comrade Captain, the infantry have arrived.'

Finally, he tore himself away from his binoculars and looked around. I tried to make out the expression on his handsome, well-bred face, guess what he thought of this marsh, and whether he rated our task as lousy or bearable. But Sitnikov was inscrutable.

Why were we here? Bastards, surely they could have told us what we were here for? We weren't soldiers, just cannon fodder. We'd been thrown into this marsh to rot, to lie and die here and not ask questions. Not once in the whole war had anyone explained a mission to me in a normal civilized manner. They sent us and off we'd go. Our job was to die, not to blather.

'Inform the Kombat that we have reached our destination and are taking up positions.' After he'd barked this order, Sitnikov grabbed his rifle, stooped down and ran toward the carriers. Once he'd got down the hillock he stood at his full height and waved his arms.

The vehicles came to a halt and the infantry streamed off

them in clusters, spreading out among the ditches and hollows. Right along the edge of the forest we could hear the cry 'Battle stations!'

I put on my headphones and called up Pioneer:

'Poker to Pioneer, do you receive me Pioneer?'

No one answered for a long time, then from the headphones I heard 'Receiving.' The metallic voice, distorted by distance and the marsh dampness, seemed familiar.

'Is that you, Sabbit?'

'Yes.'

'Did you fall asleep there or what? Just try dozing off on me, you asshole with ears, and I'll knock you out when I get back. Tell the boss we've reached our destination and are taking up our positions. Do you receive me, over?'

'Received loud and clear, you've reached your destination and are taking up positions, over.'

'Yes, and one more thing Sabbit. Find out when we'll be relieved, over.'

'Roger. Is it Poker who's asking, over?'

'No, I'm asking, over and out.'

I pushed the headphones to the back of my head and lay there awhile, waiting for it to hiss in my ears.

Everything was quiet. It suddenly seemed that I was alone in this clearing. The infantry had dispersed among the undergrowth, vanished into the marsh and frozen there, not revealing their position with the slightest movement. The dead carriers stood immobile in the dip and there was no sound from either of them.

This tense, compressed silence magnified the sense of danger. The Chechens were already here, all around, and it would kick off any second now. Tracer rounds and grenades would pour down from all sides, from the silos, the marsh, the rushes—the air would be rent asunder by rumbling and explosions, and we wouldn't have a chance even to shout or take cover.

I felt scared. My heart beat faster and a rushing noise filled my temples. Bastards, where are the Chechens, where are we, where is everyone? Why don't they tell us anything? Why did they throw us into this place and to do what? Swearing to myself, I heaved the radio onto my shoulder, got up and ran toward the carriers to find Sitnikov. I went down into the hollow and looked around. There was no one by the carriers. I went over to the nearest one and banged on the side of it with my rifle butt.

'Hey, you in there, where's the staff commander?'

The driver-mechanic's head appeared from its oily, steely-smelling depths, the whites of his eyes flashing from a filthy black face that probably never got washed clean of mud, grease and diesel: 'He's gone with our platoon commander to pick positions.'

'Where's the infantry?'

'Down there, along that pipe, lying in the ditch.'

'And where are you going to park?'

'We don't know. They said to wait here for now.'

'But which way did he go?'

'That way, to the bushes, I think.'

I went up the hillock, the way the driver had pointed, crouched down and looked around. Sitnikov and the platoon commander were standing in the bushes, surveying the area. I went over to them.

'So Sasha, you position your platoon on that knoll toward the marsh,' Sitnikov said waving his hand along the edge of the marsh. 'Put one unit with a machine gun along the pipeline and cover the rear, and put the carrier in the same place, right behind us in the hollow. The second carrier goes on the left slope of the knoll, and your field of fire is from Alkhan-Yurt to Alkhan-Kala. My vehicle will be here, covering from Alkhan-Yurt as far as the 15th. Today's password is "nine," and everyone digs in!'

'Yes, sir,' the platoon commander said with a nod.

'That's it, get cracking.'

Then Sitnikov turned to me: 'You come with me. Let's go and see what we've got here.'

We poked around by the edge of the woods for another hour and a half, picking our positions, looking around, listening. I felt tired. I was covered in sweat beneath my jacket; beads of sweat mixed with raindrops ran between my shoulder blades and cooled my heated body.

When it was completely dark, we came back to the hillock and our carrier and settled down beside a concrete beam that lay randomly in the clearing. Ivenkov was nearby, and we silently awaited the next developments. The rain intensified. We lay motionlessly by the beam, listening in the darkness.

Southern nights are pitch black and your eyesight doesn't help. At night you have to rely on your hearing alone—only its perception can help you relax, reassuring you that everything is quiet. But then your body suddenly tenses, you catch your breath between your clenched teeth, your hand steals slowly toward your rifle and silently comes to rest there. Your eyes slowly move your head toward the unexpected sound, and you try not to brush your head on your collar, try not to make a sound that might hinder your ears from gauging the situation.

Silence. The only noises that night were the dog howls of the silos and the quacking and rustling of the ducks as they moved in the rushes, just asking to be stuck on a spit. And nothing else, it was all quiet. The Chechens, if there were any in the lowland area, didn't give themselves away. Maybe they were waiting too.

The minutes stretched into years. The silence and night smothered everything; time that wasn't measured with cigarettes had lost all meaning.

Everything had died. Only we soldiers were still a little alive, despite being rooted in the cold. Like sunken submarines we lay on a shelf, our iron sides nestling closely to one another under water as we cooled off motionlessly, huddled in a pile to preserve warmth. And the night bore down on us with a mile-thick layer of expectation, our skulls cracked and collapsed, and the darkness poured inside and filled our hull compartment, leaving alive only a drop of energy somewhere in our very core. And not another sign of life around, not a single soul, only the dead.

It became increasingly hard to lie there: cramped, numbed muscles started to gnaw at my joints; cold rain penetrated my bones; my body cooled and started to shiver.

My legs were unbelievably cold, and my feet throbbed in their sodden boots, almost as if they weren't attached any more. But I couldn't flap my arms or stomp on the spot; the night and the cold shackled my movements, pressing down on my chest.

Four hours passed like this.

I moved a little, trying to slip off the safety on my rifle, but my stiff fingers couldn't feel the little flag of metal and they slipped off.

Everything was still just as quiet.

Suddenly I didn't give a damn about the prospect of fighting. I had waited for it for so long already, lying here on the ground in the winter rain. I had spent too long tensed up and nothing had happened. My physical resources were exhausted and I was about to surrender myself to total indifference. I wanted to go somewhere and warm up: into the carrier, to a fire, to a village or to the Chechens, anywhere that was dry and warm.

That's how they get slaughtered, I thought to myself, and I raised myself up on one knee. I couldn't lie like that any longer. To hell with them!

'Listen, Ventus, help me get this radio off.'

Ventus was also out of it; he pried himself off the seabed and rose through the thick freezing night. He surfaced evenly, the night streaming off the decking of his body armor, pouring off his magazine pouches, churning in the layers of eyelashes, and then receding, leaving his eyes to regain their life.

Sitnikov did not move; he kept his head firmly in combat mode as he listened to the marsh.

Ventus took the radio off my back and I stood up to my full height, bent backward, flexing my torso. My spine immediately felt better without the thirty-pound weight digging into my shoulders like a hump and cutting into my collarbones. I undid my flak jacket, removed it over my head and placed it on the ground by the concrete beam, with the warm and dry inner side facing upward. Ventus put his jacket down next to it, forming a sort of seat.

We jumped up and down, flapped our arms and ran on the spot doing silly kicks in our heavy boots. Our hearts beat faster, pumping blood into our frozen toes, and we began to glow.

'I never thought I'd do warm-up exercises in the army of my own free will,' grinned Ventus.

'Yeah, but it's pointless,' I said with a dismissive wave. 'Our stomachs are empty; we've got no calories in us. When we sit down again we'll be frozen in two minutes.'

Once we'd gotten our circulation going again we quickly sat down back to back on our jackets so as not to waste the warmth or get the jackets wet in the rain. Through my thin pants, my frozen backside caught a brief, comforting radiance from the jackets.

We lit up, sheltering the smokes inside the sleeves of our jackets. A smoldering flicker caught Ventus's face in the dark, illuminating his dirty fingers as he clutched his cigarette. I remembered how I had once spotted a guy smoking in my night-vision sight. He was far away, but every feature on his face was clearly visible, as if it had been drawn with a pencil. You can hit someone a half mile away, and it was only about that far to Alkhan-Yurt. But we were too cold and we had nothing else to warm ourselves with other than the acrid, stinking smoke of our Primas.

The carrier's hatch opened with a quiet, controlled clang. Coughing, the driver hoarsely whispered: 'Hey, boys, give me a smoke, will you?'

I had to smile. The war was of secondary importance; now human needs came first, the eternal preoccupations of the soldier: get something to eat, warm up and have a smoke. Empty stomachs and cold got the better of our instinct to survive, of duty and the war. Ghosts in army jackets rose out of the trenches, began to move and wander around looking for food. If a soldier is fed, clothed and washed he fights ten times better, there's no doubt about it.

I threw my pack of Primas at the voice. The driver groped around on the vehicle, found the pack, took a cigarette and threw it back. The pack fell short and landed in the grass. I wiped it on my pant leg.

'Shit, it's soaked through . . . Hey, infantry, are you using your night sights?'

'Do we need to?'

'Damn!' said Sitnikov. 'I'll shoot those dickheads in a minute.' He grabbed a rotten piece of wood that was lying on the ground and whipped it at the driver. 'You'd damn well better be using them. What do you think the carrier is, a hotel?

You've warmed up, now get back to your positions, and don't you even think of going to sleep!'

The driver disappeared back inside the hatch and I heard some voices as someone moved around inside. A second later the turret turned with a quiet rattle toward the mountains, sweeping its barrel as it looked into the night. Then it stopped, giving the impression of close vigilance, and turned the other way.

I grinned. In half an hour they'd probably be asleep again.

The moon, covered right up to its chin by a thick blanket of cloud, found a small gap and peeked out of the corner of its eye. The night gloom lit to gray.

My stomach rumbled. I looked up at the sky and nudged Ventus.

'It would be good to have a bite to eat now, wouldn't it, while we can see something at least? Comrade Captain, how about supper? It doesn't look like we'll be getting any action today.'

'Go ahead and eat,' Sitnikov said, without turning round.

I delved into the pocket of my webbing and started to scoop out my supplies. I happened to have four whole flat rusks, a tin of sardines in tomato sauce and a packet of raisins. Ventus only had three rusks.

'Yeah, not exactly a feast. If only we could heat up the sardines, and at least have something hot to eat.' I patted my pockets. 'Have you got a knife?'

Ventus rummaged in his pockets too and then shook his head.

'Comrade Captain. Have you got a knife?'

Sitnikov wordlessly handed me a hunting knife. It was a good one with a short, sturdy blade, a collector's piece. The handle was made from expensive wood and lay snugly in my hand.

'Wow, where did you get this, Captain? Is it a war trophy?'

'I bought it before I left Moscow.'

'How much was it?'

'Eight hundred bucks.'

I tossed the knife from palm to palm and stuck it in the can. The sharp blade sliced though the lid like paper, and greasy, tasty-looking sauce oozed from the slit, smelling tantalizingly of fish. I put the tin on the ground and got out my spoon.

'Come on, let's eat. Comrade Captain, maybe you'd like to join us?'

'You go ahead,' Sitnikov answered in a monotonous tone, still not turning round.

We took our time, scooping out the fish little by little. The war had taught us how to fool our stomachs that less is more.

After we'd taken care of the tin, we licked our spoons and took turns scraping out the remains of the fish with the rusks. My hunger wasn't sated, but the emptiness in my stomach was a little less.

'All good things must come to an end,' Ventus summed up philosophically. 'Let's have a smoke.'

We didn't manage to light up. In the bushes nearest to us a twig snapped underfoot like an exploding artillery shell, its crack hitting our straining ears and tugging at every nerve in our bodies.

I jumped involuntarily and instantly broke out in a hot sweat of fear. Chechens! I flung myself down flat on my back where I'd been sitting, grabbed my rifle, rolled over and flicked off the safety.

Ventus managed to jump over the beam and threw himself down next to Sitnikov.

Out of the bushes lumbered Igor as noisily as a bear, snagging his pants on thorns, swearing and breaking twigs and mumbling something like 'Goddamn Chechen bushes.'

I let out a stream of curses too as I picked myself up from the ground and started to brush the mud and wet blades of grass from my jacket. When he saw me, Igor threw his arms open in joy.

'Hey homeboy! How did you comms end up here? You should be back at headquarters.'

'We wanted to do some hunting, so we're picking off idiots who blunder around in the bushes,' I said.

'Are you talking about me or what?' Igor came over and gave me a gentle punch on the shoulder.

'OK, take it easy, big man. How about you give me a smoke?'

Igor, a Moscow native like me, was one of the few people I was actually close to in the battalion. We'd met back in Moscow, even before we'd left for Chechnya.

It was early one sleepy winter morning. The snow crunched underfoot, the sharp frosty air packed my nostrils and the bright streetlamps against the night gloom were hard on my eyes, which were still swollen after my farewell party the evening before.

I'd stepped down from the bus and was looking around the unfamiliar stop; the enlistment office was supposed to be somewhere nearby. A bowlegged guy of medium height stood at the stop too, trying to light up, cradling the flame of the lighter in his palm. His high cheekbones and a few gingery tufts of beard growth indicated some Tartar blood, and his angled eyes glinted with cunning.

I went over to him to ask the way. He grinned at me: 'To Chechnya, do you mean? So who are you then, homeboy? I'm Igor,' he said, holding out his hand.

Later, as we were being driven in a minibus to our Moscow region unit, Igor chattered the whole way without shutting up; he talked about his life and even pulled a photo of his daughter from his inside jacket pocket, showing it first to me, then to the driver, and then to the accompanying officer. 'Look, Major, that's my daughter.'

And from his small bag full of soldier's stuff he produced a few little bottles of vodka, one by one, to everybody's glee, repeating each time: 'So, infantry, who's for a drink?'

We lit our cigarettes and sat up on the carrier. I took a drag, and spat, wiping my frozen nose.

'Goddamn Chechnya. I'm frozen like a dog. If only it would freeze properly then at least it would be dry . . . All I've got on underneath is long johns and pants. If you wear your underlining you keel over, it's heavy as anything, really hard work. And I can't find any pants anywhere. Vasya offered me some and I didn't take him up on it, for some reason. I should have gone with him and got them.'

'You think you're cold?' Igor said, rolling up the dirty pant legs of his camouflage fatigues to reveal a bluish, goose-bump-covered leg. He had nothing on under his fatigues.

'I've been lying in a puddle for four hours without anything on under my fatigues. Imagine that! I threw out my underlining back in Goity, and my long johns. They had more lice than thread.' Igor felt the material and frowned. 'What is this raggedy shit that doesn't keep the warmth in or the water out? They could at least make jock straps for us—you could freeze your nuts off like this, isn't that right, Comrade Captain?' he said, turning to Sitnikov.

'Easy as anything.'

'Shame we can't make a fire, dry off a bit. You got anything to eat?'

'No. We've just had a tin of sardines. I wouldn't mind something myself.'

'And what about the Kombat, the bastard! He's stuck us in

this hole and forgotten about us. He could at least have sent us some grub. When they had their supper in the regiment they could have delivered some here too. Do you know when they'll relieve us?'

'We should have been relieved already. But now we'll be here until morning, whatever happens.'

We fell silent. The dank and the damp hampered my movement and I didn't feel like budging.

'Did you hear, they say Yeltsin has resigned.'

'Who told you that?'

'It's just going around,' Igor shrugged his shoulders. 'On New Year's, supposedly. They showed it on TV. He gave a speech and said his health wasn't up to it any more. Of course it's not up to it, the amount he drinks.'

'Ah, bullshit. That can't be true—a pig like that wouldn't simply give up his throne. He's a thief and a murderer. And a careerist. For the sake of power he first destroyed the empire, then he started a war and smashed parliament with tanks, and now he's simply gone and retired, just like that?'

I turned sharply toward Igor, barely controlling my anger. 'I will never forgive him for the first Chechen war, him and that pig of a defense minister, Pavel Grachyov. I was eighteen, a puppy, and they pulled me off my mother's apron strings like a clothespin and dumped me in that mess, leaving me to sink or swim. I floundered. I wanted to survive and they sent me right back there. In the two years I was in the army my mother changed from a woman in her prime into an old lady.' I shuddered with agitation. 'They've ruined my life, see? You don't know it yet, but they've ruined yours too. You are already dead—you won't have any more life. Yours ended here, in this marsh. How I waited for this war! I never really came back from the first; I went missing in action in the fields by Achkhoi-Martan.

Oldie, Anton, Baby, Oleg—none of us came back. Take any contract soldier you like, they're almost all here for the second time. And not for the money this time, but as volunteers. We are volunteers now because back then they forced us to come down here. We can no longer do without human flesh. We're psychopaths, get it? Incurable. And now you are too. Only you don't notice it here, because everyone's the same. But back there it shows right away. No, our tsar cost us too dearly to step down now—he paid for his throne with thousands of lives just so he can toss his crown around as he sees fit—'

'OK, OK, take it easy, what are you getting so worked up for? To hell with our tsar. Maybe this war will end now, what do you reckon?'

I shrugged.

'Maybe it'll end, God knows. What's it to you anyway?' Suddenly I lost interest in the conversation. My agitation ebbed away as fast as it had appeared.

'We get paid a kopek for every second of this war. That's eight hundred and fifty rubles in your pocket every day. So I don't care either way—if it ends, great; if not, that's pretty good too.'

'You're right there. But the thing is, I wouldn't mind going home. I'm tired of this lousy winter. I'm frozen, and I don't think I've been warm once when I've been asleep.'

Igor made a dreamy face, his eyes turned to the heavens. 'Yeeesss . . . They say there's no winter in Africa, but that's probably bullshit. You know what, the first thing I'll do when I get back to Moscow . . . no, vodka is the first thing, of course, I'll have a drink,' Igor grinned. 'And then after a couple of shots, I'll fill up the bathtub with hot water and I won't get out of it for a day. Heating, my friend, is a wondrous blessing, bestowed on us by the good Lord!'

'Uh-huh, quite a philosopher, aren't you?'

'What about you?'

'Me too. You become a philosopher here, like it or not.'

'No, I mean, what will you do first when you get home?'

'Oh, that . . . I dunno, get drunk out of my head.'

'And after that?'

'Get drunk again.' I looked at Igor. 'I don't know, Igor. You see, it's all so far away that it's not real. Home, beer, women, peace . . . It's not real. The only thing that's real is the war and this field. I'm telling you, I like it here—it's fun. I'm free here, I don't have any obligations, I don't have to take care of anybody or be responsible for anyone, not for my mother or any kids, no one. Just myself. I can die or survive, as I wish. If I want, I can go home, or I can go missing in action. I live and die the way I want. I'll never be this free again in my life. Trust me, I already came home from the war once. Right now you desperately want to go home, but once you're there you'll only feel down. Everyone is so petty there, so uninteresting. They think they're living, but they don't know shit about life. They're puppets.'

Igor looked at me with interest.

'Right . . . And you call me a philosopher. You think too much about the war, homeboy. Give it a rest. A fool has a much easier life. Generally it's not good for you to think, and especially not here. It's enough to send you crazy. Although you already are crazy, as you have correctly noted.'

He tapped his forefinger on his temple, slapped me on the knee and stood up.

'OK, I'm going back to our positions,' he said, flattering his ditch full of swamp water with the word 'positions.' 'We have to sort out guard duty for tonight. Dark, isn't it?'

'Did you set up trip wires?' asked Sitnikov, turning around as he woke from his contemplation of the marsh.

'Yes, sir.'

'Where?'

'Over there in the rushes,' said Igor, motioning with his arm. 'We set signal flares there, and grenades over by the water. There's no way they'll get through.'

The black Chechen night covered the marsh with an impenetrable shroud. It was quiet. Even the silos had stopped howling.

Ventus and I slumped back to back on the flak jackets, warming each other. The cold rain persisted and we couldn't sleep. Like a stubborn child, the cold kept creeping under the edge of my jacket. After ten minutes of lying in a state of delirium I'd jump around and flap my arms. I was dog tired, and although it couldn't even be midnight yet, the night had already broken me. Lying for hours in the dank marsh without food, water or warmth, only uncertainty, had squeezed out my last strength. I no longer wanted anything, or, rather, I no longer cared if I sat, lay or moved. Everything I wore was soaked through, cold and nasty, and it clung to my body, driving waves of cold into my kidneys.

Without warning, the moon sailed out in full-bodied roundness from behind a black cloud and cast instant light.

We crawled into the shade of a bush, scaring a flock of sparrows that slumbered on its twigs. The bright moonlight filled the whole valley, illuminating the water in sharp silver and bringing every object into focus.

Strange nature they have here, I thought to myself. Just now it was black as black can be, then the moon comes out and you can read the house numbers in Alkhan-Kala. No, this was definitely a dream. This marsh, river, rushes . . . It was all so distinct it could only be a dream. And I myself was soft, blurry, unreal. I shouldn't be here. I had been somewhere else all my life, in a different dream. My whole life I hadn't known there was such a thing as Chechnya. I still wasn't sure what it was, just as I wasn't sure about Vladivostok, Thailand or the Fiji Islands. I have a completely different life where no one shoots at me, where no one is killed, where I don't have to live in marshes, eat dog flesh and die of cold. And that's the life I should have always, because I have nothing to do with Chechnya, and I don't give a damn what it is, because it doesn't really exist. Because completely different people live here who speak in a different language, think differently and breathe differently. And it's logical. I too should think and breathe differently. Everything is logical in nature, everything conforms to natural laws, everything that happens does so for a reason, with some goal. So why am I here? What is the sense, what law does all this conform to? What will change back home, in my normal life, because I have been here?

On the riverbank, a quarter mile away from us, an armored carrier crawled along, the sound of its rumbling engine muffled by the damp air. It stopped. People poured out of it, scattered to the ridge and disappeared into the night as if they'd never been there.

'What the hell?' I shook off my stupor and exchanged glances with Ventus and Sitnikov. 'What's that, Comrade Captain, Chechens?'

'God knows. I can't see a damned thing,' Sitnikov said, lowering the binoculars. 'Doesn't look like Chechens, but who knows? Two days ago they did actually steal a carrier from the 15th.'

'How?'

'Hit it with a rocket, hooked it up to a tractor and towed it into the mountains. Right in these hills here somewhere, as it happens.'

The truck stood on the bank like a piece of dead metal. The

moonlight danced off the smooth barrel set against the dark body. There was no movement. It was as if the people had died and vanished in the marsh.

Sitnikov broke the spell.

'No, it's not Chechens, it's the 15th. They just switched positions.' He turned away from the marsh and switched on the light of his watch. 'It's already one o'clock, let's get some shut-eye.'

'I'll stay here Comrade Captain,' Ventus said, nodding to the carrier. 'The boys have some room, I'll squeeze in there.'

Sitnikov nodded, got up and went toward the bushes and the infantry's carrier, the same way Igor went earlier. I followed him.

The vehicle stood in a tiny hollow only slightly bigger than it was, in the middle of the hawthorn bushes. A disconcertingly large number of infantry were busying themselves all around. Damn, where did they all come from? I wondered. Haven't they put out any sentries? Fat chance of getting any sleep here. The open side hatch of the carrier cast a circle of pale light on the ground. Igor was leaning against the side, swearing as he roused the next guards.

'Come on, get a move on! You guys are like a bunch of sleepy cows. Hurry up or the Chechens will see the light. Next time I'll toss a grenade and you'll get out quickly enough! What, are you going to sleep here?' he said, noticing Sitnikov and me.

'Where else? Do you think the filthy infantry are going to live it up in the carrier while the staff commander and his radioman freeze the whole night on the hillock? Everything's frozen to hell and my nuts are clanging already. Is it warm in there?'

'No, we don't use the engine. It'd be audible three miles away across the water at night. And we're low on diesel anyway. It's like that joke, two mosquitoes fly into a gym and one says: "Brr, it's cold here." And the other one says: "No sweat, we'll warm it up with our breath overnight."'

'Have you at least got room?'

'We'll make room. We've got a whole lot of sentries out tonight,' Igor grinned, letting me go in front of him through the hatch. 'I decided to split the night into three watches of four hours, from seven to seven. It's a long time, but at least you can sleep when you're not on. The boys are pretty tired. Lay down under the turret, on those crates.'

There were a dozen of them crammed into the vehicle. They had covered the landing-force bench with rags and made a sort of bed that could fit four. Two more lay on stretchers above the bench. Sitnikov shooed the sleeping gunner from the commander's seat, and next to him the driver was snoring. Someone lay down behind them in the recess for the tarpaulin. The gunner crawled into his little seat behind the machine gun and perched there with his head resting on the ammo box. I clambered past him beneath the turret and banged my forehead on a box of bullet belts, and then the back of my head on the machine gun, snagging my jacket on the side ring mounting at the same time. I jammed myself between the sleeping platoon commander and the hull, using my weight to make a space as I settled on some ammo boxes. They were heaped up on the floor and their sharp corners dug into my ribs through my jacket. I wriggled a bit and found a way of supporting myself on four points: one corner under my shoulder, one under my backside, one under my knee and one under my foot. I put my head on the stomach of the guy who was sleeping where the tarpaulin should be. I pulled my cap down over my eyes and wrapped my rifle sling around my arm.

It was extremely uncomfortable. Two bulbs feebly lit the half-darkness inside the carrier and there were sleeping bodies everywhere. It really was a coffin on wheels, a common grave— some job they did of designing it. One person couldn't have turned around in there, let alone ten. If we'd been hit with a Fly rocket we'd all have bought it—no one would have gotten out of that crush, least of all me. I had the worst place of all, right in the middle under the turret.

I closed my eyes and teased the infantry as I dozed off.

'Hey, boys, your lookouts won't fall asleep will they?'

'No.'

'Because one Fly and they'll be writing to your mother to inform her that your service didn't quite work out . . .'

'Spit for good luck, idiot.'

I spat three times, knocked on my forehead for lack of wood, yawned and then mumbled, 'Don't wake me, don't turn me over, and in the event of fire evacuate me first,' and then I must have gone out like a light.

I woke twenty minutes later. Poked by the corner of a box, my shoulder was nagging horribly, and my bent legs were starting to get cramps. But worst of all my bladder ached; in the cold my body had expelled all the moisture it could to conserve warmth, and now I desperately needed to take a leak. Always the same, and in Chernorechye we could have set our watches by it—every fifty minutes our platoon would wake to pee.

I glanced at the infantry in the hope that someone else would wake up. But no one moved; they were all fast asleep.

'I can't get out,' I thought, despondently eyeing the heap of bodies blocking my route. 'I'll have to wait. But hell, I've just had a piss. I guess it's gotten colder.'

I passed the rest of the night in a state of half delirium.

I would plunge into a heavy sleep for five minutes and then wake up. There was probably movement in the vehicle all the time: someone coming in from guard duty, another getting out, someone waking and having a smoke, or trying to find a space. But none of this hubbub registered with me. When I woke I also tossed and turned, shifted my position and smoked. My body kept going numb on the sharp corners. It was cold, my wet things wouldn't dry and I was shivering. And the whole time I was busting for a pee.

And then I woke one more time and realized I couldn't bear it any longer. Somehow I had to get out of this frozen vehicle, jump around outside, take a leak and light a fire. I raised myself up on my elbows and looked around. Sitnikov wasn't there, and light shone in through a small opening in the commander's hatch.

I clambered over the seat, threw open the hatch and pulled myself out, whimpering like a puppy from the pain in my bladder. For fear of not making it I quickly climbed down to the ground and groaned a sigh of relief by the wheel.

'Mother of God that's good . . . Aaaah.'

The stream of urine came in two short bouts and petered out. I raised my eyebrows in surprise.

'Was that it? I really needed to go, I thought I'd pass an ocean, and that's all there was?' And then it dawned on me: 'Shit, I've frozen my bladder to a standstill!'

I grappled with the injustice of it, deeply concerned that my body, which had never let me down before, may have suffered some damage. And my bladder, too—you can't just fix that as if it were a carrier.

'What a lousy stroke of luck! The bastard Chechens, it's all their fault. Just you wait, you sons of bitches!'

It was already light outside and an early morning mist crept across the ground. The infantry sat about ten yards from the vehicle, warming themselves by a meager fire that they fed with bits of ammo boxes. A pot stood over the flames and gave off an aromatic smell.

Still swearing furiously, I approached the fire. Without looking up, the infantry platoon commander shifted over on his board, making room for me to sit down. No one else moved—the sleepless cold night had reduced us all to apathy.

'What are you swearing about?' asked the platoon commander.

'I froze my bladder.'

'Ah. It happens . . .' He broke off another board from a box and tossed it into the flames.

I pulled off my boots and placed them close to the heat. The damp leather started to steam. The warmth from the fire gradually defrosted my rigid body and I stretched out my feet and wiggled my toes, savoring the flame.

The pot belched steam into our faces. My head spun with the aroma and my stomach rumbled. I remembered that the last time I had eaten normally was the day before, in the morning. The memory awoke a sharp pang of hunger.

Sucking the air in through my nostrils, I theatrically wrinkled my nose in mock ecstasy and smiled like a clown.

'So, boys, how can I put this diplomatically . . . Is there anything to eat?'

No one stirred, no one smiled. Someone with his chin tucked into his knees replied without lifting his head:

'There's hawthorn brew about to boil.'

'Is that it?'

'Yes.'

'OK, where's the water from?'

'The marsh.'

'But it's rancid. Did you put a water purification tablet in it at least?'

'What's the point? You have to let it stand for four hours and we'd all have croaked by then.'

We hardly ever used the tablets that came with our dry rations, only when there was lots of water and we had plenty of time. Mostly we just drank the water as it came, from ditches, puddles or streams. And oddly enough no one got sick, even though every mouthful contained a year's dose of infectious microbes. No one could afford to get sick. In extreme circumstances the body focuses on just one thing—surviving—and it pays no attention to petty irritations like typhoid. Our empty stomachs digested intestinal bacilli like popcorn, sucking every last calorie out of them. In the winter we were able to sleep in wet clothes on rocks, freezing to them by our hair during the night, and none of us so much as coughed the next day.

Sickness starts later, when you get home. Your fear leaves you in screams and insomnia at night, and the tension ebbs. Then war crawls out of you in the form of boils, constant colds, depression and temporary impotence, and you spend six months coughing up the recon's diesel soot.

The pot came to boil and bubbled over. Petrovich, a forty-year-old contract soldier who was supervising the cooking, picked it up with a twig and scalded himself. Flinching, he put it on the ground and mixed the contents with the same twig.

'It's ready. Give me your mess tins.'

We held them out while Petrovich distributed the cloudy, scented liquid. He then handed the pot to a soldier sitting nearby: 'Go and get some more water for that, and bring more hawthorn.'

There weren't many mess tins so we shared them. When my turn came, I cupped the scorching-hot tin in my palms, inhaled the intoxicating aroma of warm nutrition and gulped, realizing that if I didn't give my stomach something now I would die on the spot.

The hot broth slipped down my gullet with a warm glow and landed heavily in my stomach. All of a sudden I felt sick; the brew was too potent for my hungry belly.

'Ugh, fucking awful.' I lowered the mess tin and looked at it suspiciously. 'But it smells good.' I sniffed it again and took another gulp. 'I can't drink this on an empty stomach—I'll throw up, it's too rough.'

But after the hot drink I had an unbearable urge to eat. I stood up and said: 'I'm going for a walk. Maybe someone has some food left.'

No one paid any attention to me. The infantry were engrossed with the mess tins, rolling their eyes and downing the hot sustenance.

I set off down the hillock. Now there was no one near the pipe; the soldiers had scattered and broken up into small groups and were sitting around fires getting warm. An abandoned machine gun pointed forlornly into the sky. I turned to look behind me. To the left of the bushes rose another plume of smoke. The machine gunner sat on the edge of the marsh with a second gunner, who looked familiar. They looked my way and abruptly turned away again, obviously having no need for me. A mess tin was perched on the embers and it gave off the same smell of hawthorn.

'Hey boys, what're you cooking?'

'Hawthorn.'

'With swamp water?'

'Yes.'

'I see. Is that all you've got to eat?'

'Yes.' The gunner pulled out of his boot a dirty spoon with some bits of oatmeal or clay stuck to it and stirred the can, signaling that the conversation was over. Oily spots separated on the surface of the brew. The gunner inspected the steaming spoon in the light, his dirty fingers picked off a couple of sodden lumps and he put them in his mouth.

The day started brightly. The sun rose in the sky and lit up the valley. The sun rays reflected on the remaining windowpanes in Alkhan-Yurt, and even the marsh looked picturesque as the water sparkled. The undergrowth flashed with color and I stopped in the hollow, studying the low ground and the village.

Very nice, I said to myself. To think there are Chechens down there somewhere, and war and death. The war is lying low, hiding itself in the sun, biding its time. It's waiting for us, waiting until we relax, and then it will strike. It can't do without us, without our blood and our lives. It takes its fill from us and, oh boy, is it hungry now. As I looked at this beautiful scene I remembered how once, back in the first war, I had seen a man walking across a field. He was alone, unarmed, just out by himself. It was so ridiculous. We never went out on our own, only in groups, and with armored vehicles if possible. And we never crossed a field that had been sown with all manner of explosive crap.

I watched the man walking and waited. Any moment now, one more step and there would be a blast, pain and death. I was frozen to the spot, unable to take my eyes off the striding figure, afraid to miss the moment of the explosion and the human suffering. There was nothing I could do to avert the man's end, no matter how much I wanted to, but nor could I just turn away indifferently. All I could do was watch and wait. Nothing happened in the end—a carrier came around the corner and the walking man disappeared from view.

I dreamed of this scene a few times after that. I dreamed about it a year later, when I was back in civilian life, and then a year after that. About how, in the middle of war, there's a man going about his business, walking through a minefield, a single lone figure. And oddly, I always remembered this scene in black. It was summer when it happened, the sun flooded the green earth from a bright blue sky, the world brimmed with color, life, light, birdsong and the smells of the forest and foliage. But I didn't remember any of that, not the lush green grass, the blue sky or the white sun; I just remembered this black figure on a black field in black Chechnya. And my black expectation that he would get blown apart.

I wondered whether I would remember these colors. Would my memory just retain the cold, filth and the emptiness of my stomach? I suddenly felt saddened, saddened by this wondrous day that I would have to spend racked with hunger in a stinking bog.

The ducks awoke in the rushes and began their chorus of quacking, splashing around in the water.

It would be good to shoot one, I thought, then there'd be something for breakfast. That bastard Kombat—nothing for lunch, supper or breakfast. It's just like they say, breakfast at lunchtime, lunch at supper and why don't we skip supper?

Sitnikov appeared over the hillock and stood next to me for a while, squinting at the sun and surveying the village from beneath the shade of his palm. Then he broke off a branch of hawthorn and shook the water from it. A few large, frozen berries thudded onto the ground along with the drops. Sitnikov looked at them thoughtfully, and then slowly, as if feeling awkward that he, an officer, should also want to eat, he began to pick the berries off the branch and put them in his mouth.

I went over to him, picked a berry too and took it between my lips. The heavy, sweet juice of the frozen hawthorn filled my mouth, tasting much better than the cloudy brew I'd tried. I swallowed. The lone berry seemed to clang into my empty stomach, bouncing between the folds. I felt it quite clearly, all alone in my belly, cold, and incredibly tasty and juicy. I picked another, then a third, then slung my rifle over my shoulder and began to pluck off bunches of them, ignoring the cold twigs with their long thorns, seeing only the berries as I tore at the bush.

After a while someone from the infantry joined us, first one guy, then another, until the whole platoon gradually drifted over from the fires to the bushes and stretched out in a chain along the hillock.

We ate like moose, plucking the berries from the branches with our teeth, snorting and batting last year's cobwebs out of the way with our heads. We ceased to be soldiers and forgot about the war; our rifles lay beside us on the ground, and we ravenously tore off these cold, tasty berries with our lips, moving from one grazing spot to another, leaving bare branches behind us. We felt our stomachs fill and how, after this dead night, our bodies began to bloom with life again, how we became warm and the blood started to pump through our veins.

Our teeth went black, our tongues tingled from the tartness but we kept tearing at the hawthorn, hurrying, afraid that something would prevent us from eating them all, swallowing the berries whole without chewing. But it was still too little, we could never eat enough to feel full.

We grazed like this for a long time, until we had stripped the bushes and tired ourselves. We all returned to our fires and silently lit cigarettes as we digested this low-calorie food.

A duck flew low overhead, maybe thirty feet above us, its wings beating the air. I unslung my rifle to shoot but got tangled in the sling. While I was untangling myself, the duck flew off.

'Shit, it got away!'

'Don't worry about it, you wouldn't have hit it anyway,' said Petrovich, stroking his mustache and narrowing his eyes craftily. His face assumed the expression of a hunter telling tales about big game.

'I tried shooting at them yesterday. They were flying really low, just like that, even lower than that one,' he said, showing how the ducks flew with his hand. 'I let off a whole magazine and didn't hit a damn thing. They look plump enough and you fire and fire, but they're just a rush of feathers. Now if I had birdshot it would be a different matter.'

'Yes, a duck would be pretty good right now. We've been here a day without food and water. When are we going to be relieved?' Igor said, looking at me. 'You spoke with headquarters—what does the Kombat say?'

'He doesn't say anything. Maybe we'll be relieved by evening, although that's unlikely, right before nightfall. It's more likely to be tomorrow morning.'

'Uh-huh, that means another day here. They could at least send us water.'

The air stirred once again and I grabbed at my rifle, thinking it was a duck. I realized my mistake as a heavy-caliber shell rushed high over our heads in the direction of Alkhan-Kala. We all mechanically turned our heads skyward and listened. When the rushing noise died down we turned toward the village. There was a moment's silence, then the first white house on the edge of the village distended and disappeared in a huge explosion, which sent debris flying in all directions and roof beams twirling in the air. A moment later the sound of the blast echoed across the marsh with a roar, and another second after that came the report of the heavy gun that fired the shell from the regiment in the woods.

'Direct hit!'

'Self-propelled guns, big fuckers. One shell and the house is gone.'

'Here we go, we definitely won't get relieved now.'

A heavy bombardment began and the shells fell one after another. Behind the woods and to the right, self-propelled guns were firing from somewhere in the mountains. The howl of the Grad missiles that then carpeted Alkhan-Kala came from the same place. Just off to the left of the hillock, a mortar battery piped up too, its reports distinguishable from the overall shelling. The ground underfoot trembled with every round fired.

Alkhan-Kala seemed to vanish, swept by the bombardment from the precipice on which it had stood. In its place, dust billowed up in thick black clouds, bits of dirt flew and fell and whole roofs, planks and walls hung in the air. The air shook as it was palpably torn apart by the metal, so much metal that the air and space became denser as every shard that flew into the village displaced molecules of oxygen before it and left a warm trail on your face. The blasts and shots fused in one roar that filled the air with its density, giving it a weight that pressed our heads down into our shoulders.

We stood there watching the bombardment in silence. It's at these times, when houses whirl among tons of earth in the air, fly apart in fragments and leave behind craters the size of ponds, and the ground trembles for two miles around from the impact of the massive shells, that you are especially aware of the frailty of the human body, the softness of bones and flesh and their defenselessness against metal. Heavens above, is this whole inferno just meant to kill people, or will it split the earth in two? You realize how brittle you are and that there is no way you can resist this avalanche that is tearing a whole village to shreds. And the realization of how easy it is to kill a person paralyzes you and leaves you speechless.

'Now they'll come swarming out of there, the bastards . . .'

We came to our senses and ran to our positions. Over the marsh you could hear the drawn-out, terrifying call: 'Battle stations!' I raced to the carrier, grabbed my radio and ran to join Sitnikov.

I found the captain near the concrete beam from the day before. He was lying with his elbows resting on it as he watched Alkhan-Kala through his binoculars.

Ventus sat next to him, smoking. They were both tense but showed no sign of nervousness. Sitnikov didn't turn around to me, but said: 'Call up the Kombat.'

I raised Pioneer and once again got Sabbit on the other end of the line.

'Pioneer receiving you. I'm passing you over to the commander.'

The Kombat spoke.

'Poker, this is command. OK, remain in your positions and keep both villages under observation. If the Chechens head your way you will correct the shelling. I'll be there toward evening. Do you receive, over?'

'Roger that Pioneer.' I took off the headphones as Sitnikov looked at me expectantly. 'We are to remain here and watch the Chechens, sir,' I told him.

The bombardment continued for about another hour and then began to die down. The self-propelled guns now fired one at a time, a single shell landing every couple of minutes. As the dust settled, the houses appeared through the thick swirls. I was amazed: after they had pounded Alkhan-Kala I'd expected to see a crater-filled wasteland, but the village looked almost intact. At least it seemed that way at first glance, but it was hard to say. We'd been wrong plenty of times before when we'd chosen a house in which to spend the night; often they looked undamaged, but when we entered the yard the walls were all that was left standing.

Only the right edge of the village showed heavy damage—Alkhan-Kala had taken a serious pounding there. Evidently they had fired only on this area, which was probably where Basayev and his men were, right opposite our group. If they were flushed out, our guys would have to meet them.

We lay low in our hollows, merging with the ground, staying flush with it and viewing the village along the barrels of our rifles, shifting and getting ready for battle, taking note of the landmarks in advance. We lay a long time, not making a sound that might give away our positions, waiting for the Chechens.

The Kombat arrived at nightfall, our second on this marsh. His carrier and three cars raced noisily up the hillock and stopped, making no attempt at silence.

He sat on top of the lead vehicle, rising above us like Mont Blanc in his usual arrogant pose, his arm resting on his knee, his elbow cocked and his body inclined forward, looking like an eagle. He was wearing a fancy NATO-issue flak jacket and his camouflage was not muddied. A real warrior.

'Oh. Here he is at last. Just look at him, strutting like a peacock as if he's on parade. All that's missing is a brass band—then not only the Chechens in Alkhan-Kala but the whole of Chechnya will know that Dumb Prick has arrived.'

The Kombat was not popular in the battalion. He treated us like cattle, talked down to us and used his fists a lot; he thought of us merely as cannon fodder, as drunks and morons. 'Dumb prick' was the Kombat's favorite expression, and indeed this was the only way he addressed his infantry—'Hey you, dumb prick! Get over here!'—and then he'd smack you in the mouth with a 'Take that!' We soldiers regarded him with a mutual hatred and had dubbed him Dumb Prick for the rest of his days.

One of the cars started to turn around on the hillock and take up positions. The Kombat quickly discussed something with Sitnikov, then turned to go and see the infantry; his squat figure vanished in the bushes.

Sitnikov went back toward his vehicle, followed by Ventus and myself. As he passed he told us: 'Get ready everyone, we're going back. We're being relieved.' He started to remove the Bee launcher from the carrier.

'Take everything. This vehicle is staying here—we'll ride with the Kombat.'

We took all the stuff to the other carrier. Sitting up top were two recon who accompanied the Kombat wherever he went, Denis and Anton. His arrogance had infected them as well, like a kind of flu, and they didn't bother to help us throw the launchers onto the top or give us a hand up. They just sat and smoked, waiting for their boss.

The Kombat came back a few minutes later, jumped up onto the carrier and dangled his legs into the commander's hatch.

'Let's go.'

The carrier lurched and crawled down from the hillock. Behind them the vehicles of the 9th also set off, breaking the bushes as they went before turning onto the path and heading for home. The newly arrived carriers had already taken their place.

The Kombat didn't wait for the infantry. 'Come on, step on it,' he ordered the driver.

The vehicle went faster and we felt the wind rush past us. I began to shiver; this past day had been too cold, my jacket was too damp and my stomach too empty. But our mood was buoyant. At last we were leaving this cursed marsh and going home. And even if home was only a wet, eternally muddy dugout, at least it had a stove; the rest of the battalion was there and you didn't have to spend the whole night worrying about being shot in the back from the forest. You could relax there, dry your boots and eat thin, undercooked, unsalted, tasteless, hot oatmeal. Finally I'd be able to throw off my body armor and stretch out on my back. And sleep on a bunk, not on the ground in the rain, or in a frozen carrier, but in a sleeping bag on a bunk! What bliss! You'd have to feel this with your own skin, your own frozen bladder and your armor-crushed shoulders to appreciate it. We'd been halted in the same place for over a week and had been able to set up a proper little existence there. And to be left undisturbed for a second week is an incredibly long time for a soldier.

Our carrier drove through the forest, avoiding an enormous puddle with a tractor stuck in the middle of it like an island, sunk up to its cabin in the ooze. I sat with my back against the turret, idly staring at the marsh as it receded into the past. Ventus sat behind me on the turret. The top of his boot rubbed against my neck, but I didn't bother to move away, or even to move at all.

I was thinking about nothing at all, a skill that I had developed in recent days. I had looked into the eyes of other soldiers as they were being jerked about on top of the carrier and I was amazed by their expressions, not focused on anything, not making out individual objects from their surroundings, letting everything just flow through them without being filtered by their senses. Absolutely empty, yet almost saturated at the same time—all the great truths of this world can be read in a soldier's eyes when they are turned inward; they understand everything, all is clear to them, and yet they care so little about it all that it scares you. You want to shake them and jerk them to their senses—'Hey, man, wake up!'—but their eyes will glide past your face, they won't say a thing and they turn away, cradling their rifles in a constant state of waiting, seeing and hearing everything but analyzing nothing, switching on only if there's an explosion or if tracer rounds flash past.

The first houses of Alkhan-Yurt crept into view. The hillock where we have just spent one of those never-ending days of war is now to the left and rear.

Damn, how long a day can be! We had spent just one day, a little over twenty-four hours, in this marsh and it seemed to last half a lifetime—so long and unbearably endless. I could hardly remember what it had been like before, back in civilian life. That life had become blurred, lost in the marsh that had now according to some unfathomable logic suddenly become very important, so much so that it seemed all significant events had happened here, in this marsh, where I'd spent half my life, stretching minutes into years, obscuring my memory with these minutes, letting them blot out everything inconsequential.

A tracer round flew out of the woods that now hid the hillock, silently dotting a red line just above us before it vanished in the woods on the other side. We all threw our heads back to follow it with our eyes and then looked at each other, trying to work out what it meant.

'Is that our infantry fooling around?'

'Idiots—as if they haven't done enough shooting.'

The shot came from roughly where one of the vehicles of the 7th should have been standing. They're shooting at crows for fun, I decided, and I cupped my hands around my mouth to amplify my shout: 'Hey, infantry, cut it out, you'll injure your own people.'

Right then another round flew out, much lower and more deliberate, and whined straight over our heads.

Instinctively we all dropped flat on the armor with a jerk, and our brains reacted a moment later.

'Shit, he's after us!'

'Chechens!'

'Son of a bitch sniper!'

A hot flush penetrated to the very core of my body, instantly dislodging the cold that had pulled me apart for the past day; I started to sweat and my clothing became hot and damp like a sauna. Fear.

I unslung my rifle as fast as I could, hampered by Denis who was leaning on my legs, pinning me to the armor and preventing me from finding a better position. I could feel the hard metal of the turret against my back. A bullet could just go through my chest now, hit the turret and ricochet back inside my body, ripping my lungs and heart to shreds. But Denis couldn't really move either.

Safety catch, get the damned safety catch!

Denis was already firing his sniper's rifle into the forest. He was firing blind, without aiming, his tracer rounds hitting above the source of the sniper's shot. He emptied the whole magazine in a couple of seconds and the hammer struck the empty chamber. He turned around and held his arm out. 'Give me a rifle! Get the driver's! I've only got ten rounds left in my other magazine.'

At last I slipped off my safety catch. The first burst of fire was like an orgasm, accompanied by a groan of relief. Over there, he's over there! Aim lower. The carrier jerked and jumped around . . . One more burst! Hell, I'll blow Denis's head off, I have to raise the barrel.

'Denis, get your head down!'

My rifle kicked right above Denis's ear and the muzzle flash seemed to lick the back of his head as the bullets passed a centimeter above it. 'I'll blow his head off,' the thought flashed again. Ventus's rifle thundered to the right of Denis's ear and hot shell cases tumbled off his head and shoulders. Our bodies were piled on top of each other, plastered all over the armor, and we were shooting indiscriminately with just one goal, to pin him down with lead and get him first, kill the bastard before he killed us.

'What's going on?'

I turned around and saw the Kombat half lying on the armor behind me.

'A Chechen sniper, over there, to the right of the tractor, right where we stood. Some of our guys are still there.'

But contrary to our expectations, the Kombat did not turn the vehicle round.

'Speed up, come on, step on it and take us into the bushes.'

The driver yanked the wheel sharply to the left and accelerated. With a lurch the carrier jumped into the bushes, and I managed to shelter behind the turret as Ventus piled on top of me. Thick branches hit the vehicle, ripping off a crate of sand tied on to the side, smacking our backs and arms and rasping the skin off our fingers. But the tracer shots kept coming from the woods, zipping over the top of the carrier on the right and left and hitting the trees with a dull thud, smacking the branches and clanging off the vehicle. Anton cried out, rolled into a ball and fell off the side toward the wheel.

'Comrade Major! Comrade Major!' I jabbed the Kombat in the side with my rifle barrel. 'We've lost a man.'

'Who?'

'Anton.'

'Is he wounded?'

'I don't know, probably. He grabbed his stomach and fell from the carrier.'

Once again the Kombat did not give the order to stop and instead told the driver to speed up. The carrier crashed through the bushes and emerged again on the path, sped along two hundred yards and stopped behind a barn on the edge of Alkhan-Yurt.

We had escaped the sniper fire. But behind us, where the two vehicles of the 9th had been and where Anton had fallen off injured, a skirmish had broken out. The chatter of automatic fire intensified.

We all jumped down from the vehicle, ran around the barn and crouched down, all the time looking in the direction of the firing. We had a quick powwow.

'Sitnikov, take two men and go around the right flank of the village. And you come with me through the village,' said the Kombat, pointing his finger at Denis.

The initial wave of panic had passed and was replaced with the heavy sensation of impending battle. We could still feel butterflies but there was no more fear. We became grave, acted quickly and silently, immediately understanding what was expected of us.

Ventus, Sitnikov and I ran alongside the barn to the village outskirts; the Kombat and Denis went toward the houses.

Sitnikov knelt down on one knee, while I fell on my belly and an idiotic thought flashed through my head—just don't land in a cow pattie. We both turned, following a whistling noise with our eyes. A mortar shell exploded with a bang on the spot where we'd just been standing, sending a greasy spout of mud into the sky.

'Goddamn hell, he can see us. Hey, driver, move the carrier around to the back of the barn or it'll get hit!'

The driver, who was hanging out of the hatch, dived back in and moved the vehicle.

I turned back to Sitnikov who was already climbing over a fence with the Fly launcher thumping the back of his body armor. I jumped up and climbed after him, hampered by my own jacket and the radio that dragged me downward and cut into my shoulders.

It's hard to run in a half-crouch while carrying a load of sixty pounds that makes your back and legs ache like crazy. Must keep up, must keep up, I thought. Sitnikov's back was in front of me all the time.

When we reached a house we squatted down at a corner, peering around cautiously. Around the other side was the path, and beyond it the woods. Sitnikov rocketed to his feet and ran across the road, while I took his place and waited until he'd reached the trees, covering him. Then I ran over with Ventus covering me from behind.

The fighting was in the woods, a bit farther in. Nothing

was visible through the trees, but judging from the sound it was no more than two hundred yards away. We covered the distance in short dashes, silently, straining our eyes and ears. Only occasionally did Sitnikov turn around to ask me, 'Where's Zhenya?' I would turn around too and hiss: 'Ventus, where are you?'

'Here!'

Ventus broke his way through the bushes toward us, his eyes bulging, breathing heavily, his rifle and Fly launcher trailing on the ground. He ran over and threw himself down heavily in the moss.

The infantry lay in a small clearing, separated from the village by a knee-high embankment with coils of barbed wire on top. Behind the tangle was the path, and thirty yards beyond that stood the first houses. The shooting had died down here and shifted to the right in the direction of our hillock, where the 7th were now located.

The soldiers that were concentrated along the embankment were peering into the village, scrutinizing something there. Two carriers had stopped on the right flank and were slowly moving their turrets.

Sitnikov crawled along the wire and tugged the foot of the nearest soldier.

'Where's the platoon commander?'

The soldier motioned farther on: 'Down there.'

The platoon commander was lying on his back in the center of the embankment, smoking a cigarette and looking up at the low sky. We crawled over to him and lay down beside him.

'So what's going on here? Where are the Chechens?'

'Somewhere in those houses,' he replied without turning

over, still looking up at the black clouds. 'They went quiet for some reason. Maybe we should gradually pull out, while they're not shooting?'

Without answering, Sitnikov crawled onto the bank and began to study the village. I crouched down next to him.

It seemed quiet in there, nothing moved. The empty clay houses that had been riddled with automatic gunfire showed no signs of life.

Sitnikov turned onto his side and raised himself on an elbow.

'So . . .' He didn't manage to finish his sentence. An automatic chattered in a yard just opposite us; the burst of fire passed over Sitnikov's shoulders and also hit the ground beneath his elbow. He drew his head into his body, swearing, and jumped down from the wire. Another burst came from the right in reply and zipped across the clearing, passing through the massed infantry. You could see the bullets hitting the grass between the figures plastered to the ground before they disappeared into the woods.

From the corner of my eye I thought I saw a muzzle flash in the window of a house. And then a shadow flitting from room to room. I shouted, waving my arm.

'There he is, Captain, in that window!'

'Where, which one?' Sitnikov asked, pulling the Fly from his shoulder and looking at me. There was a wild fury in his eyes. 'Well, which one is it?'

But the window was empty again and the house had fallen still; nothing moved, and I was no longer sure that there had even been a Chechen there. Then more bursts of fire came as if from nowhere, flying over the embankment and disappearing. And that was all. We couldn't pinpoint the source: the shots weren't visible and we couldn't tell from the sound, which got distorted by the courtyards of the houses.

I stared intently at the village but my uncertainty only grew. Maybe there really hadn't been anyone at the window, maybe I had just imagined it.

'Well, which one?'

'God knows, Captain, that one I think . . .'

Sitnikov looked at the window, primed the rocket and trained it at the house.

'Are you sure?'

I didn't reply, so Sitnikov lowered the weapon, loath to waste it, and instead sprayed rifle fire at the window. The burst loosed a line of clay chunks from the wall and knocked out the wooden sill, which spun in the air and then fell silently through the window opening.

And then once again I thought I could see someone in the house.

'There he is, the bastard!' No longer in any doubt, I unslung my rifle, aimed and fired a short burst at the window. Then another, and one more after that. The deputy supply officer and Sitnikov joined in right away, followed by the rest of the infantry.

At first I fired carefully at the target, but my hands were shaking after running and I couldn't hold the rifle steady. The barrel jumped around and the bullets hit low and then above the window, and in the end I started firing in long bursts without aiming.

The magazine emptied quickly. I unclipped it and took out a full one, which happened to be loaded with tracer rounds. I watched them fly through the dark window and ricochet inside the house, bouncing off something hard by the far wall and flying around the room with sparks and a hum as they tried to escape.

The house withered under the intensity of our fire, jumping on its foundation while clouds of dust and dry clay were blown from its walls and streamed to the ground like waterfalls; the earth churned at the base of the house, kicking up clumps of grass.

The infantry worked themselves up even more; some were already firing from the knee, others shot at the neighboring houses. We all felt that special intoxication you get only when things are going well, when you know you have clear superiority and the enemy can't match your firepower. There's no longer any fear—that has passed and you begin to feel your power. It makes you heady and arouses you; it draws a sweat of exhilaration, a desire to wreak full vengeance for all your fear, as you pour down fire to the left and right without thinking.

Sitnikov grabbed his launcher, went down on one knee and fired at the window. The shell flew through the gap like a fiery spot, exploding with a mighty roar inside the enclosed confinements and illuminating the house with a flash of lightning. Debris spouted onto the street and a cloud of gray smoke was belched out.

I was deafened by the sound of the rocket firing. Sitnikov had positioned the rocket clumsily and some of the back blast had struck me in the back of the head. My skull was ringing, I couldn't hear anything and the cordite vapors stung sickeningly in my throat. I leaped off the embankment, pinched my nose between two fingers and tried to swallow and to blow through my ears to clear them. Someone shook my shoulder: 'Are you shell-shocked?'

I could barely hear the voice, but from the intonation it seemed as though someone was shouting a question at me.

'No, just a bit deafened, it'll pass,' I shouted back in reply. My own voice surprised me; it was deep, as if it had come from a barrel, and it wasn't my internal hearing that had picked it up but something outside.

I blew through my ears again and shook my head. The ringing sound diminished a little, but my head still felt like it was packed with cotton wool and my thinking was fogged.

The Kombat appeared on the embankment, shooting frenziedly at the village, aiming carefully at one spot and saying something as he fired. I crawled over and lay down beside him, trying to make out what he was shooting at. Seeing nothing except the same empty houses, I began to fire in the same direction.

Hearing me next to him, the Kombat tore himself away from his rifle and elbowed me.

'You, call up Armor for me.'

'What?'

'Call Armor, you dumb prick!'

Both armored carriers answered immediately.

'Armor-185 receiving you, Pioneer.'

'Armor-182 receiving you, Pioneer.'

'Comrade Major, Armor on the line,' I said, passing the headphones and mouthpiece to the Kombat, who pressed one earpiece to his head.

'Armor, Armor, this is the commander. OK, now fire on the village, starting with the houses in front of us and slightly to the left, where the brick one is.' He motioned toward the houses as if the guys in the carriers could see him. 'Then move back and cover us. We're pulling out. Everyone, let's go!'

He returned the headphones to me and gave the order: 'Pass this down the line, we're pulling out. Small dashes, one at a time. And get Sitnikov over here.'

Sitnikov lay about ten yards to my right. I crawled over to him, tugging on the pant legs of two soldiers as I went. 'We're pulling out.'

'Comrade Captain, the Kombat wants you. We're pulling out.' Then, turning to the machine gunner lying next to him with his face buried in the ground, I yelled in his ear: 'We're pulling out, short runs, pass it on. Do you hear?'

The gunner lifted his head, looked blankly at me and buried his face in the ground again. His machine gun lay idly beside him and clearly hadn't been fired once in all this time.

The kid's stunned, I thought, and shook him. 'Why aren't you firing? I said why aren't you firing, have you been hit?'

The gunner raised his head again and looked at me with indifferent, empty eyes. I realized then that he hadn't been hit. I knew that stupid, indifferent gaze: the guy had lost it, been broken by the marsh. It happens.

A soldier who seems normal can all of a sudden barely work his legs; he moves like a sleepwalker, his head drooping as if he doesn't have the strength to hold it straight, snot pouring ceaselessly from his nose. The war can break a guy like that, and very quickly. In just two or three days he can just let himself go without even resisting, apathetically taking everything as it comes. You could beat him, kick him or cut his fingers off, and he still won't wake up or speed up, or even say anything. The only cure for this is sleep, rest and food.

I shook the machine gunner again by the shoulder, trying to get some life out of him.

'Can you hear me? Why aren't you shooting?'

The gunner said nothing, and then after a while he ventured timidly: 'Don't have much ammo . . .'

I could barely control my anger.

'What the fuck did you come here for, to fight or to stand around scratching your balls? Like hell do we need you and your machine gun! So you're running low on ammo, are you? What do you plan on doing with it, salting it and taking it home with you? What are you saving it for? Don't you see you're in battle? Now give it here!'

I grabbed his machine gun, dug the bipod into the ground and loosed off an entire belt at the village in one long burst. I angrily thrust the weapon back at the guy's broad but sagging chest and snapped: 'Take it! Now pull back. Get your sorry ass out of here and use your machine gun. Shut their goddamn mouths for them!'

The gunner silently took the machine gun from me, and without having fired a shot he crawled back into the woods, dragging the weapon along the ground. I felt another surge of fury and wanted to kick him up the backside, but in the end I just dismissed him with a wave of the hand. Idiot.

The infantry stirred at the other end of the clearing and began to pull back. One after the other the men stood up, ran six or seven yards and fell to the ground. Then the others ran after them.

The carriers started their engines in the bushes and revved up, sending clouds of diesel smoke into the air. They drove out onto the path and stopped between our positions and the village. The turrets turned toward the houses and froze, their barrels quivering like elephants' trunks sniffing out the enemy, and then they opened up simultaneously.

I had never seen a large-caliber cannon fire at close range before, and the effect was staggering. A mighty roar of fourteen-millimeter rounds muffled everything and my ears blocked up again. The impact of the sound was so powerful that I felt my body reverberating through the plates in my flak jacket. Cones of fire from the muzzles illuminated the clearing with a flickering light, and tracer rounds ripped through the walls into the houses where they exploded, shredding the roofs, tearing down trees. A vast quantity of metal hit the village with such unbelievable kinetic energy that it was dead in an instant, torn to shreds by the shells.

I felt uneasy again, plagued by the same feeling I'd had when the self-propelled guns were shelling Alkhan-Kala. Every time I heard heavy-caliber shell fire, ours or the Chechens', I got this chilling sense of unease. It wasn't fear, although fear feels just as cold. It was different, something more animal, left over from the genetic code of our ancestors. This is probably how a gopher freezes in horror when it hears the roar of a lion, and feels the power of its jaws through tremors in the ground.

I had killed before, or at least tried to kill those people who shot at me, but my killing was different, on a lesser scale and under my control. The death I administered was not grotesque—just a small hole in the body and that was it. My kind of death was fair; it gave them a chance to hide from the bullet behind a wall, just as I had hidden from their bullets. But to hide from a large-caliber cannon was impossible. This caliber could reach you everywhere; it crushed walls and killed terribly, with a roar, tearing off heads, turning bodies inside out, blowing the flesh off a person and leaving bare bones inside their tunics.

I did not feel any pity or twinges of conscience for the Chechens. We were enemies. They had to be killed to the last man, and in any way possible. And the faster and technically easier it was to do this, the better.

There was just one thing . . . What if they had large-caliber cannons too?

While the carriers were pounding the village the infantry managed to regroup in the woods. Sitnikov and I let everyone pull back first and were the last to get up from the embankment. We loosed off a few parting shots and then ran after the rest.

We went straight through the woods and came out in a clearing where a cow pasture began. We fired our last shots, skirted the woods and moved slowly down the path past the village, occasionally letting off a couple of bursts at the houses. Crouching, the infantry ran after us and then walked along in the cover of the carriers.

Just where the woods ended I ran slap-bang into Igor. He was also lagging behind, letting his unit go ahead. As usual he jabbed me playfully in the shoulder and bared his teeth in a grin.

'You alive?'

I smiled back.

'Alive. And you?'

'Me? Of course I'm alive. Heck, we took a fair beating there, no?' Igor had not yet cooled off after the firefight; he was excited and in good spirits.

'Our vehicles were behind yours. We heard you start shooting and we followed. And then, oh boy, did it kick off, automatic rifle fire from all sides. I thought we were all done for. Bastards, they came in from behind. And then there was that recon guy of yours, what's his name? Anton. We nearly shot him. We watched him run out of the bushes and try to climb up the side of our vehicle, thought he was a Chechen.'

'So what happened to him, is he wounded?'

'Nah, he just got knocked off your carrier by branches ... Fuck, we've got a long way to run yet, look.' Igor measured the distance to the turning where the Kombat's carrier stood behind the barn. The field of view ended at the other end of the village where the Chechen positions were. 'I got bushed running through the woods. Why the hell did I put on my body armor? Come on, you go first. I'll cover you.'

While we'd been exchanging news the infantry had pulled out, leaving us on our own.

'No, you go first, as far as that metal thing on the ground, and I'll follow.'

'OK,' agreed Igor. He straightened his flak jacket, crouched down and ran the fifty yards to what was either a piece of a turret crane or a bit from a silo. He came sliding down, turned to face the village, trained his rifle and waved at me.

It wasn't pleasant to leave the cover of the trees and cross the open space. A picture flashed through my head of a silent tracer flying from the bushes, heading right for me, and the hard turret, and then the ricochet inside my body. I glanced at the houses. They were very close—at this distance you could hit someone in the ear with a sniper's rifle. And if they decided to return fire you'd have no cover and they'd kill you with the first bullet.

Trying not to think about this I burst out of the trees and raced toward Igor.

We caught up with the infantry in two sprints and then started leapfrogging back with them. I was running with difficulty now; having to throw myself down and get up again each time was unbearable, my arms and legs were shaking and I cursed my ungainly flak jacket and this wretched radio. After the next run I didn't throw myself down but just dropped onto one knee, breathing heavily and grimly preparing to run again, and again after that, and then on to the bend where the Kombat's carrier was behind the barn, at least three hundred yards away.

I was desperate for a drink. The water we'd picked up the day before in the battalion as we were leaving for the swamp had run out almost immediately. The empty flask only got in my way, banging my hip, and it seemed even heavier now that it was empty.

Only with difficulty did I fend off the urge to drink from a puddle. I hadn't drunk cold water all day in a bid to stay warm, and the reserves of liquid left in my body were being squeezed out by my flak jacket, a drop at a time through every pore. Trickles of sweat flooded my eyes, my mouth dried up and my back ached so much it seemed I would never feel limber again. My sodden underwear stuck to my body and a damp heat rose from beneath my collar with every step. My rifle stretched my arms and I had the urge to empty my pockets of everything, down to the last pin. As my energies dwindled, I stopped going down on one knee; I just plodded along wearily with my head lowered.

Igor dragged himself along next to me with just as much difficulty.

The infantry had stopped running too and were wandering along, all equally exhausted.

We trailed across the field strewn with cow patties, ignoring the houses behind us that could still hold Chechens, dreaming only of getting to the vehicles, lying down and stretching our aching legs.

But the Kombat had other ideas. When we reached the bend and started to clamber up the vehicles, he unleashed a hail of abuse at us and gave the order for us to pull back farther to the positions of the 7th. They were a quater mile away, at the place where I had spoken with Vasya yesterday. Yesterday? How long ago that was, how long a day can last and never fucking end. And now we had to go somewhere else!

We sheltered behind the vehicles and resumed walking, wading through the ditch full of filthy water that the carriers had got stuck in the day before, skidding in the wet clay, sliding and struggling to pull ourselves out, unable to do so unaided but having no energy to help others.

We had only about fifty feet to go to the first trench, and we could see the heads of the 7th watching us inquisitively over the edge, when I suddenly felt I couldn't go a single step farther. Fighting through a kaleidoscope in front of my eyes, I groped my way down onto a small rut and leaned back on it, resting neatly between two cow patties. Igor fell down next to me. The infantry scattered on the ground too, just short of the trenches that the 7th had dug, a few steps beyond the bounds of human strength.

We sat there panting, unable to say a word, gulping the air into our parched mouths. Dozens of throats gasped to fill lungs with oxygen, and steam rose in the cold air around us.

But thirst was greater than our exhaustion, and licking my cracked lips I managed to croak: 'Boys . . . water . . . give us a drink.'

The soldiers of the 7th dragged out an aluminum milk can, stood it in front of us and gave us a large ladle. I threw the lid off and looked inside. The water was murky and there were weeds in it. When I dipped the ladle in, two minnows darted out from under the tendrils, circling quickly in the enclosed space, bouncing off the side and sending silt to the surface.

I looked at the soldiers.

'Where's the water from?'

'From over there,' a pockmarked sergeant told me, nodding toward a near-stagnant stream that looped across the pasture. I followed it with my gaze. The stream came from the same woods we had just left. From the marsh. I shouldn't have waited and just drunk from the ditch, I thought, and dismissing it all I lowered my head to the ladle.

Never in my life had I drunk anything more delicious than this brackish marsh water. I drank it in huge gulps, freezing cold and with weeds too, and occasionally I let down the ladle to take air and then gulped from it again. A little minnow banged against my teeth, but I didn't stop, I couldn't, and I swallowed it live.

I drank the liter-sized ladle down in one gulp. The water made me sweat instantly and I wiped my chin on my sleeve, recovered my breath and dipped the ladle in once more.

After I had drunk my fill I passed the ladle around and flopped down again in front of the trench. I lit up and finally stretched out my screaming legs, feeling an unbelievable but already diminishing exhaustion in my muscles. The fog and roaring in my ears passed, my energy started to return and I came back to life.

The infantry perked up too. They finished off the ten-gallon can in two minutes and then sat down on the ground and lit cigarettes.

Men of the 7th climbed out of the trenches and came over to us to ask about the fight. And the infantry fluffed up their feathers and, with the casual air of seasoned soldiers, recounted their 'battle.' This was the first taste of action for many of them and it had gone well, with no casualties, and now that they had rested they were filled with the feeling that it wasn't so terrifying; the fighting had been a piece of cake this time, and maybe it would always be that easy. They had fired and been fired at, bullets really had whistled over their heads and they'd have something to tell the folks back home. They felt like real rangers who had walked through fire and water. The adrenaline that their fear had driven out of them in huge quantities now churned in their blood, and their energy flooded back. I looked at them with a smile and listened to their chatter.

' ... The Kombat and I were running, looking around, and this Chechen appears from a house porch to see what's happening. So the Kombat whips off his rifle and goes for him. The guy falls down and crawls around the house to croak, and the Kombat keeps firing at him, must have loosed off a whole magazine. He's got a big smirk on his face, very pleased with himself. "Huh, dumb prick," he says ...'

'... These recon were checking out the routes to see where we could get out of the village. There weren't many of them, see, so they didn't stop to mess around, they even shot the hell out of the bushes. That's their tactic. They crawl up, hit them with a grenade launcher and pull out. When we were going to reinforce the 15th outside Oktyabrskoye they burned out a carrier doing just that ...'

'... I fell from the carrier and there were bullets going *whack-whack* in the branches, right over my damn head. Man did they start up then! I crawled behind the bushes and then I saw our guys lying over in the clearing ...'

No one was paying any attention to the village now. The battle had finished, the Chechen recon we'd run into had gone; they'd either pulled out or holed up somewhere. So we relaxed. We lay on the wet ground in front of the trenches, without digging in or camouflaging ourselves, and we just sat around in a group. *Which you do not do in war, under any circumstances.*

The Chechens immediately punished us for this carelessness. We all heard the whistle.

It started in the village and grew in strength, cutting through the exhaustion in our brains and throwing us onto the ground.

'Incoming!'

'Get down!'

'They aren't letting us pull back, bastards!'

We landed in the ruts. My fatigue dissolved instantly and my body was flushed with heat once again.

The first shell exploded a fair distance away from us, on the pasture. But behind this one a few more flew out of the village and exploded closer and closer as they advanced on us.

I was in a vulnerable position. I lay exposed on a slope, presenting a perfect trap for shrapnel, and I was entirely visible from all sides. The next shell hit the ground like a fat raindrop;

a shower of clay clods rained down from the sky, smacking me painfully on the back of the head.

I desperately wanted to shrink, become tiny, congeal into a ball and disperse into the ground, merging with its protective lap. I even managed to picture a tiny burrow where I would be safe from shrapnel and bullets, protected on all sides as I peered out with one eye. With every fresh explosion my desire to be in the burrow grew stronger and stronger, and with my eyes pressed tightly shut, afraid to open them before I died, I groped around in the grass for a way in.

But there was none. My body no longer responded to me; it did not want to crawl into hiding but instead became huge, filling the field, presenting a target that couldn't be missed. I would now be killed.

I shouldn't have come to Chechnya. I shouldn't have come.

Oh dear God, just make it so that I'm no longer in this hell-hole Chechnya, whisk me home so that the next shell finds only an empty space. I swear I'll beg forgiveness from all those I've wronged or failed in this life, that I'll love the whole world from now on and donate all my army wages to Chechen orphans, whatever it takes, just get me out of here. And dear God, do it right now, because here comes another.

This time it was certain death and there was nothing I could do in those rapidly contracting fragments of the only second that remained—the shell would hit much faster than I could think to race into the ditch with Igor, who had made it, faster than it took me even to move a finger—here it comes now—I leaped up with a throaty scream of defiance and fear, eyes bulging and seeing nothing but the ditch I was dashing for, slipping on the wet grass, tumbling headfirst into a cow pattie.

The shell dropped way beyond us and blew up on the other side of the pasture. No one moved.

Igor and I started to shift and shake off the mud. I pulled my face out of the pattie, looked around through one crazed eye and mumbled, 'Got away with it.'

My head was still empty. All I could hear ringing in my ears was the whistle of the shell, my shell, short, sharp and piercing, flying toward me again and again out of the village, coming right at me. I automatically cleaned the fresh, liquid mess from my hands, and I felt no trace of disgust; I was ready to dive straight back into shit if the need arose.

Beside us the infantry platoon commander was brushing himself off just as dismally. Standing at his full height he slowly picked off blades of grass from his pants, one by one, and dropped them on the ground. Then he held one of them in his hand, twirled it in his fingers and said thoughtfully: 'It's actually my birthday today.'

I looked at him in silence for a few seconds, and then suddenly I began to laugh.

At first I tremored quietly, trying to contain it, but then I gave in and started to roar, louder all the time. Hysterical notes crept in, and with my head thrown back I flopped down on my knees facing the low, clouded sky, threw my arms out and howled, purging my fear with laughter, the smothering fear of a bombardment, when everything is out of your hands and you have no way of protecting yourself or saving your life, and you just lie there facedown on the ground, praying that you'll get away with it this time too. It's not the rousing fear you feel in battle, but a lifeless fear, as cold as the grass you are pressing yourself into.

Igor crouched down beside me and lit up. He looked at me without saying anything for a while, then poked me in the shoulder.

'Hey, homeboy, what's up with you?' Fatigue weighed heavy

in his voice, making it dry and hoarse. He too had been scared, and fear ravages you, sucks the energy out of you and makes it hard even to speak.

I couldn't answer him; I carried on heaving with laughter, unable to stop. Then after I'd caught my breath, I managed to say something, punctuating my words with more chuckles.

'Birthday! Exactly! Don't worry, I'm OK, my head's still on my shoulders. You know what?' I said, wiping my tears and feeling the cow dung smear across my face. 'I just remembered. Today is the fifth of January . . . the fifth . . . of January,' I said, still snorting.

'So what?'

'Well, it's my Olga's birthday today too, see?' I said. 'Today's the fifth of January, they've just celebrated New Year's back home—belated Happy New Year's to you, by the way—and now they're sitting around a table celebrating, all dressed up, drinking wine and eating tasty food. All they do is party and they have no idea what a bombardment is like. And people are giving my girl flowers . . . They've got flowers there, imagine! Flowers! And here I am, covered in crap, with lice scuttling on my nuts, it's a scream all right!' and I burst into laughter again, falling onto my back and rolling from side to side.

The thought of flowers staggered me. I could clearly picture Olga sitting at the table covered with a white cloth, with a glass of fine white wine—she loves dry white wine and doesn't drink cheap stuff—surrounded by enormous, beautiful bouquets. She has a big smile on her face as she listens to her friends' birthday wishes for her. The room is full of bright light and the guests are wearing ties, making merry and dancing; their day's work is over and they are free of problems. They don't have to think about finding food and warmth, and instead they choose flowers for a girl. In that world there is time to work and time to have fun. And a person gets food and warmth right there in the maternity ward, along with a birth certificate.

It was only here that people got killed regardless of the time of day.

Sitting in that trench it seemed to me that there was war everywhere, that everyone was out to kill everyone else, that human grief permeated every corner of the world, right to the door of my own home, that there was no way it could be otherwise.

And yet it turns out that there is a place where people give flowers.

And that is so strange, so stupid and so funny.

Olga, Olga! What happened to our lives, what happened to the world, how did I come to be here now? Why must I now kiss a rifle instead of you, and bury my face in crap instead of in your hair? Why?

After all, these constantly drunk, unwashed contract soldiers, smeared in muck, are not the worst people in the world. We have atoned for a hundred years of sin in that marsh. So how come this is all we get for our pains? I just couldn't get my head around it all.

My darling, may everything be well with you. May you never in your life know what I've known here. May you always have a celebration, a sea of flowers, and wine and laughter. But I know that you are thinking about me now, and your face is sad. Forgive me for this. You are the brightest; you are worthy of the very best.

Let me be the one who has to die in a marsh. Lord, how we are different! Only a two-hour flight separates us, but what completely dissimilar lives we lead, we who are two identical halves! And how hard it will be to connect our lives again.

Igor took the last drag on his cigarette and ground it out. He became pensive; I could tell he was thinking of pretty dresses, perfume, wine and dancing. Then he looked at me, at my ragged jacket and filthy face, and grinned: 'Damn right, Happy New Year.'

I didn't manage to eat that day. As soon as we returned to the battalion, I jumped down from the vehicle and headed for my tent, where I came face to face with the platoon commander as he was on his way out. He quickly greeted me and asked about the fight, and then he gave me a new assignment—to go as radioman with the fat lieutenant psychologist.

The psychologist used to be a platoon commander in charge of repairs, or maybe he was just twiddling his thumbs in the rear somewhere, because basically he was no good for anything. But later, when they sent the regiment to Chechnya, it turned out that according to regulations each battalion had to have a psychologist. If any soldier starts losing his head at all the killing, he can come and bleat about his psychological incompatibility with the war and the army in general. And theoretically the kind psychologist would put his arm around the weary soldier, bemoan his lot with him, calm him with sedatives and send him to a Crimean sanatorium for rehabilitation. But all we got were bums like the fat lieutenant who served no purpose anywhere else. As it happens, no one ever came to him for help, because the only thing he could do to set a crazed head back in place was administer a hard punch on the jaw. And his fists were plenty big enough for that. He was also an energetic fellow who would get bored if he had nothing to do, so he would run all sorts of errands.

This time they gave the psychologist the following task: Get to Alkhan-Yurt, find the battalion water tanker that's been ambushed and burned out by the Chechens and tow it back to the repair company. And also find out what happened to the driver and the escort soldier—see if they are alive, and, if not, find their bodies and bring them back.

Three of us went: the psychologist and I, and Sergei, the driver of the tracked carrier we were in.

It wasn't very comfortable riding on the carrier. Although it was quite a bit wider than a wheeled carrier and completely flat, it jolted sharply when the tracks made turns, and I felt like a pancake sliding and jumping in a greasy frying pan as I tried to grab on to the fittings on its armor.

And here I was once again, traveling through this dismal field in the rain, with the sound of the tracks churning up the muck, with mud flying up into my face and landing on top of the vehicle. My jacket was still damp, for the nth month in a row, and my boots were sopping wet again. And for God knows how many months now my things had been filthy. And it was cold—God, how I was sick of this eternal, bastardly cold; if I could spend just one day in the warmth, to warm through my bones. And I was hungry.

We huddled together in our turned-up collars and smoked. There was that turning again, the Federal Highway and the sign RUSSIANS ARE PIGS. How sick I was of all this—I just wanted to go home!

This time we didn't turn toward the silos but in the other direction, to the left. We stayed on the highway and turned off to Alkhan-Yurt, and then crept along another quarter mile, keeping close to the houses until we reached a mosque. It was newly built but already shot to pieces. This was where the zone of destruction began. Not one house was intact; most had just two or three walls and a pile of debris in the middle, or just one wall, like a person blown inside out by an explosion, with strips of wallpaper trailing outside in the wind.

We were stopped by some interior ministry troops at the mosque; they were clustered in the building's empty loading bay, pressed against the inside of the fence. No one could get any farther. Around the corner, Chechens held the rest of the village, and they had dug in in large numbers. All day long the area boiled with shelling. The explosions came one after the other, the charges falling as constantly as the incessant cold rain. Somewhere farther on, nearer the river, there was uninterrupted shooting, and the chatter of automatics rose above the general barrage.

There was no life in the village; the streets were deserted and the locals were nowhere to be seen. The houses stood dead. Only the interior troops huddled beside the fence and crawled along the ditches. Occasionally, after peering cautiously around the corner, they would run across the open ground.

The psychologist and I immediately fell into the rules of the game. Lying on our stomachs, we flattened ourselves to the carrier. Hanging slightly off the side, the psychologist shouted at the interior troops:

'Hey, boys! Somewhere here they burned out our water tanker. Have you seen it?'

'Yes,' answered one small soldier who was dwarfed by his flak jacket. 'There it is, we towed it out,' and he pointed down the street.

We looked to where he was pointing. Beyond the bend, in the no-man's-land, stood a huge pile of rusty, charred metal. The psychologist turned to the soldier in bewilderment:

'No, not that one, ours was new.'

The soldier looked at him as if he was an idiot. The psychologist suddenly realized that he had said something stupid and flushed with embarrassment. It had been new, then it got old, something that happens fast in war. It just takes a while to sink in sometimes. Same with a person: one minute he's alive, the next he's dead.

'Listen, can we tow it, do you think?' he asked the soldier.

'Yes. I told you we towed it. We just dumped it there. What do you want it for? You'll never repair it.'

'We have to recover it so we can write it off as lost in battle. Do you know where the driver is?'

'Gone back to the regiment. He was wounded, so was the other guy with him. They left together.'

'I see.' The psychologist turned away from the soldier and stuck his head into the driver's hatch. 'Sergei, head over that way, do you see it over there?'

The carrier's tracks crackled on brick debris strewn on the asphalt as it slowly drove over to the wrecked tanker and turned around to back up. Sergei began to reverse with the psychologist guiding him, kneeling to get a better view. Still lying on top, I took off the radio to get ready. When the psychologist waved his arm and Sergei stood up in the hatch, I would have to jump down and hook a chain onto the tanker.

Interior troops lay in a ditch that ran past us to the left, watching our maneuvering with detachment. Beyond the ditch stretched a field sown with corn, and a lone farmer's house stood in the middle of it. Tracer rounds flew out of the house every four or five seconds in the direction of Alkhan-Yurt, the red dashes etched against the woods in the evening light. The streams of fire crossed the road about fifty yards ahead of them and flew in a mass beyond the river, vanishing among the house roofs and the plumes from the explosions.

I suddenly realized that we were right in the thick of the fighting. That patch we had occupied in the marsh was only the frilly edge of the pie, while this place was right in the middle, with all the berries.

A Chechen sniper was firing from the farmer's house without trying to conceal himself. Interior troops were moving about in packs here, while somewhere else the Chechens were doing the same. They were being buffeted by the explosions, but our guys were over there too. You couldn't see them from where we were, but the Chechen sniper in the house could, and he was firing at them. And the troops here could see the sniper but no one bothered with him. They had been lying in their ditch for so long, with so much fire pouring overhead, that no one gave a damn about a lone sniper. Nor did I, or Sergei, or the psychologist. We weren't supposed to be fighting here; we'd only come to pick up our water tanker, which had apparently been shot up from that very house where the sniper was now. The Chechen could see us too, but he wasn't firing at us, evidently concentrating on a more attractive target. His tracer fire disappeared over the river toward a spot visible only to him. And in that spot our guys saw only the sniper, who had become the most important and fearful thing on earth for them, and they desperately wanted someone here to kill him. But no one touched him, because to kill him or dig him out of the house would be difficult—all they could do is keep him pinned down for a while, but then there would be a firefight when he started shooting back, and he'd kill someone for sure. And no one wanted that. But he wasn't shooting at us yet so there was no need to bother him unnecessarily.

Meanwhile, the war was raging all around and as usual nothing made much sense. Everyone was doing his thing—the sniper was popping off rounds, the interior troops were fighting across the village, shells were exploding, bullets were flying, the psychologist and I were towing a wreck, and the wounded driver and the other guy were walking home somewhere, like schoolboys after lessons. Everyone was stewing in this war, and now that there was a brief lull no one wanted to shatter it. Everything just ticked along like normal; it was humdrum even.

God only knows what lay in store and what was going on in the sniper's head, so we did well to take care.

'Comrade Lieutenant, you should get down, the sniper's pretty active over there,' I warned the psychologist.

The lieutenant looked at the house, followed the tracer with his eyes, lay down on the armor and waved his arm.

'OK, stop!' And looking at me, he shouted, 'Hook up!'

The interior soldier had been right, there was nothing left of the tanker: the bare hubs of the wheels, their rims sprouting wires from the charred tires; the gaping mouth of the half-open, bullet-scarred hood; the riddled, mangled cabin. It had been fired on at close range by several weapons and God knows how the driver and the other guy had survived. One of them had left dried blood on the metal cabin step.

I hooked on the tow cable, waved to the psychologist and jumped onto the carrier. Sergei hit the gas and the tanker dragged itself back home behind us, its twisted, charred metal groaning as it went.

For us the war was over for the day, and we left.

Behind us tracer fire kept on zipping over the river, the interior troops remained in their ditches and Alkhan-Yurt heaved with explosions. It was still raining.

The mortar dangled out of the side of the army car, bouncing as we went over ruts. The blind, hooded eye of its barrel stared into the sky, and I felt the urge to spit into this blind eye.

I sat smoking on the low bench in the car, propping myself up on the side with one leg. My head was empty of thoughts. Everything that took place around me—the foggy gray morning, the drizzle, the same damned field day after day, the path, the same highway, Alkhan-Yurt—drifted past my consciousness without lingering in it.

I was driving to Alkhan-Yurt once again, this time with a mortar battery. We were on our way with two army cars with two crews to reinforce the infantry, heading back into the gloom where we had yesterday emerged from battle and where I had drunk greenish water with minnows in it, and laughed myself silly as I remembered the birthday.

Again we turned off the highway, through the massive puddle, past the antitank platoon's house and the site hut, where Korobok had been stripped to the waist and shaving in a piece of mirror propped on a board. I wanted to say hello to Vasya, but there was no sign of him. Maybe I could have picked up those pants.

The cars stopped when we reached the forward positions of the 7th. The mortar crews poured out of the back and like ants they secured the bedplate, uncovered the mortars and positioned them. They did it all so swiftly and smoothly, without needing to be ordered, that I was surprised—I had never seen such coordination. The battery commander had done a good job on them, I thought to myself—the mortar men were already half set up before I'd even sucked the last nicotine from my cigarette.

The commander was a dry, muscular guy with a long, high-cheekboned face and a resolute, cruel disposition; he never doubted the correctness of his actions and was prepared to kill readily, and even happily. Now he stood by the army car studying Alkhan-Kala through his binoculars. He called me over.

'Tell the Kombat I'm ready to fire. And check the coordinates. Now we'll give these bastards a good going over.'

I called up Pioneer.

'Slab to Pioneer, do you receive me? Please confirm coordinates.'

'Pioneer to Slab. Abort shoot, I repeat, abort shoot and return to base.'

'Please repeat. How abort?'

'Slab abort shoot and move out.'

I took off the headphones, not understanding anything, and looked at the mortar commander: 'Are we waiting for something, Comrade Captain?'

'How do you mean waiting?'

'Our orders are to abort firing and return home.'

'Home? You must have misunderstood. Tell them I am in position and ready to fire. Ask if the earlier target coordinates remain or are there new instructions?'

The soldiers stood around listening to our conversation, smoking, and looking at me expectantly. I knew that they loved their work. They were sent to the front line more often than anyone else, to reinforce other units. And when they returned they were excitable and talkative. The mortar crew was like a separate unit. While we in the battalion sat stuck in our dugouts in the second line of defense, dying of boredom, the mortar guys raced around Chechnya doing their thing, fighting and shooting at the enemy and reveling in it all. And they prided themselves in their work, saw themselves as real military daredevils. They would hang out only with each other and were basically strangers in the battalion, living separately from the rest of us. It was a truly battle-ready unit with a brutally entrenched hierarchy, and they carried out orders unquestioningly, regarded their commander as a god and trusted him implicitly. He reciprocated the trust and would fuss over them, find food and organize steam baths for his unit. Eventually he was able to use his authority to shape his battery the way he thought an army should be, and he didn't let other commanders near his soldiers, teaching them like good dogs to heed only his instructions.

Right now they were waiting for the commander to give

them their orders, and they could not understand what the delay was. And he in turn was waiting to hear his orders from me. He couldn't grasp why there was a holdup either.

I called up Pioneer again, and once again I heard the order to abort. 'He says abort,' I told him with a shrug.

The commander boiled over.

'Who does he think I am, some kid he can send running back and forth like this? First we're supposed to shoot, then we're not!'

He suddenly fell silent and turned to his soldiers. His face darkened.

'Take aim! Fix on old coordinates!'

The soldiers ran to their positions and spun the handles of the sights.

'First crew standing by!'

'Second crew standing by!'

The commander didn't answer. He was glued to his binoculars, studying Alkhan-Yurt in silence as if he was trying to make out Chechens there.

An infantry lieutenant appeared from the trenches of the 7th, came over and stood beside the commander, who still didn't respond. The lieutenant adjusted his rifle on his shoulder and stood for a while in silence, also looking at the village. Then he asked: 'Are you going to fire?'

'I thought I'd loose a couple of rounds off.'

'Our guys are there,' the lieutenant said, nodding toward the woods and beyond, to where the marsh was.

'Where?' The commander tore his eyes away from the binoculars and looked at him inquiringly.

'Over there, beyond the woods. The marsh starts after that and our platoon is there.'

'Is that right? And I have orders to fire on there. So now what?'

'I don't know. There are Chechens in Alkhan-Kala, but it's pretty quiet there now.'

'I see . . . Well, it's a bit far to Alkhan-Kala, we wouldn't hit it—it's not as if I have field guns.'

The commander turned to the mortar crews and said in a calm, cooled-off voice, all traces of irritation now gone: 'Abort shoot. Let's pack up.'

While the grumbling crews covered up the mortars and loaded them back on the army cars, the commander and infantry lieutenant lit up and chatted. I went over too, got a light and stood beside them. It was the usual soldier's chitchat.

'So, what happened yesterday?' the mortar commander said, frowning at the platoon leader through a cloud of smoke. 'I heard the Kombat overdid it a bit here, is that right?'

'Yeah, he ran into some Chechens and got fired on while he was on his way to the same marsh.'

'What was he going there for?'

'No idea.'

'He was relieving us,' I said. 'We were there with the 9th and he brought us our replacements.'

'So what happened then?' the commander said, looking at me expectantly.

'Not much . . . A bit of shooting and then we all went our separate ways. Their recon came out of the village and ran into us. First a sniper started up and then they dropped a few mortar rounds on us.'

'Anyone killed?'

'No.'

'Just some locals,' the infantry lieutenant said. 'They came to us from the village today and asked us not to shoot, said they were going to hold a couple of funerals. An eight-year-old girl and an old man. As soon as our guys started firing here they tried to shelter in a basement but they didn't make it.'

The lieutenant recounted this calmly, as if he were talking about burning his oatmeal at breakfast.

'A cannon shell went through the house wall and blew up inside. The girl died instantly and the old man died in the hospital in Nazran.'

I looked in silence at the platoon leader, my eyes fixed on his calm face. I felt my cheeks suddenly flush with heat! Shit, that's all I needed. I remembered the firefight, how the infantry lay down on the embankment in the clearing and how two bursts flew from the village. And how I had shouted: 'There he is, the bastard!' although I wasn't sure if there was anyone at the window. But to lie there under fire was too terrifying, just as it was too terrifying to get up from the ground and run toward the shots from the village. And so I shouted.

There was no one at the window, that much was clear after the first bursts. The Chechens had made their presence felt and pulled out. But the Kombat still ordered the carriers to shoot up the village because he was afraid and wanted to buy his life with the lives of others. And we had eagerly carried out the order, because we were also afraid.

But if I had not shouted out the Kombat would have given the order to fire on the village a minute later, and the girl and her grandfather would have managed to find shelter in the cellar.

Yesterday I murdered a girl. I suddenly felt sick. And there was nothing I could do about it: there was nowhere to go and beg forgiveness. I had murdered them and it was irrevocable.

Now I would be a child killer my whole life, and I'd have to live with this. Eat, drink, raise children, be happy and sad, laugh and cry, be ill, love. And . . .

And kiss Olga. Touch this pure, radiant creation with hands that have murdered. Touch her face, eyes, lips, breast, so tender and vulnerable, and leave greasy traces of death on her clear skin. These hands, these damned hands! I should cut them off and discard them—I will never get them clean now.

I stuck my hands between my knees and started to rub them on my pant legs. I understood that this was psychosis, madness, but I couldn't help it. It seemed my hands had become sticky, like when you've eaten food in a dirty café in the sun. Murder had stuck to them, the vilest kind of murder, and I couldn't get it off.

I didn't even notice when we arrived back at the battalion. I don't know how I got to my tent and sat down next to the stove. I only came to my senses when Oleg handed me a mess tin with oatmeal:

'Here, eat this, we saved it for you.'

'Thanks.'

I took the tin and absently started to wolf down the cold oatmeal. Then I stopped.

'Remember how the Chechens hit us by Alkhan-Yurt yesterday? You know what . . . it turns out we killed a girl when we fired back. An eight-year-old girl and her grandfather.'

'It happens. Don't think about it, it'll pass. If you're going to put yourself through hell every time it happens, you'll go out of your mind. People here kill and get killed. They kill us, we kill them. I've killed too. It's just war. Our own lives aren't worth a thing here, let alone someone else's. Don't think about it, at least not until you get home. Right now you're still too close to her. She's dead and you're alive, but you're both still rotting in one place—only she's below ground and you're above it. And the difference between you may only be one day.'

'Yes, just one day. Or maybe one night.'

I put down my mess tin and spoon with a clank and walked out of the tent without saying anything, closing the flap behind me.

The night was amazingly clear. The universe had sunk onto the field and embraced us soldiers like babes in arms—eternity favors those in battle.

It would be cold tomorrow.

I thought about the skirmish of the night before, the girl, her death. I imagined how she and her grandfather were making their way down to the cellar when the shooting started. It was gloomy in the house. The old man opened the hatch into the cellar and held out his hand to her, getting ready to help her down the stairs. And then a tornado erupted around them, smashing through the wall, bricks spinning in its wake, drowning their screams in a huge roar and flash as the shells exploded inside. She was killed immediately as the blast tore into her belly and she fell facedown in front of him, her innards blown against the wall behind her. Her head was wrenched around and snapped back on her slender neck. Her eyes were still open, the dead pupils showing from under her eyelids. And the old man was injured. He crawled up to her through a stream of her blood and shook her lifeless body and howled and cursed the Russians. And then he died in Nazran.

For the love of God please forgive me. I never wanted this to happen.

I slipped the safety off my rifle, cocked it and stuck the barrel into my mouth.

Another day ended.

The next morning we left that field. The temperature had dipped during the night and snowfall had thrown a clean, white mantle over everything, covering it in crystals of frost. Chechnya had gone white-haired overnight.

The regiment formed on the highway in a giant column that stretched for half a mile. I sat motionless, my rifle sling wound around my wrist and both of my hands tucked into my sleeves. I was already freezing cold; my wet jacket had turned stiff and frozen and it stuck to the top of the carrier. We had a long drive ahead, at least four hours in convoy.

The communications carrier stood just opposite the turning to the marsh, from where the vehicles of the 7th were slowly withdrawing onto the highway. I recognized Misha's carrier, and there was Vasya, sitting up on top, hemmed in on all sides with antitank rockets. I waved at him and gave him a crooked, joyless smile. Vasya waved back.

The fighting had stopped during the night and left Alkhan-Kala quiet again. It seemed we must have nailed the last Chechens, although no one had any news to this effect. Basically we never got much news at all, and it was often only through the television that we found out what had happened to our regiment, or to ourselves. But the fact that we were pulling out meant it was all over here. Maybe they even got Basayev.

The column set off and we headed toward Grozny. The platoon leader said we'd now be taking up positions opposite the cross-shaped hospital, the one that had been nicknamed 'purgatory.' And evidently we would be the ones to take it.

To hell with the hospital.

To hell with all of them!

The main thing for me was to survive and to think about nothing. I had died here, or at least the person inside me had, together with a last glimmer of hope in Nazran where the old man had died. And a different soldier had been born in my place, a good one—empty, devoid of thought, with a coldness inside me and a hatred for the whole world. With no past and no future.

But this stirred no pangs of regret, just a sense of ruin and anger.

May they all go to hell.

I did not know what lay ahead: the storming operation in Grozny; the cross-shaped hospital; the mountains; Sharo-Argun; Igor's death—Igor was killed in the mountains in early March—and the sixty-eight other dead guys. I didn't know yet that the battalion would have its ranks cut down by half in one night, or that Yakovlev would be found gutted in that awful cellar, and the hatred and madness and that damned hill . . . And there were still four months of fighting ahead of me.

But I kept my word: I thought about that Chechen girl only once more the whole time I was at war, and that was in the mountains when a boy of about eight got blown up on a minefield.

We took him on a carrier to a helicopter. I placed the boy's shattered leg across his knee, the white bandages contrasting unnaturally against the backdrop of black Chechnya, and I held it there when we hit ruts, while the boy's unconscious head bounced up and down with dull thuds on the armor, *bang-bang, bang-bang.*

17/ The Storming Operation

It's quiet. Day has broken but the sun still hasn't risen and the cloudless sky in the east is illuminated by pink reflections. That's bad—it'll be another bright day, perfect for snipers.

We sit in the cellar of the command building, warming ourselves by a fire and devouring our dry rations. We're a bit scared, jittery; it's as if we're suspended in weightlessness, just temporary life-forms. Everything is temporary here: the heat from the fire, breakfast, the silence, the dawn, our lives. In a couple of hours we will advance. It'll be a long, cold, hard slog, but still better than the uncertainty we face now. When it starts everything will be crystal clear, our fear will abate and yield completely to the strong nervous tension that is already starting to overtake us. My brain is lapsing into soporific apathy and the urge to sleep is strong. I just want it to start. Then I am awoken by a rumbling that squeezes my ears. The air shakes, like jelly on a plate, the ground trembles, the walls, the floor, everything. The soldiers get up, keeping close to the wall, and peer out of the window. Only half awake, I don't understand what's going on and I jump up, grabbing my rifle.

Have the Chechens started shelling us? I wonder. One of the boys turns around and says something. He is speaking loudly, his throat visibly straining to force out the words, but the noise muffles his voice and I can't hear anything. From his lips I read the words: 'It's started.'

It's started. Now I really am scared. I can't stay in the gloom of this cellar any more. I have to do something, go somewhere, anything but stay sitting here.

I go out onto the porch and the rumbling intensifies so much that my ears hurt. The infantry press themselves against the walls and hide behind the carriers, all of them in helmets. The commanders stand at the corner of the HQ house: the Kombat, the guys from regiment headquarters, all craning their necks as they look around the corner in the direction of Grozny, where the explosions are coming from. My curiosity wakens and I too want to see what's going on. I go down the steps and have moved only ten paces when a sturdy piece of shrapnel the size of a fist slams down at my feet and lies there, hissing in a puddle, its jagged blue-charred edges flashing up at my eyes. Right after comes a shower of hundreds of tiny pieces of shrapnel bouncing off the frozen clay. I shield my head with my arm and run back into the building, tripping and flying inside as I cross the doorstep. I have no more desire to go outside and I make my way down to the basement, to a breach in the wall where light is shining through. A crowd stands at the opening, half of them inside and half outside, exclaiming from time to time: 'Wow, look at that, they're giving them a pounding! Where did they get antiaircraft guns? Look, there's another one!' I look out cautiously and see soldiers standing with their heads tipped back as they gaze into the sky. I go up to a platoon commander I know and ask what's going on. He motions upward and shouts above the roar: 'The Chechens are firing at those Sukhoi jets bombing the city.'

Sure enough, the black clouds of explosions are erupting around a tiny plane spinning in the clear sky, first above it and to the right, and then closer and closer. The plane goes into a dive to escape the barrage and then returns and rakes the area with its rocket launchers before flying off.

Everyone suddenly crouches down and somehow I end up on the ground when a burst of heavy machine gun whips through the air, followed by an explosion, and once again metal showers down from the sky, clattering on armor, walls, helmets.

We hear swearing and shouts: 'Those morons in the artillery can't shoot for shit, falling short again!' Beside me hunches Odegov, our mortar man. For some reason he's grinning as he shows me a thumb-sized piece of shrapnel: 'Look, this just hit me in the back!' he tells me.

'Are you hurt?'

'No, it stuck in my flak jacket!' he marvels, turning around. Between his shoulders there is a hole in his jacket.

'Odegov, that's a bottle of vodka you owe me!' A day before the storming operation, when he was pulling the metal plates out of his jacket to lighten it, I advised him to leave the Kevlar plating since it doesn't weigh much and would protect him from flying shards. And so it did—the plating saved his spine.

The next salvo rushes overhead and the shells fly into the city. You can't see anything down there because of a large embankment in the road ahead blocking the view. I go up to the second floor and run into the Kombat who's leaning over a map on the table discussing something with the company commanders. The Kombat glances at me and I make like I'm busy with something and duck out of sight into the next room. Yurka, the 8th company commander's orderly, is there sitting in a rocking chair, smoking and looking out of the window like he's watching TV. Another rocking chair beside him is empty. I wait around the corner for ten minutes and nothing is happening, no sniper fire, so I join him and light up. And there we sit, rocking gently, watching the bombardment while we smoke, as if we're at the cinema. All we're missing is popcorn.

The scene in the city is indescribable. In fact, there is no city: all that's visible is the road and the first row of houses in the private sector. Beyond that it's an inferno, a maelstrom of explosions and smoke, total hell. The gunners are laying down a carpet of fire and the shells land just over the road, about a hundred yards from our positions, sending a mass of shrapnel flying in our direction. Beams and boards hurtle through the air together with sections of wall and whole roofs.

I've never seen a bombardment like this. There won't be anything left but a wasteland, which is a good thing in one sense. Let the artillery flatten the hell out of everything, and then we'll march into the city, whistling as we go, cigarettes in our mouths, lazily kicking aside the bearded bodies. Then again, if no roofs are left intact, where are we going to sleep tonight?

The commander of the 8th company summons Yurka and me with shouts from headquarters. I'm sent for the radio and go with them as their operator. The operation officer, who's sitting by a bricked-up window, tells us the 506th regiment is moving in. The 506th will advance first, followed by us and then by the interior ministry troops who'll do the final mop-up. I look over the officer's shoulder through the firing slit expecting to see something fantastic, a thousand soldiers with faces contorted with fury, running like they do in the films and shouting 'For Stalin! For the Motherland!' But it's all a lot simpler than that, ordinary even. An infantry battalion of the 506th regiment lies in a single line on the embankment. There aren't many of them, maybe a hundred men prostrated along the slope, waiting for the shelling to shift right into the city, so they can get up and follow the shell bursts. The bombardment duly moves, and they get to their feet and run over the brow of the embankment, disappearing one after the other down the other side. They run awkwardly, stooped down, each one carrying more than sixty-five pounds of gear: cartridges, grenades, rocket launchers, flame throwers, weapon mounts, ammo belts, machine guns. No one shouts 'Hurrah!' Instead they labor their way forward silently, indifferent and accustomed to death, once again dragging their bodies from the ground and hurling themselves at flying metal, knowing that not all of them will survive.

The operation officer points out of the window, greatly amused by the sight of one guy trying to clamber up the embankment, impossibly weighed down with gear and bent beneath a grenade launcher. Protected behind the brick wall, the officer is laughing for all he's worth and I feel an instant and intense hatred well up inside me. *Those are your men going to their deaths and here you are laughing at them, you piece of shit!*

I watch the frail little figures stand and run over the embankment to where they will be killed, torn apart, crippled, and I am suddenly terrified, racked with an unbelievable fear that makes my knees tremble. I am scared for them, for human life as a whole. How can I watch the infantry attack while I stay behind? It's enough to drive you crazy. I feel like a deserter who has betrayed his brothers. How can they run to their deaths while I'm safe here? I must go with them, run over the embankment too. I know I won't be scared over on the other side, all thoughts will just vanish leaving just flashing pictures in my brain: *A rut. Get down. Run. Shoot. There he is. Give a burst of fire. Another. Another. Got him. Run. Fall.* There, over the embankment, everyone's equal—all of the soldiers have the same chance, and fate will decide who is to live or die. Back here, though, all I can do is clench my fists until they are white and repeat to myself like a clockwork toy, 'Just don't die boys, don't you dare die!'

Within twenty minutes we get our first dead guy, a '200' case, as we call those destined for the zinc coffins. They've wrapped him in a cape, and they bring him out on a BMP tracked carrier. It appears under the bridge, drives through a hole in the fence and pulls up in the yard of the command house. Twenty minutes later there are already ten wounded lying by the carrier, their snow-white bandages contrasting with their black, haggard faces and crazed eyes. The injured smoke agitatedly and lean on each other as they climb into the vehicle. It turns around and sets off for the hospital. The dead guy shakes around on the top, his feet bouncing in time with the vehicle's motion.

Twenty more minutes pass and the 506th return. On the other side of the road the artillery has not done its job properly; the Chechen fire is too concentrated and the infantry can't take the houses. Their commander withdraws the company and the little figures run back across the road and lay down on the embankment again. The artillery fire resumes and we wait.

The shelling shifts once more and the infantry renew the attack and vanish over the embankment. They seem to have better luck this time. I run to the 8th company, which is clustered in platoons along the fence, smoking during the wait, and find the company commander. He's repeating the task to the platoon commanders and they're nodding back. Then the order comes over the radio to move out.

We go with the 2nd platoon, seven of us altogether: the platoon commander, Yurka, me, Mikhailych the machine gunner, Arkasha the sniper, Denis and Pashka. We gather at the hole in the fence, ready to rush through at the order.

'Let's go!'

We run through the gap and cover the hundred yards or so to the bridge without trouble—it's dead ground, and no one can see us. We get held up at the bridge where a sniper's nest sits on the embankment beside one of the supports, a pit built up with sandbags. It's the perfect spot; he's in the shadows and his field of vision couldn't be better. Mikhailych fires a burst toward him and spits: 'That's where he was sitting, the bastard. I must have let five clips off at him and I still couldn't flush him out. He's gone now, bearded scum. Too bad!'

A long straight road leads off immediately after the bridge. The 506th and the Chechens are about a quarter mile from us. Not even the devil knows what's going on down there—either the Chechens are counterattacking or they're just blindly firing away in rage. Either way, you can't get down the road; tracer rounds are flying past the houses and smacking into the fence, whizzing in clusters under the bridge and whining around as they strike the supports, showering us with plaster. One burst flies right over our heads, and we duck down. 'Fucking hell! Forward, go, go, go!' We run out from underneath the bridge and turn left off the road behind the houses. The bullets don't reach us here and we can stand up again.

In front of us lies a small irrigation canal, and just beyond it is the first line of row houses in the private residential sector. There aren't many, the row stretches about two hundred yards left and right, and our job today is to take them.

The worst place is on the left by the 1st platoon, a huge open area with a school in the middle. The best place is on the right, by the 3rd platoon, with the embankment behind you, more embankment to the right and then the 7th company farther down. The company commander tells me to radio for the situation with the platoons. Likhach, the commander of the 1st platoon, says they are in real trouble: it's three hundred yards to the school and the Chechens are holding it. He is pinned down in a ditch beside the road, with snipers firing at the slightest movement. The 3rd platoon commander reports that his area is quiet; the houses are empty and can be occupied right now.

There's no answer from Pioneer, the reconnaissance platoon. We have a bad feeling about this and I keep trying. Eventually they answer and tell us we are pissing them off, that they have no idea where they are, although they think they can't be far from Minutka Square. The place is teeming with Chechens who are roving around in groups, but keep missing Pioneer; the 506th is now way behind them and they are still advancing. Without a word, the company commander gets out the map and looks at it, cursing. It's God knows how far to Minutka, halfway across the city. It's way behind the enemy front line and how they ended up there is a total mystery. The company commander takes the headphones from me, calls up Pioneer and with a stream of abuse tells them to get back here. Meanwhile, we send Mikhailych and Yurka off to scout and wait for them to come back. Ten minutes later they tell us we can advance; it's all clear.

We cross the irrigation canal, walking along a thin board that bows beneath our feet. On the other side there are some fences and one has a hole in it. The platoon files that way with Malakhanov on point. He's a big lanky half-wit who is forever losing his rifle and getting hauled up before the special panel and slapped with a charge of selling weapons. He reaches the hole and flips aside a piece of slate with his foot. There's a loud bang as a trip-wired grenade explodes. We run over to Malakhanov, who is just standing there, wiping his muck-spattered face and blinking in disbelief.

'Where are you hit?' Dumbstruck, he swivels his head around to inspect himself and shrugs. We examine him from top to bottom—not a single hole, not even a scratch. Unable to believe our eyes we check him out again. Nothing, he's in one piece. The guy was born lucky, and as they say, the Lord must indeed protect children and idiots. And Malakhanov is an idiot for sure; no one has any doubt about that. Only a total cretin would kick stuff around like he did. Malakhanov keeps blinking, like he still doesn't understand what happened. We swear at him, he nods and turns around, goes through the hole and runs straight into a second trip wire—*Boom!* Smoke engulfs his body and billows out of the hole in layers. Holy hell, how about that for a turn-around? He got away with it once but this time he'll have lost his legs for sure, at the very least. You don't get two miracles in a row. When the smoke clears our jaws drop: Malakhanov is standing in exactly the same pose, wiping his face, his eyes still batting in disbelief. On his right palm at the meaty base of his thumb a shard of shrapnel has nicked him and slightly torn the tissue. And that's all! Other than that there's not a scratch.

We bandage him in silence. The platoon commander is the first to shake off his stupor and unleashes a barrage of abuse at Malakhanov; he takes his rifle from him and tells him to get his ass back to the rear, to the medical post, the hospital, the special department, wherever the hell he likes. The commander doesn't want any trace of this idiot here any longer and tells him he has no wish to have to write to his mother informing her of the death of her moron son.

Carefully, scouring the ground beneath our feet, we climb through the hole into the yard. There are no more trip wires—Malakhanov has taken care of them all. The yard has an apple orchard, a barn and a house, which despite six hours of shelling is oddly more or less intact apart from a few broken windows. We go inside and find two rooms, a large working oven and a load of beds with pillows and blankets. Yes, today we will sleep like people, in the warm and on beds.

The company commander says we'll set up the command post here and orders us to comb the remaining houses, just in case, although it's clear they are also empty. We split up in the yard, half of us to the left and half to the right. We take only a few steps before mortar shells start raining down with a vile whistle and hammer the backyards. We scatter into the ditches and curse our mortar men and their useless firing. I call up the Kombat. 'Our guys are mortaring us—get them to cease firing!'

'Our mortars aren't firing.'

'Yes, they are! And pretty accurately too; they are coming right down on us!' I yell.

'If you've got mortars landing on you, it's the Chechens,' he shouts back.

He's right, damn him, it is the enemy. Now I feel ashamed— what was I panicking for? It's probably better to be killed by enemy shrapnel than to get nailed because of some thick-headed gun layer from your own side. But it seems the Chechens can't see us and are just firing randomly, their shells dropping from a fair distance. We regain our senses and crawl through the adjacent yards to poke around in the cellars and pantries and inspect the houses.

I get the cottage across the street. Before I run over I peek out from between the doors of the gate and gauge the situation. Projectiles of all sizes are whistling, whizzing and crackling overhead. Ducking down, I race across the street and into the yard of the cottage, which is surrounded by a tall brick wall. The yard is large and has a wealthy air about it. To the left I see a dark entrance down to the cellar, to the right another wall that divides the yard in two.

I hear someone poking around on the other side, moving some bits of glass. I take a grenade from my pocket, prime it and get ready to throw it over the wall. 'Who's there?' It's one of the guys from Likhach's platoon, looting some jam. I should check out the cellar myself, scavenge some vitamins. By now we are all sick to death of that empty, half-cooked oatmeal they give us.

In the cellar I find shelves of different glass jars full of all kinds of unusual jams made from melon, grapes, nuts, plus a three-quart jar of honey and four ten-quart canisters of pickles. Not a bad haul, I say to myself, and decide to carry this booty straight back to our guys. There are plenty of opportunists like me who would take off with all this free stuff in a flash.

No sooner do I come out of the cellar than I hear the familiar whistle of a mortar shell overhead. I throw myself face-down on the ground, although I know it's too late to do anything; they've got me and I'm already dead. It's not easy to drop. Fear has rendered my body empty and light. The shell hits the ground before I do ('Look at him, he didn't get down in time—now he's got shrapnel in his legs and belly,' they'll say later) and explodes with a short, sharp burst, battering my ears with the shock wave and then . . . nothing. No shrapnel, no dirt raining down, no smoke. But it did blow up in the yard, of that there's no doubt. I raise my head, look around and realize what's happened. The shell landed two or three yards from me, but on the other side of the wall dividing the yard. Lucky.

I run around to the other side to see what's happened to the guy over the wall. They are already helping him out; his sweater hangs in tatters around his shoulder blades, and a streak of blood is seeping through the field dressing from his shoulder to his spine. His face is pale, he looks weak and he's clearly in a bad way—it's a serious wound. I radio the tracked carrier to evacuate the '300,' as we call the wounded guys, and it arrives a couple of minutes later. I watch them put him inside and find myself thinking that it was a pity the shell didn't blow up on my half of the yard. I would happily go to the hospital now, to all those nurses and clean sheets. It's only a fleeting thought and a second later I shake it from my head, shoulder my rifle and go back to our house.

Everyone is assembled and the place is a hive of activity. The boys are making shooting slits with bricks, hanging drapes over the windows, firing up the stove and unloading all their booty onto the table. When everything is done we sit down to eat. And our supper today is unprecedented: tomatoes and cucumbers, bread and canned stewed meat, buckwheat, butter, honey, different jams and tea. It's a staggering fortune and our stomachs turn over with anticipation at the sight of it. We last ate in the morning at the command house, and not even a crumb has passed our lips since then. It's now almost evening and dusk is falling. Our spoons glimmer as we dive into the spread.

At the height of supper Likhach enters the room, stands in the doorway and watches us eat with strange, feverish eyes. We invite him to join us at the table but he just stands there motionlessly and says, 'I've been wounded.' It doesn't need bandaging, they already did that, he tells us. He took a piece of shrapnel in the thigh during the day but refuses to go to the hospital, says there's no one to turn the platoon over to. The company commander tells him to go to the medical point and report his wound. Likhach says he's just been there, and he stands at the door in silence for another minute, turns and goes out. We watch him leave; he's acting oddly, as if he's got shell shock too. Although, if we'd been hit in the thigh, we'd probably be acting oddly too. When he's gone we get back to the food, and to finish the six of us polish off three quarts of honey with our tea.

While we eat it gets completely dark outside. We divide up watch duties for the night; two of us at a time will do three-hour stints. Yurka and I get from one to four o'clock, the worst, as we'll have to break our night's sleep into two halves.

Mikhailych and Arkasha take first watch while we get undressed and lay down on clean, crisp sheets. My God, how long it's been since I slept like a human being! I've grown so unaccustomed to it, and it's kind of hot under the blanket, that the pillow seems useless and the bed too soft. Altogether rather uncomfortable, nothing like a sleeping bag under a bush. Uncomfortable, but nice nonetheless, clean and fresh.

Mikhailych barely touches my sleeve and I wake. It's ten to one. I rouse Yurka and we get dressed and go to the lookout point in the hall. The windows are blocked solid with bricks although two have gaps left for small firing slits where machine guns have been set up. In front of each stands a rather plush armchair and a bedside table made of Karelian birch, with boxes of bullet belts on top. The boys have done well; they've set up the place nicely, and you could easily spend six hours in a lookout like this. We sit down in the armchairs and put our feet up on the windowsills, with one hand on the butt of the machine gun and a cigarette in the other. Just like the Germans in war films—the only thing missing is a harmonica. We joke about this, pretending to be Wehrmacht soldiers: '*Ja, ja, natürlich.*'

When we tire of this we look out through the firing slits. The picture on the outside is much worse and we see that the position has been set up very unprofessionally. We're locked in by a thirty-yard strip of the yard and we can't see beyond that. Fence to the left, gardens to the right and the next house straight ahead. You could approach us standing up and cut us down at your leisure, for we have no field of vision. Only to the left of the open gate can you see a bit of the road and the windows of a house standing at an angle on the other side.

If they'd been smart they'd have put the lookout over in that house. One machine gun over there, one here, and no son of a bitch could slip past. I tell this to Yurka, who looks over at the house, estimates the distance separating it from us, looks at the machine guns and then surprises me by saying that our lookout is excellently situated. I look at him in puzzlement and see fear etched on his face. He clearly has no desire to enter that house at night and sit there for an hour and a half on his own, cut off from the rest of the platoon, and then have to crawl back. What's more, if it kicked off now he wouldn't be able to get back. Thirty yards is a long way to go under fire and he'd have to shoot his way out on his own, drawing all the enemy fire toward him.

Yurka knows that I see his fear and starts to mumble about how over there we'd have to sit on the bare floor in the cold and not on these soft, comfy armchairs, how the field of vision here is more or less OK. The other boys are close by too, so why bother going over there? So that's settled, we're staying in this comfortable but badly set up lookout, because I'm not going over there on my own either.

A stream of tracer rounds flashes by from the Chechen side. I take my night-vision sight and go outside. Everything is unusually green but pretty clearly visible through the aperture. Over on the other side of the street the twigs of an apple tree quiver in the wind and it seems there is someone in the window. But it's only my eyes playing tricks. I see the 3rd platoon's carrier. The driver is moving around near the vehicle, fixing something. He's about a hundred and fifty yards away, but in such visibility I could put a bullet in his ear. The thought unnerves me and I tear myself away from the night sight and crouch down behind the wall. A green light is still flashing in my eyes and for a while I can't make out anything until my pupils accustom themselves to the darkness. Then objects start to emerge and I see the stairs, the doorstep and the door. I go back inside and sit down in my armchair. Yurka and I sit in silence for the rest of our shift, listening to the darkness and keeping close watch.

At ten to four our night vigil comes to an end and I wake Denis and Pashka. They appear yawning and say nothing as they flop heavily into the armchairs, their eyes still half closed. I'm sure they'll fall asleep the moment we shut the door. I look at the backs of their shorn heads and remember how about five days ago two guys from the next company had fallen asleep at the lookout. It was during the day and all they had to worry about were snipers: after all, who's going to crawl around enemy positions in broad daylight? And since they were shielded from telescopic sights by piles of earth they relaxed and fell asleep, their heads resting on their chests, the napes of their necks turned up to the sun. Then two Chechens crawled out of the ruins and, without even bothering to hide, walked up to them, shot both soldiers in the back of the head and strolled off with their rifles and some boxes of ammo.

I look at Denis and Pashka. I should shake them, chat for ten minutes so they wake up properly, but I don't; sleeping time is too valuable to waste on idle talk. To hell with them. After all they'll be the first to bite it if anything happens, and they might manage to at least yell first.

Next morning, the dank misty dawn meets us in silence. We go out of the house and take a leak as we listen for the sounds of nature. There are none; it's quiet outside, as if there's no storming operation going on at all. A garden, apple trees, mist, silence. Back home at our country cottage, if you get up a bit earlier at the end of August, when the trees have not yet shaken off the night cold and the puddles are covered with a brittle crust of ice, you can witness the same chilly silence. And it smells just the same, of shriveled leaves, of morning and autumn.

Taking advantage of the lull, we decide to have a bath. We take turns: two of us heat up water, two snort and splash over tubs set outside on stools and two stand alongside with rifles. We hurry—today we'll have to advance again and it's already seven. Sure enough, before we even have breakfast we get the order to prepare to move out. The company commander orders me to summon the platoon commanders to the command post, and I call up Likhach and Pioneer. There's no contact with the 3rd platoon. The company commander sends me over there to find out what's wrong.

The 3rd platoon's command post is located to our right, in an elegant house two streets down. I stuff five grenades into my webbing, six rifle magazines, ten packs of bullets and a spare radio battery in case theirs has run down. I hop up and down, tighten my belt and adjust my webbing, flex my shoulders. Not bad, it feels comfortable enough.

I cross the gardens to reach the first street, my rifle at the ready in case some bearded fighter has been sitting in the cellars since last night, laying in wait for some lone soldier like me. I climb over a stack of firewood behind the barn and jump into the next yard. It's neat and well tended, the stone ground covered in sand. A Lada the color of wet tarmac stands under a carport. It looks new, and only its windows are broken. I go over to the car; it's bare inside, there's nothing to take and no keys to start it. But the house is in good shape and doesn't seem to have been looted. I should take a look on the way back for blankets, socks, gloves and other warm things that can take the edge off the soldiering life.

I look out of the gates, on my guard: if anything happens here there's no one to help me. With one eye I check out the street and I keep an ear out for anything going on behind me in the yard. Both places are quiet. I have to run across the street but I can't force myself to leave the yard. After the peace of the early morning this seems far more terrifying than it did yesterday, when we were constantly showered with shrapnel. During this short peaceful morning I have managed to shed the continual readiness to die; I have relaxed and I am now loath to throw myself headfirst back into cold death.

Finally, I steel myself, draw my lungs full of air, exhale sharply and run out of the open gates in sprints. The street seems to be very large, enormous, like it's thousands of miles wide, a whole continent covered in very fine smooth asphalt without a single rut that might afford protection. Slowly, like a slug, I am crawling into the sights of some sniper. That's probably what I look like through a telescopic sight—a small, helpless slug trying to escape death in the middle of a huge street.

I rocket through the gates on the other side but it remains quiet behind me, no one shoots. They didn't get me this time. I straighten my webbing, adjust my grip on my rifle and carry on. Fear has given my mood a boost and I start to whistle a song.

I cross the second street more confidently. I've greeted death again and things have now settled into their usual rhythm.

In the distance I can see the 3rd platoon's large brick house. They are all in the yard and I can make out familiar faces, Zhenka, Drum and some of the other boys. We haven't seen each other for ages and I'm glad they're OK. I ask why they didn't answer the radio calls. Their battery is shot. We change it and I call up the company commander to check contact. The sound is fine and I have to get back fast; we're moving out in ten minutes. I relay the order to the 3rd platoon commander, and before I go I look around for Zhenka and Drum. Drum waves and smiles. I wave back, straighten my webbing, duck down and run back the way I came. A burst of fire echoes from the Chechen lines, then another. Our guys shoot back and a firefight ensues. Then a mortar joins the fray. The day has begun.

18 / Argun

We are halted for the fourth day in a row at the canning factory in Argun. It's the best place we've been so far during our deployment and we feel completely safe inside the fence that skirts the perimeter.

The trouble with this war is that we are in a permanent state of encirclement and can expect a shot in the back at any moment. But here we are sheltered.

Two automatic mounted grenade launchers are positioned inside the administration building and cover the whole street from the gates. There are two more launchers on the roof of the factory's meatpacking section and a machine-gun nest on the second floor of the gatehouse. This way we completely control the surrounding area and feel relatively secure. We relax.

April has arrived and the sun is already beating down. We walk around practically naked, wearing only our cutoff long johns and army boots, and we are alike as brothers. And brothers we are, for there's no one in the world closer than emaciated soldiers with lice-bitten armpits, sun-browned necks and otherwise white, putrefying skin.

The battalion commanders leave us in peace to get our fill of food and sleep. Yesterday they even fixed up a steam bath for us in the old sauna room in the guardhouse and we sweated away there for almost an hour. They issued us with fresh underwear into the bargain, so now we can enjoy two or three blissful louse-free days.

Fixa and I sit on the grass by the fence and wait for two Chechen kids to reappear. In the sunshine we bask in long-forgotten sensations of cleanliness and warmth. Our boots stand in a row and we wiggle our bare toes and smoke.

'Bet you five cigarettes I can stub out this butt on my heel,' he says.

'Think you'll wow me with that one, do you?' I reply. 'I'll do the same trick but for two cigarettes.'

The skin on my soles has grown as hard as a rhino's from my boots. I once drove a needle into my heel for a bet and it went in more than a centimeter before it hurt.

'You know, I reckon the brass is being too wasteful in handing over our guys' bodies to the families,' Fixa muses. 'They could put us to far better use after we're killed; they could make a belt sling from a soldier's hide. Or you could knock out a pretty good flak jacket from the heels of a platoon.'

'Uh-huh. And you could make a whole bunch of them from the guys who died up in the hills. Why don't you tell the supply officer? Maybe he'll give you leave for the smart idea,' I suggest.

'No, I can't tell him, he'll just sell the idea to the Chechens and start trading in corpses.'

A gentle breeze plays over our bodies and we laze ecstatically as we wait for the kids to show up.

The knot of nervous tension inside me just won't loosen up after the mountains, and fear keeps churning away somewhere below my stomach. We need to unwind. The two signal flares that we're swapping for marijuana are stuffed into the tops of Fixa's boots. We already gave three flares to the Chechen kids as an advance and now we're waiting for them to come back with the promised matchbox of weed.

There's a small gap in the fence at this corner and a little market has sprung up. The kids sit all day on the other side and soldiers go to and fro on ours to offer their wares: canned meat, diesel, bullets. Half an hour ago the battalion cook stuffed a whole box of butter through the gap. Fixa wonders if we should give him a beating but we can't be bothered to get up.

We get an unexpected treat of meat. The infantry caught and shot a guard dog, roasted it over a fire and gave us two ribs. It turns out that some of the infantrymen are from Fixa's home region. It's a good thing to have common roots with guys in your unit. Only when you are far from home do you realize what a bond you have with someone who wandered the same streets and breathed the same air as a child. You may never have met before and are unlikely to meet again later, but right now you are like brothers, ready to give up everything for the other, a Russian trait through and through.

We chew the tough meat, and bitter-tasting fat runs down our fingers. Fantastic.

'A spring onion would be good now—I love meat with vegetables,' says Fixa. 'But most of all I love fried pork fat with potato and onion. My wife cooks it just how I like it. First, she fries the fat until the edges curl upward and the grease oozes out. It has to be well fried or it will stew like snot and won't be tasty. And when the fat starts to sizzle in the pan she adds thinly sliced potato and fries it lightly on one side, and then the first time she stirs it she adds salt and onion. The onion has to go in after the potato or else it burns. And then . . .'

'Shut up, Fixa.' I suddenly have a craving for pork fat and potatoes and I can't listen to any more gastronomic revelations. 'There's no pork here. They're Muslims and they don't eat it.'

'Oh, you've just noticed, have you? You won't find pork here in a month of Sundays. How are they supposed to have pork fat if they can't even wipe their backsides with paper like human beings, I ask you?'

This aspect of local Chechen culture engenders particular hostility in Fixa, and in the rest of us too. Quite apart from anything else, our soldiers resent the Chechens because they wash themselves after doing their business, rather than using paper.

In each house there are special jugs with long spouts made from some silvery metal, and inscribed with ornate Arabic script. At first our boys couldn't figure out their purpose and used them for making tea. When someone finally told them, they freaked out. The first thing they do now when they occupy a house is kick these jugs outside or fish them out with sticks.

Actual faith doesn't matter one bit to us, be it Allah, Jesus or whoever, since we ourselves are a godless bunch from birth. But these jugs embody the difference between our cultures. It seems to me that the political officer could distribute them instead of propaganda leaflets, and we'd rip Chechnya to shreds in a couple of days.

'My cousin served in Tajikistan and told me the Tajiks use flat stones after the toilet,' I say as I inspect the dog rib in my hand. 'It's still the Stone Age there, they don't know about toilet paper or even newspaper. They gather pebbles from the river and use those. Each outdoor toilet has a pile of stones beside it like a grave.'

'So what's it like in Tajikistan? Bound to be better than here. What else does your cousin say about it?' asks Fixa.

'Nothing. He's dead.'

My cousin died just two days before he was due to be demobilized. He volunteered for a raid at the border. The patrol was made up of green conscripts who still didn't know anything and so my cousin stood in for some young kid. He was a machine gunner and when the shooting started he covered the group as they pulled back.

A sniper put a round into his temple, a rose shot, as we call it: when the bullet hits the head at close range the skull opens up like a flower and there's no putting it together again. They had to bind up my cousin's head for the funeral or it would have fallen apart right there in the coffin.

'Yeah,' says Fixa. 'It's all just one war, that's what I think. And you know what else, Chechnya is just for starters—the big war is still to come, you'll see.'

'You think so?'

'Yes. And I also think I'm going to make it through this one.'

'Me too,' I say. 'Maybe since my cousin was killed I believe I'm going to survive. Two Babchenkos can't die in battle.'

We finish the ribs. We've gnawed off all the gristle and soft tissue and all that's left in our fingers is two inches of hard bone that we can't chew down any farther. We put the stumps in our cheeks like lollipops and, lying on our backs, suck out the last traces of fat. Our sucking is the only noise for the next fifteen minutes. Finally even this pleasure ends; the ribs are bare.

Fixa wipes his hands on his shorts and gets out a notebook and pen that he brought along specially.

'So tell me where we've been again. I just can't remember the names of these villages.'

'OK. You joined us at Gikalovsky, right? So, Gikalovsky, then Khalkiloi, Sanoi, Aslambek, Sheripovo, Shatoi, and . . .' I pause for a moment, trying to get my tongue around the next one, ' . . . Sharo-Argun.'

'That's right, Sharo-Argun. I remember that all right,' Fixa mutters.

'You don't forget something like that in a hurry.'

'I'll draw a gallows beside Sharo-Argun,' he says, sketching awkwardly in the notebook. His fingers are not comfortable with a pen; he's more used to handling steel. Before the war he wielded a trowel and shovel as a builder, and now a rifle and grenade launcher.

I lean over and look at the crooked gibbet and the figure hanging from it. Sharo-Argun. What a terrible name. We lost twenty men there—Igor, Pashka, Four-Eyes the platoon commander, Vaseline, the list goes on.

There are lots of places like that in Chechnya: Shali, Vedeno, Duba-Yurt, Itum-Kale, all names of death. There's something shamanistic about them, strange names, strange villages. Some of my comrades died in each one and the earth is drenched in our blood. All we have left now are these odd, un-Russian words; we live within them, in the past, and these combinations of sounds that mean nothing to anyone else signify an entire lifetime to us.

We take our bearings from them as if from a map. Bamut is an open plain, a place of unsuccessful winter assaults, a place of cold, of frozen ground and a crust of bloodstained ice. Samashki—foothills, burning armored cars, heat, dust and bloated corpses heaped up by the hundred in three days. And Achkhoi-Martan, where I had my baptism of fire, where the first tracer rounds flew at me and where I first tasted fear.

And not forgetting Grozny, where we lost Fly, Koksharov, Yakovlev, and Kisel before them. This land is steeped in our blood; they drove us to our deaths here, as they will continue to do so for a long time yet.

'You should draw an ass instead of a gallows,' I tell Fixa. 'If you imagine the earth as an ass, then we are right in the hole.'

I shut my eyes, lie on my back and put my hands behind my

head. The sun shines through my eyelids. Hell, I don't even want to think about it, the mountains, the snow, Igor's body. I'll get to it later, but for now everything has stopped—for a while at least. Right now we are alive, our stomachs are filled with dog meat, and nothing else matters. I can lie in the sun without fearing a bullet in the head and it's wonderful. I suddenly recall the face of the sniper who was gunning for me in Goity. For some reason I wasn't afraid then.

Then I remember the photo we found near Shatoi of the little Chechen boy. He's only about seven, but he's showing off with a rifle in his hands while mom stands alongside, beaming at her grown-up little son. How proud she is of him, so full of joy for the holy warrior who already knows how to hold a rifle.

There will be even greater pride in her eyes when he severs the head of his first Russian prisoner at the age of seventeen. At twenty he'll attack a column and kill more people, and at twenty-two he'll run his own slave camp. Then at twenty-five they will hunt him down from a helicopter like a wolf, flush him into the open and fire rockets at him as he darts between shell craters, splattering his guts all over the place. Then he'll lie in a puddle and stare at the sky with half-open, lifeless eyes, now nothing more than an object of disgust as lice crawl in his beard.

We've seen warriors like this, grown up from such boys, from cubs into wolves. And to think my mother would have flayed the skin from my back with a belt if I'd ever thought to pose with a weapon when I was a kid.

Enough, no sense in dwelling on this now. Later. Everything later.

Fixa and I lie in the grass in silence, neither of us feels like talking. The sun has tired us out and we daydream, maybe doze off for a while, it's hard to say—our hearing stays as sharp in sleep as when we're awake and registers every sound, from the twittering of the birds to soldiers' voices, stray gunshots and the chugging of the generator. All harmless noises.

We don't rise until the sun sinks beneath the horizon. It gets chilly and the ground is still damp. I'm covered in goose bumps and I want to cover up. My cold stomach aches. I get up and pee where I stand. The stream of urine quickly wanes but I get no relief, my belly still hurts. I'll have to go to the medic.

The Chechen kids never showed up. We wait another half an hour but they still don't come. Evidently our signal flares went to the fighters' beneficiary fund free of charge.

'Some businessmen we are, Fixa,' I say. 'We should have got the grass first and then paid. We've been had. Come on, let's go.'

'We should have brought our rifles, that's what, and held one of them at gunpoint while the others went for the weed,' he says.

'They still wouldn't have showed up! They're not fools; they know we won't do anything to them. Would you shoot a boy over a box of grass?'

'Of course not.'

We follow the fence back toward our tent, brick debris and shrapnel scrunching under our boots. There has been fighting here at some time, probably in the 1994−96 war. Since then no one has worked at the factory or tried to rebuild it. These ruined buildings have only been used for keeping slaves.

I suddenly remember Dima Lebedev, another guy I transported coffins with in Moscow. His armored car ran over a mine near Bamut and the whole unit except Dima died instantly. He said he saw his platoon commander fly up like a cannon ball as the shock wave tore off his arms and legs, and dumped his trunk on the ground, still in its flak jacket.

Dima was heavily concussed and lay there for almost a day.

The Chechens that emerged from the undergrowth after the blast thought he was dead and didn't bother to put a bullet in him. He came around at night and ran straight into another group of fighters who took him with them into the mountains and kept him at a cottage with six other conscripts.

Their captors would beat them, cut off their fingers and starve them to get them to convert to Islam. Some did, others like Dima refused. Then they stopped feeding him altogether and he had to eat grass and worms for two weeks.

Each day the prisoners were taken into the mountains to dig defensive positions and finally Dima was able to escape. An old Chechen took him in and hid him in his home, where Dima lived with the family like a servant, tending the cattle, cutting the grass and doing chores. They treated him well, and when Dima wanted to go home they gave him money and a ticket and took him out of Chechnya to the garrison town of Mozdok, moving him at night in the trunk of a car so the rebels wouldn't get him.

He made it home alive and later corresponded with his old master, who even came and stayed with him a couple of times. That's what Dima called him—master—just like a slave. He was scarred forever by captivity. He had submissive, fearful eyes and was always ready to cover his head with his hands and squat down, shielding his stomach. He spoke quietly and never rose to an insult.

Later his master's nephew came to his home, knocked his mother around, abducted his sister and demanded a ransom for her release. I wonder, maybe he even kept her here in the basement of this factory with dozens of other prisoners.

'Tell me, would you really have finished off that wounded guy back in the mountains?' Fixa suddenly asks. We stop walking. Fixa looks me in the eyes and waits for an answer.

I know why this is so important to him. He doesn't say so, but he's thinking: *So would you finish me off then, if it came to it?*

'I don't know. You remember what it was like, it was snowing, the transport couldn't get through for the wounded and he was going to die anyway. Remember how he screamed, how awful it was? I just don't know . . .'

We stand facing each other. I suddenly feel like hugging this skinny, unshaven man with the big Adam's apple and bony legs sticking out of his boots.

'I wouldn't have shot anyone, Fixa, you know that, and you knew it then in the mountains. Life is too precious and we would have fought for it to the very end, even if that kid had puked up all his intestines. We still had bandages and painkillers, and maybe by morning we could have evacuated him. You know I wouldn't have killed him, even if we had known then for sure that he would die anyway.'

I want to tell him all of this but don't manage to. Suddenly there's a single shot and a short burst of rifle fire immediately followed by a powerful explosion. A cloud of smoke and dust envelops the road by the gatehouse, right where our tents are pitched.

My first thought is that the Chechens have blown up the gate.

'Get down!' I shout, and we dive facedown onto the asphalt. We freeze for a moment and then hurl ourselves over to the wall of the transformer box where we lie motionless.

Damn it, no rifle: idiot that I am I left it in the tent, now of all times. I'm never without my weapon! Fixa is also unarmed. We've completely dropped our guard at the factory; we thought we could take it easy and go a hundred yards from our position without rifles.

Fixa's eyes dart around, his face is pale and his mouth agape. I can't look much better myself.

'What do we do now, what do we do?' he whispers in my ear, clutching my arm.

'The flares, give them here,' I whisper back, petrified with fear. Without a weapon I am no longer a soldier but a helpless animal, a herbivore with no fangs or claws. Now they'll pour through the breach, take us right here in nothing but our shorts and butcher us, pin our heads down with a boot and slit our throats. And there's no one else around—we are alone on this road by the fence. They'll get us first and kill us before the battalion comes to its senses and returns fire. We are dumb tourists.

I look around. We'll have to make a run for the warehouses where the vehicles are parked, and where there are people.

Fixa pulls the flares from his boots and hands me one. I tear open the protective membrane and free the pin. We hold them out in front of us, ready to fire them at the first thing that appears on the road, and we freeze, holding the pull strings.

It's quiet. The shooting has stopped. Then we hear voices and laughter from the direction of the gatehouse. They are speaking in Russian, with no accent. We wait a little longer and then get up, dust ourselves off and go around to find the battalion commander, supply officer, chief of staff and some other officers milling around, all half drunk. They've dragged a safe out of the admin building, fixed a stick of dynamite to the door and blown it in half. It's empty. One officer suggests blowing up a second safe in the building in case there's anything in it, but the battalion commander is against the idea.

'Morons,' Fixa growls as we pass by. 'Haven't they had enough shooting yet?'

Our own injuries are minor. I tore up my knee slightly on a piece of brick when I threw myself down and Fixa has a long scratch on his cheek. What bothers us more is that we are filthy again and the steam bath has been wasted. We go into our tent and bed down.

That night we come under fire. A grenade flies over the fence near the transformer box where Fixa and I had prepared to defend ourselves. A second grenade explodes, then tracer rounds illuminate the sky. A few bursts pass over our heads and the bullets whine in the air. It's not heavy fire, maybe two or three weapons. The sentries on the roofs open up in reply and a small exchange ensues.

Three signal rockets rise from the other side of the fence, one red and two green. In the flickering light we see the figures of soldiers running from tents and clambering up to the tops of the buildings. While the flares hang in the air, the fire in our direction intensifies and we hear a couple of rifle grenades being launched.

We crouch by our tents and watch the sky. No one panics as it's clear that the only danger from this chaotic night shooting is a random hit. The fence shelters us and there are no tall buildings near the factory; since our attackers can fire only from ground level the bullets just go overhead. Our tents are in a safe place so we don't run anywhere. We can only be hit by shrapnel from the rifle grenades, but they explode far away.

The fighters could inflict far more damage if they fired through the gates, but either they didn't think of this or they don't want to risk it. Our lookout post is in the admin building where the two grenade launchers and a machine gun are set up, and it would be hard to get close on that side.

We sit watching the light show as green streams of tracer fire course across the sky. Then the guns fall quiet as suddenly as they started up. Our machine guns on the roofs pour down fire in all directions for another five minutes and then they also cease. It is now silent apart from the background chugging of the generator.

We have a smoke. It's great outside and no one wants to go back inside the stuffy tents where kerosene lamps are burning. We are almost grateful to the Chechens for getting us out. The moon is full, it's nighttime, quiet. Garik comes down sleepy-eyed from the roof of the meatpacking shop where our grenade launcher is mounted. He slept right through the shooting, the moron. Pincha was on duty with him but he stays up top, afraid that Arkasha will give him a thrashing.

'Why weren't you shooting?' I ask Garik.

'What was I supposed to shoot at—you can't see anything beyond the fence. And we didn't want to drop any grenades; we might have hit you.'

He knows it sounds unconvincing but he also knows we won't do anything about it. None of us was wounded so there's nothing to get worked up about.

'Enough of your stories,' says Arkasha, the oldest and most authoritative among the privates in our platoon. 'Do you want to spend two whole days up there? I can arrange that for you, no sweat.'

Garik says nothing, knowing he can land himself in hot water. Arkasha can indeed see to it that they spend two more days on the roof.

Fixa nudges me. 'Those were our flares, did you notice? One red and two green, just like the ones I gave the boy. Definitely ours. Return to sender, you could say.'

'I'd have preferred it if they'd just tossed the matchbox to us,' I mope.

The commanders step up the guard for the rest of the night and we sit like cats up on the roof. Fixa, Oleg and I join Garik and Pincha, while Arkasha, Lyokha and Murky head over to the admin building.

I know they'll just go to sleep as soon as they get there. Nor do we have any intention of peering into the steppe all night, and we take our sleeping bags up to the roof and bed down between two ventilation shafts.

The generator chugs away below us. In Argun lights glimmer at a few windows; it seems they've already hooked the place up to the electricity. All is quiet out in the steppe, not a single person is to be seen, no movement. Chechnya dies at night; the Chechens lock themselves into their homes and pray that no one comes for them, that no one kills or robs them or drags them off to the Russian military detention center at Chernorechye. Death rules the nighttime here.

On the horizon the mountains stand out as a dark mass. We only just came from there. That's where Igor was killed. I fall asleep.

Replacements arrive, about a hundred and fifty crumpled-looking guys who are trucked in to our battalion from Gudermes. They stand bunched together in a crowd in front of the gatehouse, on the square that we have dubbed the parade ground. They carry half-empty kit bags: all the things they had with them have been bartered for drink on the way.

This group is no use as soldiers; there isn't a single bold or cocky one among them, and not even one who is physically strong. Each new batch of replacements is worse than the last. Russia has clearly run out of romantics and adventurers, and all that's left is this worthless scum who have nowhere to go apart from the army or prison. These guys on the parade ground have darting, lost eyes set into swollen, unshaven faces and seem to blend into a monotonous, gray mass. And they stink.

We stand by the tents and bluntly survey the new recruits. It's a dismal sight.

'Where the hell do they get them from?' says Arkasha. 'We don't have any use for this sort here—all they can do is guzzle vodka and piss their pants. We have to talk to the commander so he doesn't take any of them on.'

'What do you want, for them to send us linguists and lawyers?' replies Oleg. 'Those types aren't very likely to come here. All the clever, good-looking ones have managed to wriggle out of this war, but since the draft board has to meet its quotas they just shunt whatever's left in our direction.'

We're short of people in the platoon but Arkasha is right, there's no place for this rabble; we'll manage somehow without them.

Two are assigned to us anyway, slovenly specimens of an indeterminable age, rat-like, unreliable. They immediately dump their kit bags in the tent and make themselves scarce, mumbling something about vodka. We don't hold them up.

'Maybe they'll get chopped to bits at the market—it'll be less hassle for all of us,' says Pincha, digging dirt from between his fingers with his knife.

Arkasha has come up with the idea of breaking into the trailer that the supply officer tows behind a Ural truck all around Chechnya. It's constantly guarded by cooks; what they keep in it is anyone's guess, but you can be sure it's not state bank bonds.

To effect the burglary we plan a full-scale military operation. Arkasha's plan is simple. It came to him the night we were being bombarded, and in this instance the arrival of the replacements will only be to our advantage.

When it gets dark we emerge from our tents, turn left along

the fence, make our way to the fence opposite the parking lot and jump into one of the useless sentry trenches the cooks have dug for themselves there.

In front of each trench a firing slit has been cut in the fence and the embrasure lined with turf. Judging from the fortifications they are preparing to defend the stocks of canned meat to the bitter end.

Lyokha and I get two hand grenades and pull the pins, while Arkasha wraps his rifle in three ground cloths and aims it into the bottom corner of the trench.

'Ready?' he whispers.

'Ready.'

'Now!'

We toss the grenades over the fence and they explode with a deafening clap in the night silence, or maybe it just seems that loud, such is the tension. Arkasha looses a few bursts into the ground.

The muzzle flash is invisible inside the ground cloths and the sound seems to come from the earth. It's impossible to tell where the firing is from—it seems like it's coming from all sides at once.

Lyokha and I throw two more grenades and I fire a signal flare.

The overall effect is extremely realistic.

'That'll do!' says Arkasha. 'Let's get out of here before they wake up!'

We manage to run about ten yards before the machine gun on the roof comes to life. I'm suddenly afraid that in his stupor the gunner will take us for attacking Chechens and cut us down in the wink of an eye.

Meanwhile, cooks emerge from every nook and cranny and lay down a withering barrage of fire. We also fire a few bursts in the air, our faces hidden in the crooks of our arms and averted from the illuminating muzzle flashes.

No one pays us any attention. The whole battalion is now dashing around in disarray and within a minute gunfire issues from all corners of the factory grounds.

The new recruits stoke the confusion, shouting 'Chechens, Chechens!' as they run toward the fence with their rifles, indiscriminately spraying bullets from the waist and generally behaving like children. To make matters worse they're firing tracer rounds, which ricochet and whiz all over the place, perfectly creating the impression that we are being attacked.

We freeze for a moment, dumbstruck. Little did we suspect that four grenades and a couple of rifle bursts could stir up such pandemonium. It must be said, a battalion is a force to be reckoned with.

We make our way amid the chaos to the trailer. There's no guard. Arkasha breaks the lock.

It's pitch black inside and we hastily grope around the shelves, chancing upon cans and small sacks and packages that we sweep into an open ground cloth. I come across a heavy, bulky object wrapped in paper. I stuff it inside my shirt and fill my pockets with more cans, spilling something in my haste, sugar maybe. Speed is of the essence.

'Give me a hand boys, I've got something here,' says Arkasha. I feel my way over to him. He is holding something by two handles, big and heavy, covered with a tarpaulin.

'It's butter,' exclaims Lyokha. 'Just look how much that bastard has stolen.'

'Right, let's get out of here,' Arkasha orders. It's almost as dark outside and the only light is from the muzzle flashes up on the roof. There's still a fair bit of shooting but the commotion is gradually dying down.

Someone is approaching the trailer, panting his way toward us with the stench of onions on his breath. It looks like some sneaky character has also decided to take advantage of the melee. Arkasha lashes out blindly in the dark with his boot and the man yelps and falls.

'Let's get out of here!' I hiss and we bound and stumble our way back. The wooden chest with the butter is unbelievably heavy; it painfully thumps my ankle bones and slips from my fingers, but we're not leaving it behind. It's impossibly awkward to run with all this stuff—apart from the chest we have cans bouncing around in our pockets, and I have to hold the package inside my shirt with my spare hand to keep it from falling out.

We reach the warehouses and find a small ditch that we dug earlier and lined with ground cloths. We dump the chest in it with our cans and packages and cover it all with more ground cloths that we've brought with us. Finally we scatter chunks of brick and lay a sheet of metal over the top. Then we hurry back up to the roof.

The shooting has almost stopped. We race across the roof toward the gatehouse, jump down to ground level by the meatpacking shop and wander leisurely back to our tents. I jab Arkasha with my elbow and he bumps me back with his shoulder. We grin at each other.

The next morning they order the whole battalion onto the parade ground. The commander tells us how last night, while the battalion was repelling an attack, some swine broke into the transport park's storage trailer and stole food from his comrades. There is to be a search of all personal property and vehicles while we remain on the square.

'Like hell it was from our own comrades,' says Arkasha. 'Our comrades would never have seen this butter. We should regard ourselves as battalion delegates for sampling food products intended for us. Later we'll tell the guys how delicious the food is that we are supposed to get.'

They keep us standing there while the supply officer personally shakes down every tent and armored car, throwing everything out onto the ground as he overturns bunk beds and knocks
over cooking stoves.

His lower lip is swollen and he is in a foul temper. He's the
one Arkasha kicked, right in the face. We were damned lucky
that he didn't grab his leg and pull off his boot. They'd have
beaten us half to death for this, but now it's impossible to identify us.

We smirk at the contorted face of the supply officer and
smile among ourselves. The stolen goods are well hidden in the
ditch and there is no evidence.

The search continues for six hours and we grow thirsty as the
sun beats down. I read somewhere that the Germans used to
force concentration camp inmates to stand in the sun half the
day for fun, much like this.

But we're in good spirits nonetheless. Covered in ground
cloths in that ditch by the warehouses a chest full of butter
awaits us, and we'd happily stand on the square a whole week
for that.

'OK boys, I invite you all for tea,' says Arkasha. 'I promise each
of you a butter sandwich that weighs two pounds. Pincha even
gets a double portion.'

'Wow,' says Pincha. 'But where's the butter from?'

'Let's just say there's no more left where it came from,' grins
Arkasha, winking at Lyokha and me.

Eventually they dismiss us. As was to be expected, the supply
officer didn't find a thing. Nor did he expect to—any fool knows
that no one would keep stolen stuff in his tent. He just wanted
to get his own back for the split lip.

For the rest of the day we wander idly around the factory but
stay away from the hole. That night we are all put on guard

duty again. Toward morning we leave our positions and make our way to the warehouses. Arkasha shines his flashlight in the ditch as Lyokha and I retrieve the booty.

Our raid has yielded eighteen cans of various foodstuffs, bags of sugar, four sets of dry rations, a hefty chunk of pork fat that must weigh five pounds—the package that was in my shirt—two loaves of bread, six cartons of cigarettes and in the chest . . . a generator! It's the exact same one we looted near Shatoi, a beautiful plastic-cased Yamaha, complete with that crack in the housing. It stands in the ditch covered with ground cloths as if this were its rightful home.

'It's butter, it's butter!' Arkasha says, angrily mimicking Lyokha. 'Can't you tell the difference between butter and engine oil?'

'Actually I can't, I've been pretty much unable to tell the difference between any smells recently. My nose is probably clogged up with soot. And anyway, it was in a case and doesn't smell too much of anything.'

He's right, the supply officer has kept the generator in good condition—clean and dry and not one new dent in it.

'Never mind, we can sell it,' I say. 'The Chechens would give their arm for something like that and still think it was a bargain. For them a generator is like manna from heaven, and this one will power up twenty homes. Have you seen how they mount a Lada engine on a stand and turn it into a dynamo? This is a factory-made generator and a diesel one at that.'

'Risky,' says Arkasha. 'We can't get it past the fence and it won't go through the gap. We'll leave it here for the moment—maybe we'll think of something.'

Until dawn we carry some of the stolen goods to our tent and stash the rest in a personnel carrier driven by a pal of ours. We put two cans at a time in our armpits and walk through the yard with bored expressions, yawning as if we were just out for a stroll and a breath of air. We carry the pork fat and cigarettes inside our shirts.

Later we divide the spoils equally. We give Pincha an extra can of condensed milk to make up for the lost butter. It's his birthday in a week and he stashes the can away, almost swooning with happiness—it's the best present he's ever had. He says he won't open it before five a.m. on Friday, the time he came into this world. He's lying of course; he'll wolf it down tonight, unable to wait.

That evening we have a feast and no one goes to the vehicle park for the usual gruel. Pincha eats his fill of pilfered canned meat and noisily stinks up the tent all night.

The Kombat has caught two recruits from the antitank platoon up to no good. It turns out they had passed some boxes of cartridges through the fence to the Chechen kids, then drunk a bottle of vodka and fallen asleep by the gap.

Half an hour later the Kombat chanced upon them and gave them a beating, and then kept them overnight in a large pit in the ground. Today their punishment is to be continued and they march us onto the parade ground again. We know too well what will happen now.

At the edge of the square they've dug an improvised torture rack into the ground, a thick water pipe that has been bent into the shape of a gibbet. At the Kombat's orders, the platoon made it during the night by placing the pipe against two concrete blocks and using an armored car to bend it in the middle. Two ropes now dangle from it.

The antitank gunners are led out, hands bound behind their backs with telephone cable and dressed in ragged overcoats and long johns. Their faces are already swollen and purple from the beating and there are huge black bruises where their eyes should be, oozing pus and tears from the corners. Their split lips can no longer close, and pink foam bubbles from their mouths, dripping onto their dirty, bare feet. It's a depressing sight. After all, these are not tramps but soldiers, ordinary soldiers; half of the army is like these two.

They stand the soldiers on the square. The two raise their heads and look through the gaps in the swelling at the ropes swinging in the wind.

The Kombat grabs one by the throat with his left hand and hits him hard in the nose. The soldier's head snaps back to his shoulder blades with a cracking noise. Blood spurts. The commander kicks the second one in the groin and he falls to the ground without a sound. The beating begins.

'Who did you sell the bullets to?' screams the Kombat, grabbing the soldiers by the hair and holding up their swollen faces, which quiver like jelly beneath the blows. He traps their heads between his knees in turn and lashes them with blows from top to bottom.

'Well, who? The Chechens? Have you killed a single fighter yet, you piece of shit, have you earned the right to sell them bullets? Well? Have you even seen one? Have you ever had to write a letter of condolence to a dead soldier's mother? Look over there, those are soldiers, eighteen-year-old kids who have already seen death, looked it in the face, while you scum sell the Chechens bullets. Why should you live and guzzle vodka while these puppies died instead of you in the mountains? I'll shoot the fucking pair of you!'

We don't watch the beating. We have been beaten ourselves and it has long ceased to be of any interest. Nor do we feel particularly sorry for the gunners. They shouldn't have gotten caught. The Kombat is right, they have seen too little of the war to sell bullets—only we are entitled to do that. We know death, we've heard it whistling over our heads and seen how it mangles bodies, and we have the right to bring it upon others. And these two haven't. What's more, the new recruits are strangers in our battalion, not yet soldiers, not one of us. But most of all we are upset that we can no longer use the gap in the fence.

'Cretins,' spits Arkasha. 'They put the gap out of bounds. They got themselves caught and ruined it for all of us. So much for selling the generator.'

He is more bothered than any of us. Now he'll have to go to the local market to satisfy his passion for trading. We don't like it at the market—it's too dangerous. You never know if you'll come back alive. You can only buy stuff from the Chechens at the side of the road, when one of you jumps down from the armored car and approaches them while the platoon trains their rifles on them and the gunner readies his heavy-caliber machine gun.

The market is enemy territory. Too many people, too little room to move. They shoot our guys in the back of the head there, take their weapons and dump their bodies in the road. You can walk around freely only if you take the pin out of a grenade and hold it up in your fist. It was a whole lot more pleasant to trade through the fence on our own ground. We were the ones who could shoot people in the back of the head if need be.

'Yeah,' says Lyokha. 'Shame about the gap. And the generator.'

The Kombat works himself into an even greater rage. There's something not right with his head after the mountains and he is on the verge of beating these two to death.

He lays into the wheezing bodies with his feet and the soldiers squirm like maggots, trying to protect their bellies and kidneys, a vain hope with their hands tied behind their backs. The blows rain down one after another.

The Kombat kicks one of them in the throat and the soldier gags, unable to breathe. His feet kick convulsively and he fights to gulp in some air, eyes now bulging through the swelling.

The rest of the officers sit in the shade of a canvas awning near the gatehouse, watching the punishment as they take a hair of the dog from a bottle of vodka on a table in front of them. Their faces are also swollen, but from three days of continual drinking.

Our political education officer, Lisitsyn, gets up from the table and joins the Kombat. For a while they flail at the gunners with their boots in silence—the only sound is their puffing from the exertion.

We understood long ago that any beating is better than a hole in the head. There have been too many deaths for us to care much about trivia like ruptured kidneys or a broken jaw. But all the same, they are thrashing these two way too hard. We all thieved! And every one of us could have wound up in their place.

Thieving is both the foundation of the war and its reason for continuing. The soldiers sell cartridges; the drivers sell diesel; the cooks sell canned meat. Battalion commanders steal the soldiers' food by the crate—that's our canned meat on the table that they snack on now between shots of vodka. Regimental commanders truck away vehicle-loads of gear, while the generals steal the actual vehicles themselves.

There was one well-known case when someone sold the Chechens brand-new armored cars, fresh from the production line and still in the factory grease. Military vehicles that were sold back in the first war and written off as lost in battle are still being driven around Chechnya.

Quartermasters dispatch whole columns of vehicles to Mozdok packed with stolen goods: carpets, televisions, building materials, furniture. Wooden houses are dismantled and shipped out piece by piece; cargo planes are filled to bursting with stolen clutter that leaves no room for the wounded. Who cares about two or three boxes of cartridges in this war where everything is stolen, sold and bought from beginning to end?

And we've all been sold too, guts and all, me, Arkasha, Pincha, the Kombat and these two guys he is beating now, sold and written off as battle losses. Our lives were traded long ago to pay for luxurious houses for generals that are springing up in the elite suburbs of Moscow.

The blows eventually cease. Those two jackals step back from the gunners, who lie gasping facedown on the asphalt, spitting out blood and struggling to roll over. Then the armaments officer steps forward and helps Lisitsyn lift one up, raise his arms and tie his wrists in the noose. They tighten the rope until his feet dangle a few inches above the ground, suspending him like a sack, and string up the second guy the same way. They do it themselves as they know that none of us will obey an order to do it.

'Fall out,' shouts the Kombat, and the battalion disperses to its tents.

'Bastards,' says Arkasha. It's not clear who he means: the gunners or the Kombat and Lisitsyn.

'Pricks,' whispers Fixa.

The soldiers hang there all day and half the night. They are opposite our tents and through the doorway we can see them swaying on the rack. Their shoulders are pressed up to their ears, their heads slumped forward onto their chests. At first they tried to raise their bodies up on the rope, change their position and get a little more comfortable. But now they are either asleep or unconscious and they don't move. A pool of urine glistens beneath one of them.

There is a hubbub inside the command post as our commanders down more vodka. At two in the morning they consume another load and tumble out onto the square to administer a further round of beatings to the dangling gunners, who are lit up in the moonlight.

The officers place two Tapik (TA-57) field telephones under the men and wire them up by the toes. The units contain a small generator, and to make a call you wind a handle, which produces a charge and sends a signal down the line.

'So do you still feel like selling bullets?' Lisitsyn asks and winds the handle of the first phone.

The soldier on the rope starts to jerk and cry in pain as cramps seize him.

'What are you yelling for, you piece of shit?' Lisitsyn screams and kicks him in the shins. He then rewinds the Tapik and the soldier howls. Again Lisitsyn lashes at his shins. And so on for maybe half an hour or more.

The officers of our battalion have turned into an organized gang that exists separately from the soldiers. They truly are like jackals, and so that's what we contract soldiers call them. We in turn are called 'contras,' or sometimes 'vouchers,' as we are there to be spent. And the two camps hate each other for good reason.

They hate us because we drink, sell cartridges and shoot them in the back in battle, because every last one of us yearns to get discharged from this lousy army. And since we want nothing more from it than the money it pays us for each tour of duty, we don't give a damn about the officers and will screw them over at every opportunity. They also hate us for their own poverty, their underfed children and their eternal sense of hopelessness. And they hate the conscripts because they die like flies and the officers have to write letters informing the mothers.

What else can you expect of the officers if they themselves grew up in barracks? They too used to get beaten as cadets, and they still get beaten at their units. Every other colonel of ours is capable of little more than screaming and punching, reducing a lieutenant, captain or major to a moaning, disheveled wretch in front of junior ranks. Nor do the generals bother to mete out penalties to the colonels any more; they simply hit them.

Ours is an army of workers and peasants, reduced to desperation by constant underfunding, half crazed with hunger and a lack of accommodation, flogged and beaten by all, regardless of the consequences, regardless of badges of rank, stripped of all rights. This is not an army but a herd drawn from the dregs of the criminal masses, lawless apart from the dictates of the jackals that run it.

Why should you care about soldiers when you can't even provide for your own children? Competent, conscientious officers don't stay long and the only ones left are those with nowhere else to live, who cling to empty assurances that they will be allocated an apartment someday. Or those who cannot string two words together and know only how to smash in the teeth of some young kid. They make their way up the career ladder not because they are the best, but because there is no one else. Accustomed from the very bottom rung to beating and being beaten, they beat and are beaten right to the top, teaching others to follow suit. We learned the ropes long ago; the ways of the gutter are the universal language in this army.

Lisitsyn gets bored of winding the Tapik. He puts a flak jacket on one of the gunners and shoots him in the chest with his pistol. The round doesn't pierce the jacket but the impact rocks the body on the rope. The soldier contorts and gasps, his lungs so close to collapse that he is unable to draw breath. Lisitsyn is about to fire again but the Kombat averts his arm, worried that in his state of drunkenness he will miss and hit the wretch in the belly or the head.

We don't sleep during all of this. It's impossible to doze off to these screams. Not that they bother us; they simply keep us awake.

I sit up in my sleeping bag and have a smoke. It was much the same in Mozdok. Someone would get a beating on the runway and I would sleep with a blanket over my head to keep out the light and muffle the cries and I'd think, great, it wasn't me today. Four years have passed since then and nothing has changed in this army. You could wait another four years and forty more after that and it would still be the same.

The yelling on the parade ground stops and the officers go back to the command post. The only sound now is the moaning of the gunners. The one who was shot at wheezes heavily and coughs as he tries to force some air into his chest.

'I'm sick of their whining,' says the platoon commander from his sleeping bag. 'Hey, shitheads, if you don't settle down I'll come and stuff socks in your mouths,' he shouts.

It goes quiet on the square and the platoon commander falls asleep. I pour some water in a flask and go outside. Arkasha tosses a pack of cigarettes after me.

'Give them a smoke.'

I light two and poke them between their tattered lips. They smoke in silence, no one speaks. What is there to say?

An illumination flare rises in the sky over the police post near the grain elevator, then a red signal flare. A firefight starts. Short, chattering bursts of rifle fire echo across the steppe and then a machine gun opens up on the roof of the elevator. Our 8th company is holed up on the twenty-second floor, and from there they can cover half the town. The fighters have no hope of dislodging the police after one of our guys, Khodakovsky, mined the stairs for them.

The machine gunner has spotted some fighters and looses off short, targeted bursts. After a while the exchange peters out and the police troops send up a green flare to give the all-clear.

The cigarettes burn down. I stub them out and give the gunners a drink of water. They gulp it greedily. I remember that we still have some rusks in our rations—now they'll have to suck them like babies as they probably have no teeth left. The battalion sleeps.

At the morning parade the two gunners are beaten again, but not as viciously as yesterday. They no longer squirm and just hang there, moaning quietly. Afterward the armaments officer unties the ropes and they fall to the ground like sacks of flour. They can't stand or lift their swollen arms. Their hands have gone black and their fingers are twisted. The Kombat kicks them a few more times, then takes their military ID cards and tears them into shreds.

'If I catch one more son of a bitch with cartridges, I'll shoot him without trial. That means every last one of you, old and new. Is that clear?'

No one replies.

'Throw this trash out of the gate,' he orders, nodding to the two prostrate forms. 'Don't give them money or travel documents—they don't deserve it. They can find their own way home. I don't need shit like that in the battalion.'

The gunners are carried out and dumped on the street. They turn their heads and look up at us as the gates close behind them. They have no idea where to go or what to do. There's no way they'll make it to Mozdok. The fighters will probably get them right here in Argun. If I were them I'd try to reach the police headquarters and ask the guys there to put them on a convoy to Khankala.

The police troops won't refuse since our guys helped them last night. But even then they'll be unable to fly out of Khankala and they'll be left to wander around until they get taken prisoner. We stand in silence. The Kombat turns and goes back to the command post.

The gunners sit at the gates like abandoned dogs until night falls. At dawn I take up my lookout shift in the admin building and the first thing I do is glance onto the street. They're gone.

One morning the battalion gets a visit from the top brass. We've just gotten up and are washing ourselves from hollow support blocks, knee-high piers for propping up the metal walls of the unfinished meatpacking shop. Each one holds about a gallon of greenish water from melted snow, no good for drinking but fine for a rinse.

A captured Mitsubishi off-roader drives in followed by two armored personnel carriers loaded with humanitarian aid packages. It belongs to Colonel Verter, the regiment commander.

Colonel Verter steps down from the silver jeep and the battalion is hastily ordered to fall in as if the alarm had been sounded. We come running, still dressing.

'I wonder what's up?' says Pincha, leaning on Garik as he wraps a puttee around his leg. The cloth is black with filth and stinks to hell. Even though we're used to all manner of stench we wrinkle our noses, unable to fathom how he managed to foul his puttees so badly. We've only recently had a steam bath and since then all we've done is sunbathe half-naked. Then again, Pincha always walks around in several layers of clothing and boots and his feet are usually so dirty you could plant potatoes between his toes. Arkasha tells him he should scrape off the dirt from his feet and sell it as shoe polish. That always amuses us.

It's forty-five minutes before morning parade and no one knows why we have been marched outside. We stand for a while, guessing what might have happened, then a rumor spreads along the ranks that the regiment commander has brought medals and will decorate those who have distinguished themselves.

Medals are good news and we brighten visibly. We don't say as much but we all hope to get one and return to our homes in full splendor. We didn't give a damn about this in Grozny or up in the mountains where the only thing we wanted was to survive. But now peace is within reach and we want to go back to civilian life as heroes.

I nudge Lyokha and wink. He'll certainly be hanging a 'For Bravery' medal on his chest today, having been twice commended by the platoon commander before we even left Grozny. He grins back.

They carry a table covered with a red cloth to the center of the parade ground and arrange lots of little boxes and award certificates on it. The medals cover almost half the surface, enough, it seems, for all of us to get one.

It starts to drizzle. A few drops spatter on the covers of the booklets and smudge them. Two soldiers pick up the table and move it against the wall for shelter, placing it next to the torture rack. We are to be decorated with a gallows as a backdrop!

Pincha thinks our first award ceremony might have offered a little more pomp and circumstance and that the colonel could have arranged a military band.

'I've seen medal presentations on TV and there's always a band playing a brass fanfare,' he says. 'Otherwise there's no sense in awarding the medals. The whole point is that you're presented them to a fanfare.'

'Yeah, right,' I scoff. 'And maybe you'd also like the president to kiss your ass while they give it to you?'

'That's not a bad idea,' says Pincha, with a thoughtful look in his eyes. 'I reckon every last one here should be able to pin a medal on his chest. Ever been in Chechnya? Well then, dear private, please accept this "Merit in Battle" medal. Were you there during the storming of Grozny? Then have "For Bravery" too. What, you even served in the mountains? Then you must also have the "Order of Courage." '

'You know they only give "Courage" to those who are wounded or killed. The most you can hope for is "Merit in Battle—First Class." '

'Well, that's not bad either,' Pincha concedes. 'But in that case I expect a fanfare with it.'

'Do you know how many regiments there are just in our army group?' Garik asks. 'No band could attend all those medal presentations. And how do you know they even have a band?'

We then argue whether the army group has a full military band. Pincha and Fixa are adamant that such a large formation must have one, or at the very least a small company of musicians. How else could they have celebrated the 23rd of February, Defenders of the Fatherland Day in Khankala? There was bound to have been a parade of some kind and you don't have a parade without a brass band.

Garik and Lyokha don't think there is a band in Chechnya. But either way, everyone agrees with Pincha that some extra sense of occasion is appropriate today.

Still the question arises: If there's no band, how do they give generals a proper send-off if one of them gets killed?

'Generals don't get killed,' says Oleg. 'Have you ever heard of even one of them dying here? No, they all sit tight in Moscow.'

'What about General Shamanov?' objects Pincha. 'He's down here and drives around the front line. He could easily get blown up on a mine. And Bulgakov, he was up in the mountains with us, wasn't he?'

'Shaman won't get blown up,' I chip in. 'I've seen how he travels. He has two armored personnel carriers riding with him and two choppers buzzing around overhead all the time. And even though he only rides in a jeep you can be sure the engineers have swept the road ahead. No, Pincha, it's not so easy to blow up an army group commander. Colonels, sure, they get whacked. I've seen a dead colonel with my own eyes and even heard about colonels being taken prisoner. But generals are another matter.'

'But they come down from Moscow for inspections here, don't they?' persists Lyokha. 'Some generals or other from GHQ fly in and bunches of them get flown around in choppers. They could easily get shot down in the mountains.'

'I somehow don't recall a single inspection by generals in the mountains,' I say. 'Seems to me they just come down in order to collect their war-zone per diem, and even then they go no farther than Khankala or Severny—they count as forward positions too.'

'How is Khankala a forward position?' asks Pincha, confused. 'It's well in the rear.'

'It might be the rear for you, but in the generals' expense claims it's the front line all right. Each day they spend there counts as two, and then they get the presidential bonus of fifteen hundred rubles a day in wartime, plus extra leave. Three trips to Chechnya and they get another "Courage" for their chest.'

'I stopped in Severny on my way back from the hospital,'

Lyokha tells us. 'It's great there now, not like a couple of months ago. Nice and peaceful, green grass, white-painted curbs, straight roads. They hooked it up to the electricity recently and now Severny lights up like a Christmas tree in the evening. They even have women there, officers get posted there with their wives. Just imagine, in the evening couples wander around the lanes under streetlights, just like back home. The soldiers there don't carry weapons with them and they get hot food three times a day and a steam bath once a week. They don't even have lice—I asked while I was there. They built a modern barracks there, you know, just like in the American movies. They even have porcelain toilets with seats, white ones—I kid you not! I went specially to use them. And boys, you won't believe me, but they even have a hotel for those inspections we've just been talking about. Televisions with five channels, hot water, showers, double-glazed windows . . .'

We listen, mouths gaping, spellbound by his description of the Severny base and airport on Grozny's outskirts as if we were hearing a fairy tale. White porcelain toilets, mess halls, double glazing. It seems fantastic that Grozny can have a hotel. We saw this city when it was dead, when the only residents were rabid dogs that fed on corpses in cellars. And now it has a hotel—that surely can't be true?

Severny is only a stone's throw from Grozny's Minutka Square, where the heaviest fighting took place, and from that cross-shaped hospital where we lost masses of guys. This is a city of death, and as far as we are concerned there should never be any luxury there so that what happened is never forgotten. Otherwise this whole war amounts to nothing but a cynical slaughter of thousands of people. It's not right to build new life on their bones.

We've just returned from the mountains where our battalion suffered a 50 percent loss—you couldn't even raise your head without being shot at. Up there they are still killing and shooting down helicopters, while in Grozny our commanders are apparently taking hot showers and watching TV. We are willing to believe in white porcelain toilets, but a hotel for the generals is going too far.

'You're making it up,' says Murky. 'It can't be true.'

'Oh yes it can, I saw it myself.'

'Saw it yourself, did you? You, the same person who tells us that herds of generals prance around in the mountains like antelopes? Well, that at least can't be true—they'd never leave the hotel.'

'I still want to know what happens when they bump off a general,' Pincha says, returning to the topic. Lyokha's account has made no impression on him—he took it all for a fairy tale and nothing else.

'If a general dies, do they pay his widow an allowance or not? And how do they pay it? Do they bring it around to her house, or does she stand in line with the rest of us in a cashier's office at the base and write letters to the newspapers saying "Please help me, my husband was killed and the state has forgotten me"? There were lots of women like that back at my regiment, struggling through all the red tape after their men got killed.'

Pincha's right. When we signed our contract to serve in Chechnya we saw women like this too. We got an advance before we moved out, and we waited for the money in the same line as they did. Out of respect for the mothers who gave up their most precious possessions for their country—the lives of their sons—we always let them go ahead of us in this line for the state's attention. They waited there to receive some elementary compassion and sympathy and yet they got nothing in return, not even money for a funeral.

These women got brushed off everywhere by the bureaucrats. Now the mothers of Fly and Yakovlev and the others are probably also fighting their way through red tape to get some basic rights.

'Of course they don't stand in the same line. You can be sure a general's widow gets her payments in full and right away,' says Fixa. 'After all, we're talking about a general, not some worthless Pincha, the likes of which they can heap up by the hundred every day and not care. But we don't have that many generals. They have to be bred, trained in the academy, educated. I bet the president himself knows them all by name. Yes, I bet he does.' Fixa pauses to consider his latest revelation. 'Hmm, I wonder what it's like when the president shakes your hand . . .'

Arkasha finally puts an end to the discussion.

'It doesn't matter if you're a general or a colonel,' he says. 'What's important is the position you hold. To be the widow of the chief of the military accommodation authorities or the widow of a general in command of some military district deep in Siberia are completely different things, even though the district commander is higher in rank. And like hell does the president know them all by name—we have countless generals. Up at the defense ministry they wander around like orderlies and clean the latrines—since there are no ordinary soldiers there, the generals have to get on their knees with rags and mess up their dress pants. I heard this from a colonel who asked us to help file a complaint on his behalf. A general beat him up and broke his tooth so he snitched on him, told them how the general was using stolen materials to build himself a house and had soldiers sweating away for him on the building site. They have their own system of hazing in the ranks, you can rest assured.'

I don't believe him—it seems unlikely that they have violent hazing even in the ministry. Then again, why not? Generals are not cupcakes; they were once lieutenants themselves. A couple more wars like this and our Kombat will become a general too; he'll get promoted and cudgel us all from up there instead. And what's so special about it?

At last Regimental Commander Verter comes out onto the parade ground accompanied by the Kombat. We fall silent.

'Greetings, comrades!' he shouts, as if addressing a parade on Red Square and not some depleted battalion in Argun.

'Greetings, sir,' we reply halfheartedly.

'At ease,' he tells us, even though it hadn't occurred to anyone to stand at attention.

The colonel talks to us about drunkenness. He calls us bastards and pissheads and threatens to string us all up by our feet from the rack so ingeniously devised by our Kombat. He fully approves of this innovation and will advise commanders of other battalions to draw from our experience. And just let any soldiers dare complain to him about nonregulation treatment—he intends to fight drunkenness and theft in the ranks!

After this he goes on at length about the duty we have fulfilled in the mountains and how the Motherland will not forget its fallen heroes and other nonsense. He strides up and down on stiff legs, his beer belly thrust forward, and tells us what fine fellows we are.

'Calls us crap, then sucks up to us,' Murky comments.

'You know what?' says Arkasha, narrowing his eyes. 'He's on his way up. He's just been appointed deputy division commander and that means he'll be a general. And for a successful antiterrorist operation in Chechnya, Colonel Verter has been put forward for the "Hero of Russia" medal. A guy I know at GHQ saw the letter of recommendation.'

'No way!' exclaims Oleg. 'He's a coward! He's only been to the front once. He got half the battalion killed for some lousy hillock and he still didn't manage to take it. His kind should be shot—no way can he become a general and get the "Hero of Russia" on top.'

'Sure he can. It may be a lousy hillock to you but in his reports it's a strategically important height, defended by superior enemy forces. And we didn't throw ourselves at them head-on for three days, we executed a tactical maneuver as a result of which the enemy were forced to abandon their positions. It's all a matter of presentation. Don't be so naive. The war isn't fought here, but in Moscow, and what they say goes. Don't you agree that you're a hero? I suppose you'll refuse a medal now?'

No, no one intends to turn down any medals. If each of us helps heave a handful of colonels and generals up the career ladder, then let them give us something for our trouble in return.

'I wonder what Verter will do with his Mitsubishi after the war,' Pincha says.

'Don't worry your pretty head about it, he's not going to give it to you,' replies Arkasha.

'Now that would be a fine thing. I wonder how he'll get it out of here. On a transport plane probably.'

After the colonel's address the awards begin. He stands at the table below the rack and in a wooden voice starts to read out the decoration order of the army group commander.

We wait impatiently. Who will be first? Who does the Motherland see as the best and most worthy among us? Maybe Khodakovsky—he never got a scratch but was one of the first to reach Minutka Square during the assault on Grozny. And he fought like a true warrior in the mountains. Or Emil, our Dagestani sniper who crawled fifty feet one night to the enemy trenches and fired on them at point-blank range. He killed thirteen and came out unscathed, earning himself a commendation for 'Hero of Russia' from the Kombat. Or maybe one of the mortar men—they heaped up more dead than all of us.

After he reads the order, the colonel takes two steps back and allows the Kombat forward to the table to hand out the decorations. He takes the first box, opens up the medal certificate and draws a deep breath. We freeze in anticipation. Who will it be?

'Private Kotov, step forward!' he announces loudly and solemnly.

At first I don't have a clue who this Private Kotov is. Only when he passes through the ranks and trots up to the table with an embarrassed smile, raising a clumsy salute, do I realize it's Kot, the cook from the officers' mess. He cooks for the Kombat, lays the table and serves up the dishes.

The Kombat probably just happened upon his medal first by chance. He might have shown a bit more care; the first person in the battalion to get decorated should be the best soldier or officer.

The medals go next to the staff clerk, then the transport chief, and then to someone from the repair company. We lose all interest and ignore the ceremony—it's clear enough what this is all about.

'Everyone who was in this stinking war should get a medal,' says Lyokha. 'Cooks, drivers, clerks, everyone, just for being here. Every last one of us has earned that much.'

'Right enough,' says Arkasha. 'And Kot above all.'

Standing beneath the gibbet, the Kombat awards a medal to the next 'outstanding' soldier. It suddenly strikes me that he perfectly embodies our state, a gibbet behind his back and medals in his hand for lackeys. For he is the highest authority on this strip of land inside the fence. For us he is judge, jury, prosecutor and parliament rolled into one. Here and now, he is the state. And so it turns out that the state has screwed us over yet again, heaping favors on those who are closest to it and who sucked up to it best.

Khodakovsky and Kot now both wear the same 'For Bravery' medal, although the first could have been killed a hundred times in the mountains and the second risked death only by overeating.

The only one in our platoon to get even a second-class 'Merit in Battle' is Garik, and then only because he worked for a month as a clerk at headquarters. After he is decorated he resumes his place beside us, shifting with embarrassment. He wants to take off the medal but we don't let him—he earned it.

We no longer believe in these decorations; to us they are just worthless metal. We are far more likely to receive a smack in the mouth from our country than an award that actually means something.

'Hey, Fixa,' I say, elbowing him. 'It's a shitty country we live in, isn't it?'

'Yep, it's shitty all right,' he answers, picking a blister on his palm.

After the decoration ceremony we are addressed by a representative of the Soldiers' Mothers Committee. A feisty, cigarette-puffing woman of about forty, she is bubbly, big-boned and still pretty. She has a commanding, chain-smoker's voice and can hold her own with us in her swearing.

We take to her at once and smile as she tells us simple things, like how this war has ravaged all of us and how peace is not far away, how we must hold on just a little longer, and how folks back home are thinking of us and waiting. And as proof of this, she says, she's brought us presents. She then distributes to every one of us a cardboard box with lemonade, biscuits, candy and socks. It's a great haul.

Later they prepare a sauna for the regimental commander, the officers and the female guest. They steam away a long time before the procession finally troops out and the half-naked officers sit in the shade beneath the tarpaulin and start on the vodka. A towel periodically falls from the representative of the mothers' committee, giving us a flash of her ample white body. She's not in the least bit shy and soon we forget our own shyness.

Even Arkasha refrains from joking. We like her and no one dares to cast judgment on this woman who came to war bearing gifts for the boys. She is the only person in months who has spoken to us as though we're people and we forgive her unconditionally for the things we'd never forgive the regimental commander: the half-naked fraternization with the officers; the drunkenness; the box with aid intended for us that stands on their table. After all, she could sit tight in Moscow and not risk taking a bullet here. Yet she has chosen to rattle her way down here in a convoy from Mozdok without expecting anything from us in return.

Before she leaves she gathers phone numbers and addresses, offering to call home or write for us and tell everyone we're alive and well.

She calls us all boys and even 'sonny.' Arkasha's pockmarked face creases in a smile and he gives her his phone number, telling her they might even meet after the war.

I come up to her and give her my home number too. When she hears I'm from Moscow she snaps a quick photo of me, hugs a dozen of the nearest soldiers and then leaps nimbly into an armored vehicle as the convoy pulls out.

A cloud of dust swirls for a while beyond the fence and settles and we stand like orphaned children by the gates as they close. It really does feel like our mother has left, our common mother, and we soldiers, her children, have been left behind.

'Fine woman,' says Arkasha. 'Marina's her name. Her son is somewhere here and she's driving around to different units looking for him. I feel sorry for her.'

The regimental commander is still here and they put us on the roofs on reinforced guard—the brass have to see that we are carrying out our duty properly.

We clamber up onto the meatpacking shop, kick away rusty shell fragments that have lain here since some barrage and seat ourselves on black-tarred roofing sheets that are baking hot from the sun. We have four of the aid boxes with us and spread out the grub on jackets.

'In the name of the Russian Federation the flesh of Private Fixa is hereby decorated with the "Order of the Stoop—Second Class," with lifelong entitlement to dig near electricity lines, stand under crane booms and cross the road when the light is red,' Arkasha announces ceremonially and presses a biscuit onto Fixa's chest.

Lyokha sings a fanfare, wipes a tear from his eye and gives the grinning Fixa a fatherly clap on the back as we salute in unison. Then we dive into the food, scooping condensed milk into our mouths with biscuits and washing it down with lemonade. Our fingers get sticky and we wipe them on our sweaty bellies, munching away with smiles on our faces. Emaciated, unwashed soldiers in huge boots and ragged pants, we sit on the roof and gorge ourselves. We've never had it so good.

'Enjoying that?' Fixa asks me.

'You bet. Are you?'

'Couldn't be better.'

Two cans of condensed milk, a bag of biscuits, a dozen caramel candies and a bottle of lemonade. That's our total reward for the mountains, for Grozny, for four months of war and sixty-eight of our guys killed. And it didn't even come from the state but from mothers like our own, who scrimp and save the kopeks from their miserable village pensions that the state still whittles away at to raise funds for the war.

Well, to hell with the state. We're contract soldiers, mercenaries who fight for money, and we need nothing more from it. We'll go into battle right now if need be, and they can pin their medals onto their backsides to jangle like ornaments on a Christmas tree.

Fixa wipes his milk-smeared hand on Pincha's pants and daintily takes a postcard from one of the boxes. It bears the Russian tricolor flag and the gold-printed words: 'Glory to the Defenders of the Motherland!' Afraid to smudge it, he holds it in two fingers and reads aloud:

'Dear Defenders of the Motherland! Dear Boys! We, the pupils and teachers of sixth class B of school 411, Moscow Eastern District, extend our heartiest congratulations to you on the Defenders of the Motherland holiday. Your noble feat fills our hearts with pain and pride. Pain, because you are exposed to danger every minute. Pride, because Russia has such courageous and strong people. Thanks to you we may study in peace and our parents may work in peace. Look after yourselves and be vigilant. May God protect you. Come home soon, we await your victorious return. Glory be yours!'

'Are we supposed to be the strong ones here?' Pincha asks, spraying crumbs from his mouth.

'Yes pal, it's about you,' answers Garik.

'Good postcard,' says Fixa.

'Bad one, it's on glossy paper,' I disagree.

'I mean it's well written, you fool.'

There is a slight tremble in Fixa's voice and his eyes are misty. What's up with him, surely he's not touched with emotion? Can it be that this tough guy from Voronezh, who usually has no time for frilly sentiment and understands only the most basic things like bread, cigarettes and sleep, things that are as simple as he is, has been moved by a postcard from a bunch of kids? Well, I'll be damned.

I take the card from him and look at it. It's nothing like those despicable cards they sent us before the presidential elections in 1996. For a while they stopped calling us bastards and sons of bitches and started to refer to us as 'dear Russian soldier' and 'respected voter.' These were our first elections, and for three of us in my unit they were also the last. They didn't get to cast their ballots and died in the first Chechen war before they could fulfill their civic duty.

'This school is in the east of the city, not far from where I live. If you like, after the war I'll drop by there and thank them,' I tell Fixa to make him happy.

'We'll go there together,' he says. 'We'll go to the school together. We have to, don't you see? They remembered us, collected money, sent us aid packages. What for? Who are we to them?' He pauses. 'It's a shame Khariton is gone—I shouldn't have driven him on at the hill, shouted at him. Nor should you,' he tells Arkasha. 'What did you hit him for? He was just a kid. Why did you hit him?'

Arkasha doesn't reply. We sit in silence. Fixa is crying. I fold the postcard in half and put it in my inside pocket. At that moment I really believe I will visit that school after the war.

After the glut of sweet food we suffer a fresh epidemic of dysentery in the battalion. Our stomachs are unaccustomed to normal food and we are stricken twice as badly as the previous time. The inspection pits in the garage are full to brimming and black clouds of flies circle above them.

Oleg says this outbreak is our bodies reacting now that the danger has passed; we've relaxed and now sickness is kicking in.

'The same thing awaits us at home,' he says. 'You'll see, we'll come home from the war decrepit wrecks with an A to Z of illnesses.'

I think there's another reason. The battalion is squeezed into a small area and those same flies buzzing over the pit settle on our mess tins when we eat.

We crouch half-naked in the meatpacking shop, the only place left we can still use. We sit this like half the day; there's no point in putting on our pants since dysentery sends you running continuously. Sometimes you can't force anything out, other times you jet blood.

'False alarms are a symptom of acute infectious dysentery,' says Murky, flipping through a medical encyclopedia he found in Grozny and has carried with him across Chechnya, establishing erroneously that we have symptoms of typhoid, foot-and-mouth disease, cholera and plague. Now the encyclopedia itself befalls a terrible fate, being made of soft pages like newspaper, and within two days only the binding is left. Dysentery is the last disease that this fine medical reference book diagnosed in its time.

'Remember how they made us crap on paper?' Garik asks with a grin.

'Oh God, yes,' Oleg laughs back.

Before we were sent to Chechnya, the regiment would file out of the barracks twice a week and, company by company, drop its pants after placing a piece of paper on the ground. While a pretty young woman medic walked through the ranks they made us defecate and hand her our excrement to be analyzed for dysentery. The cattle must go to the slaughter in good health, and our shame at this act bothered nobody.

Now no one shows us such concern. All they do is give us some kind of yellow tablets, one pill between three of us. We

take them in turns but this treatment has no effect whatsoever.

'Heavy caliber, take cover!' warns Fixa before loosing off a deafening burst in the pit. Arkasha responds with a smaller caliber,
Murky fires single shots. But Pincha outguns us all, straining
long and hard before producing a report that would shatter all
the windowpanes in the area if any had still been intact.

'Tactical nuclear warhead with enriched uranium, explosive
power equivalent to five tons of TNT,' he says, smirking.

'That's prohibited weaponry, Pincha,' protests Arkasha with
a belly laugh.

At night the battalion resounds with deep rumbling and
moaning. The sentries do their business right off the rooftops;
it's too exhausting to run down twenty times a night. The night
sky is illuminated by bright stars and gleaming white soldiers'
backsides. Walking under the roofs is hazardous.

My bleeding starts again and my long johns are permanently
encrusted with blood. We all have it. Your rectum swells up and
protrudes several centimeters. Half your backside hangs out
and you sit resplendent like a scarlet flower. Where are we supposed to find wiping material? We strip the remaining scraps of
wallpaper from the storerooms and rasp at our poor backsides,
inflicting further harm on ourselves and sending blood gush-
ing from our pants.

War is not just attacks, trenches, firefights and grenades.
It's also blood and feces running down your rotting legs. It's
starvation, lice and drunken madness. It's swearing and human debasement. It's an inhuman stench and clouds of flies
circling over our battalion. Some of the guys try to heal themselves with herbal folk remedies that end up making many of
them even sicker.

'This is our reward from the Almighty,' Arkasha says. 'The

whole battalion has flowers springing from their asses—that's our springtime!'

'What did we do to deserve this?' moans Pincha.

I find a roll of paper towels in the admin building and hide it in a pile of trash, using it only when there's no one else around. It wouldn't last the platoon even half a day, but now I'm OK for a while at least.

In a bid to fight the dysentery the battalion commander imposes a strict regime of mess-tin cleaning. Now after each meal a duty soldier washes the platoon's mess tins. There's no water here and we wash them in the same water we use for washing ourselves each morning. Flakes of soap and grease float in the green water with mosquito larva, and we have to scoop away the flora and fauna with our hands to gather enough water for tea.

Because of the shortage people start pilfering water again, and our position by the gates gives us a strategic advantage. As soon as the water truck drives in we block its path until we have filled every container we have.

Arkasha and Fixa have found an old bathtub somewhere and we also use that. The supply officer threatens to have us shot, but still we carry out the tub every morning to go water collecting.

In the recesses of the unfinished meatpacking shop we find more concrete support piers with hollows full of murky water. We keep our find a secret, but people catch on and we have to mount a guard. It comes to blows as we jealously protect our source.

'We'd be better off fighting again,' says Fixa. 'At least then there's no problem with supplies.'

That's true enough. The commanders think about us soldiers only when we are being killed by the hundred. After each storming operation they fall us in and tell us what heroes we are and give us normal food and water rations for two or three days. Then once again we get half-cooked gruel for breakfast and a smack in the mouth for lunch.

'But these lulls are still good,' says the platoon commander, washing his feet with a kind of dried-fruit water they call 'compote' that we are supposed to drink. 'Warm, dry and nowhere to go. Not even for washing water. Look at this brew: it isn't even sticky because it's peacetime.'

Peacetime compote is indeed different from the stuff they serve during the fighting. What they give us now in this slack period can be used for anything. You can drink it, wash in it or use it for soaking your underwear because it doesn't contain a single gram of sugar or dried fruit; the supply officer traded both commodities for vodka. He does the same during times of combat, just not so often, the conscientious fellow.

One day a jeep carrying police officers is shot up near the village of Mesker-Yurt. We are alerted and set off in two carriers, a platoon of infantry and our three gun teams.

The first vehicle churns up great clouds of dust, making it impossible for those of us following behind to breathe or open our eyes. The dust grates on our teeth, blocks our noses and coats our eyelashes, eyebrows and hair in a gray film. We cover our faces with bandanas but they don't help and still we can hardly breathe. Fucking weather: impenetrable mud in winter and vile summer dust that turns into dough when it rains.

The jeep stands on a road between fields and has been almost completely destroyed. The fighters waited in the undergrowth and hit it with a rocket launcher. One side has been blown apart; mangled metal and a seat hang out with a pair of dangling legs and some other lumps of flesh. The four guys inside were torn to pieces. The attackers evidently raked the jeep with several rifles after the explosion and the other side is peppered with holes where bullets and shrapnel exited.

The local police arrive and there is nothing for us to do except guard the investigators. We leave after a couple of hours.

That evening we are sent again in the direction of Mesker-Yurt. A paramilitary police unit has located the same rebel group that killed the officers earlier. They've holed up in the village after the attack and were waiting to ambush us, but we never came.

I can't mount my grenade launcher on the personnel carrier; my hands don't respond and the bedplate won't go onto the bolts. My body is like cotton wool, my fingers can hardly feel the nuts and I fumble to tighten them. I look at them and can't focus properly. I sense that I should not go to Mesker-Yurt today. I'm scared.

Fear fills me gradually, rising in my body like a wave and leaving an empty space behind it. This is not the hot, rushing fear you feel when you suddenly come under fire, this is different, a cold, slow-moving fear that just doesn't recede. Today, near Mesker-Yurt, I will be killed.

'Go and get two cases of grenades,' the platoon commander orders.

I nod and go to the tent. The cases weigh thirty pounds each and I can't carry two at once; they are slippery and there's nothing to hold them by. I empty my backpack and stuff one case inside and put the second under my arm and run out of the tent to see the column already driving out of the gate. The platoon commander motions me to stay behind.

I watch them disappear toward Mesker-Yurt and suddenly I am seized by a powerful trembling. I feel chilled to the bone, my arms are weak, my knees give way and I sit down sharply on the ground. Blackness clouds my sight, I see and hear nothing and I sit uncomprehendingly, on the verge of vomiting. I haven't felt such terror in ages.

Fixa is standing near the gate.

'How come you didn't go?' I ask.

'I got scared, you know?' he replies.

'Yes, I know.'

He gets his cigarettes out. My hand is trembling so hard I can't even strike a match. What the hell is the matter with me? Nothing like this has ever happened before. I have to get a grip. The column left while Fixa and I stayed behind and are out of danger.

Our guys come back at night. Mesker-Yurt was taken but our battalion was deployed in the second security cordon around the village and didn't take part in the fighting. The police paramilitaries did all the work and lost ten men.

We didn't take any casualties that night, but I still feel that it would have been my last. I want to go home.

I live with fear constantly now. It began that day and doesn't abate. I am scared all the time. The fear alternately turns slowly like a worm somewhere below my stomach or floods through me with a hot flush of sweat. This is not the tension I experienced in the mountains but pure, animal fear.

One night I beat up Pincha for leaving the lookout post before he was relieved, and then did the same to two new guys. They didn't hit it off with our platoon and sleep separately in the cook's armored car. Then the pricks go and brew tea right on the windowsill of the lookout post. Their fire flickers away for all to see and is visible for miles, giving away our position and maybe drawing the attention of snipers. And I'm the one who has to relieve them.

I can no longer sleep. I don't trust the sentries and spend

most nights in the admin building or on the parade ground. I always keep my chest harness stuffed with loaded magazines that I've traded for food and cigarettes. I have about twenty-five magazines and it still seems too few. I also empty a few clips of bullets into my pockets and hang about a dozen grenades from my belt. It's still not enough. If they storm us I want to be fully armed.

One night I relieve the guys on the lookout. I stay away from the window and stand motionless in the room around the corner for four hours, freezing at the slightest sound outside.

It seems I am alone and that while I am skulking in the admin building the Chechens have silently butchered the whole battalion and are coming up the stairs for me. I hate the generator as it drowns out every other sound. I try not to breathe and strain to hear what's going on in the building.

Sure enough, they're already inside. Chunks of brick grate underfoot as someone makes his way up the stairs. The Chechen turns on the stairwell and puts his foot on the last flight. Nine more steps and he'll reach my floor. My heart stops beating. I don't want to shoot because I'll give away my position. I may take out one of them, but the rest will know I'm here and they'll get me with grenades. I won't be able to run away or hide anywhere; they're all around.

'I want to go home,' I say out loud and draw my knife from the top of my boot. The blade gives off a dull gleam in the moonlight. I clutch the weapon with both hands in front of my face and tiptoe slowly to the stairs, keeping my back close to the wall, trying to step in time with the Chechen.

He's now on the second step. I also take a step. We move our feet simultaneously. Third step, fourth, fifth. He has four more steps to go, three, two...I leap forward and lash out wildly around the corner with the knife, striking a deep gash in the wall and scattering crumbs to the floor. A chip bounces down the stairs and hits an empty can with a clink. There's no one there. I take several deep breaths.

The stairwell is deserted. The Chechens are already in the room, of course. While I was fighting ghosts in the stairwell they've occupied my position, climbing up the heap of trash outside and swinging themselves stealthily through the window. Now they are fanning out to the corners. I can't hide any more, so I unsling my rifle, slip off the safety and tramp my way noisily toward the room. I kick a brick and it flies off to one side with a deafening crash. My footsteps are probably audible from the street. I give a sharp shout.

My plan is simple. They will hear me coming along the corridor and run out of the room one by one, only to be picked off by me. But then I beat them to it, burst in, squat down and circle the room like a wolf, training my rifle ahead of me. No one. I'm still alive, thank God!

I stand in the corner again and listen into the night. I can't see anything from here but snipers can't see me either. And in this corner I have a better chance of surviving if a grenade comes through the window. I crouch down, cover my head with my jacket and switch on the light on my watch. Thirteen minutes of my shift have passed. Another three hours and forty-seven minutes at the lookout.

I hear footsteps on the stairs and freeze. Five more steps. I draw the knife from my boot.

I stop talking to people altogether. I don't laugh or smile any more. I am afraid. The desire to go home has become an obsession. That's all I want and I can think of nothing else.

'I want to go home,' I say as we have supper in the tent.

'Shut up,' says Arkasha.

He gets more wound up than the others by the mention of home. He is not due for demobilization, he has no medals and, in any case, if he goes home they'll probably lock him up because of an old bribery charge against him from his civilian days.

We've been halted in Argun for too long and the tension is now being displaced by fear. This spell of rest and recuperation can't last forever—something has to happen. They'll either send us home or march us back into the mountains.

'I don't want to go back into the mountains,' I say. 'I want to go home.'

'They can't send us back into the mountains,' Fixa assures me. 'We've done our stint. There are so many different units, so they just send new brigades up there. No, we won't go into the mountains any more. And we can annul our contract any time we like, don't forget.'

'I want to go home,' I repeat.

Arkasha throws an empty can at me. I don't react.

We wait.

I have ulcers on my thigh and pay a daily visit to the medics to get them dressed. They refuse to heal and continue to grow, having now reached the size of a baby's palm. Smaller ones dot my arms.

There are two new nurses at the first-aid point, Rita and Olga. Rita is a redhead, well built and with a drink-toughened voice that was made for firing off her earthy locker-room jokes. She's one of us and the boys go crazy over her. But I like Olga more.

Olga is small, quiet and over thirty, with a good figure. She hasn't had an easy time here—women like her have no place among drunken contract soldiers. She's a real lady and remains one even in the midst of war. She hasn't started smoking or swearing, and she doesn't sleep with the officers. The little white socks she wears never fail to fascinate me, femininely dainty and always clean. God only knows where she manages to wash them.

I visit her every day for treatment. She removes the old bandages and inspects the wounds, bending down over my thigh. I stand naked in front of her but it doesn't bother either of us. She's seen countless unwashed guys encrusted in blood and I am in no condition to flirt with a woman anyway.

But it's still pleasant when her cool fingers touch my thigh and her breath stirs my body hair, bringing me out in goose bumps. I close my eyes and listen to her tapping gently on the skin, and I will my leg to rot further so she will have to care for me a little longer. Olga's tender touch is so much like peacetime, and her palm is so like the palm of the girl I left behind in my prewar past.

'Why don't you wear underwear?' she asks one day.

'They don't issue us any,' I lie. In fact I am simply ashamed of my lice-ridden long johns and before each visit I remove them and hide them in a corner of the tent.

She spreads ointment on my festering thigh ulcers and pork fat on my arms to contain the others. Two weeks later they start to heal.

We hear a three-round burst of fire. Someone screams over at the infantry personnel carriers.

'Rifles on safety!' I hear Oldie shout. We run over.

It turns out some drunken driver forgot to put his rifle on safety and accidentally pressed the trigger. All three rounds hit home. One ripped off a contract soldier's jaw. He sits on the ground, blood streaming from his smashed mouth into a large, fatty pool on the earth. He doesn't make a sound, just sits there and looks at us, arms hanging limply before him. The pain hasn't set in yet and he doesn't know what to do.

The staff commander tends to him, injects him with painkiller and tries to bandage what's left of the jaw. Jagged splinters of bone tear the gauze as he binds the wound. The soldier starts to jerk so Oleg grabs him by one arm and pins him to the ground while Murky holds the other.

The other two bullets did far more damage, hitting Shepel in both kidneys. He lies on top of the armored car while Oldie bandages him.

The soldier's breathing is labored and uneven but he is conscious. Even in the light of the moon his face looks deathly pale.

'Shame,' he gasps. 'Shame it ended like this, I almost made it home.'

'Nothing has ended, Shepel,' Oldie tells his friend. 'Do you hear me, nothing has ended! We'll get you to the hospital and everything will be OK. Come on pal, you'll see.'

He applies bandage after bandage, several packages, but he can't stop the bleeding. The blood flows thickly, almost black in color. It's bad. Shepel no longer speaks. He lies with his eyes closed and breathes heavily.

'I'll kill that son of a bitch,' Oldie screams.

The personnel carrier leaves for Khankala with the injured men and Oldie goes with them.

'That's the most goddamned unfair death of this whole war,' Arkasha says as he watches the vehicle disappear into the darkness. 'To go through so much and die here, in the rear, from a stray bullet.'

His fists clench and unclench and the muscles in his cheeks twitch.

'What an unfair death,' he whispers into the darkness. 'So unfair.'

They don't let the carrier through at the checkpoint into Khankala. Shepel lies on the top dying while some duty lieutenant demands the password, saying he can't open the barrier without it. This rear-unit rat who's spent the whole war in this field wants the password and couldn't care less that our comrade is critically wounded.

He is afraid to let them through, afraid that the brass will find out and that there will be consequences for him. They are all afraid that for any screw-up they will get sent to the front lines. And then they will be the ones bleeding to death on top of a carrier while someone else blocks the way to the hospital.

Oldie doesn't know the password and starts shooting in the air in fury, sending tracer rounds over safe, snug Khankala with its cable television and double glazing. He fires and screams and begs Shepel to hold on a little longer. They get through the checkpoint and to the hospital, but Shepel dies a few hours later. We had failed to stem the bleeding.

They don't let Oldie out of Khankala and would surely have thrown him into one of the infamous *zindan* pits in the ground that captives are often kept in. But there aren't any pits in Khankala because there are plenty of journalists here and they consider it an unacceptable form of torture to keep soldiers in pits, although torture in my opinion is something quite different.

So to avoid antagonizing civilians the command has generously allocated some wheeled trailers as detention cells. There are lots of these trailers here, a few for holding our soldiers and the rest for captured Chechen fighters.

One of those housing Chechens was dubbed the 'Messerschmitt' after some genius painted a white swastika on its side.

At night harrowing screams rise from the Messerschmitt as our interrogators extract confessions.

Oldie has landed himself in an unenviable situation. Shooting in Khankala is a serious blunder. The rear commanders were scared witless when he unloaded tracer rounds over their heads and now they want to avenge their embarrassing display by pinning a drunken rampage charge on him.

We manage to visit him in Khankala after talking our way onto a transport run with sick cases. While our medic delivers them to the hospital we look for the trailer where Oldie is locked up.

This place is completely different than how we remember it. Khankala has grown to an incredible size. It's no longer a military base but a town with a population of several thousand, if not tens of thousands. There are untold numbers of units here, each with its own perimeter fence, and you can get lost if you don't know your way around. But it's remarkably quiet, as if you are on a farm. The soldiers wander about without weapons and they stand upright, having rid themselves of the habit of stooping like they do at the front. Maybe these guys have never even heard a shot; their eyes betray neither tension nor fear, they are probably not hungry and perhaps they have no lice. This really is the rear.

It's a cozy little world, segregated from the war by a concrete wall. This is the way the army should be: ideal, astounding order. And it's just how Lyokha had described Severny to us, although we didn't believe him at the time: straight, blacktopped roads, green grass and white-painted curbs, long parades of new one-story barrack houses, a metal Western-style mess hall with a gleaming semicircular corrugated roof, clean toilets and saunas. Everything neatly swept and sprinkled with sand, a few posters here and there, and portraits of the president gazing down at you every three feet.

And there are streetlamps that work, casting light onto officers as they stroll with their wives. Lyokha was right—they actually bring them down here to live. Some of them even have their children with them, and they grow up here in Grozny.

We walk around Khankala, calling out Oldie's name. People stare at us: we are superfluous here in this place in the rear, where everything is subordinate to strong army order. The neatness of it all infuriates me. We walk around like plague victims and survey these well-fed soldiers with hatred. Let just one of them say a single word or try to stop or arrest us and we'll kill the bunch of them.

'This place is a goddamned rats' lair,' spits Fixa. 'Shame we don't have a grenade launcher—we could stroll around and take care of these people with a few bursts. Oldieee!'

'Oldieee!' I follow.

Finally Oldie's unshaven face appears at a tiny barred window in one of the wagons. Fixa gives the sentry some cigarettes and we have a few minutes to talk. We can see only half of his face. We smile at one another and light up. I climb up on the wheel and pass him a smoke and the three of us puff away in silence. We don't know what to say; we are loath to ask how it is in there and what they feed him. What does that matter now? It has to be better than in the mountains.

As it turns out, it's quite bearable in there. There are a few mattresses on the floor, he has a roof over his head, it's warm and dry—what else do you need? They don't even beat them here because of the journalists. They should have sent a few journalists into the mountains, or to us in Argun when Lisitsyn shot at the soldier on the rack—that would have been a hoot! Then they would know what real torture is. But with them it's all *zindan* this and *zindan* that. I think they just like the word.

'It's like a rest home here,' Oldie says with a grim smile as he tells us of his daily life. 'Mountain air, three meals a day. Pincha would love it. No oatmeal here; they give us proper food from the officers' mess hall. Today, for example, I had meatballs and pasta for lunch.'

'Oh really? Nice setup you have here,' says Fixa.

'Can't complain.'

I look at his face through the bars and smile. I don't have any particular thoughts, I'm just happy to be here with him, and happy that we're together again. I can't imagine being demobilized without him, or how I will live later without all of them—Oldie, Fixa, poor Igor.

'Shepel died,' Fixa tells him.

'I know. I'll find the guy who did it.'

'We'll find out who it was, Oldie, I promise.'

'No, I'll find him myself. I have to do it, don't you see? If I don't find him, then the deaths of Shepel, Igor, Khariton, Four-Eyes, all of them, will cease to have any meaning. Then they've simply died for nothing. All of them could just as easily have been killed by some drunk with no retribution, no one bearing any responsibility. If I don't find him then all these deaths are a kind of dreadful crime, plain murder.'

He is absolutely calm as he says all of this. His expression hasn't changed and retains the same good humor as if he were still telling us about the meatballs he had for lunch. But I know this is not just talk. He will find and kill this guy and he is fully entitled to do so.

The value of a human life is not absolute and Shepel's life in our eyes is far more valuable than the life of some drunken driver who never had a single shot fired at him, was never pinned down by sniper fire, never used his hands to stanch flowing blood and never saved anyone's life. So why should he live if Shepel died? How could it be that this person who never experienced the horrors Shepel did was able to go and kill him in a drunken stupor and stay alive himself?

It doesn't seem right. There is no other punishment apart from death because anything less is still life, and so it's no punishment. To shoot a swine of an officer in the back is in our eyes not a wicked deed but simple retribution. Swines shouldn't live when decent people die.

Oldie and Shepel were good guys; they immediately hit it off though they weren't from the same town.

'I understand. We won't touch him,' I tell him.

'Did you come here with the medic?' he asks.

'Yes.'

'Have we got many wounded?'

'None, just sick. The war is coming to an end now.'

'Too bad, I really wanted to go home,' Oldie says.

'We won't leave you behind. If need be we'll tear this shitty Khankala to pieces, but we won't leave you. You're coming home with us.'

Oldie makes a tired gesture. He has let himself go since he's been here. Maybe Shepel's death broke him somehow, or maybe he's just worn out by it all.

'To hell with all of them,' he says. 'It doesn't matter any more. The main thing is that we are alive. I don't care about anything else. After all, a few years behind bars is still a few years of life, isn't it?'

'They can send you down for seven years on these charges, you know.'

'So what . . . it doesn't matter any more.'

We smoke another cigarette and then it's time to go. We push a few packs of smokes through the window and head back to the hospital where the transport is waiting for us. Fixa and I turn and see Oldie watching from the window.

We won't leave him behind.

The battalion leaves for Kalinovskya where we are to be discharged. For us, the war is over.

It starts to rain. The tires of the vehicles squeal on the wet asphalt and rainbows glimmer in the spray thrown up by the wheels. I open the hatch and stick my face out under the rain. Large drops fall straight and evenly on my skin. The sun hangs heavily on the horizon and our column casts long shadows in its rays.

And that's it. Peace. This warm, damp day is the last day of our war.

Shepel is dead, and so many others. I remember all of my comrades; I remember their faces, their names. At last we have peace, boys—we waited for it for so long, didn't we? We so wanted to meet it together, to go home together and not part company until the whole platoon had been to everyone else's home. And even after that we would stay together, live as one community, always close, always there for each other.

What will I do without you? You're my brothers, given to me by the war, and we shouldn't be separated. We'll always be together. We still have our whole lives ahead of us.

Hey Kisel, Vovka! How's it going Igor, Shepel?

I stand up to my waist in the hatch. The runway is deserted. Warm rain falls. Large raindrops roll down my cheeks and mix with tears. I close my eyes and for the first time in the war I cry.

19/ A Soldier's Dream

Snow fell the whole night. It fell in soft, large flakes, and when we wake up we can't find our friends because they are all covered in snow.

It grows light and we wait for the sun to appear. The night is ending. Our hands tremble slightly, and we feel chilly as the nervous tension ebbs away and our bodies relax.

The most frightening part is over; we have survived another night and that means we have another day ahead of us. Nighttime means cold, and we hate and fear the night. The climate in the mountains fluctuates wildly: by day it is sixty degrees, the sun shines, and at night it can easily snow, blow a chill wind and send the temperature falling to the teens. We take the jackets from the wounded, who are evacuated to the rear. The jackets get soaked through under the snow, and if you zone out for ten minutes to lean against the armor, you find yourself frozen to the surface, even your hair.

Nighttime means fear. As dusk falls you feel everything inside you grow cold and hard, feel it knot in a lump and mobilize itself for action. Your brain starts to work more precisely, your eyes see better and your hearing tunes in. The tension is acute; you expect something to happen and you are ready for anything. Then the fear recedes to a deeper place beneath your stomach, turning over from time to time, but faintly, leaving behind just the tension.

Nighttime means loneliness. No lights around, no sounds, no movement. A huge, endless sky above you where you know a plane with lights and passengers inside will never fly. There is no one around, you are quite alone. And even if there are a hundred of you, you are still alone. All of you are alone.

There is no life around either; you yourself are life and comprise your whole world. You are a little soldier in the middle of enormous Chechnya under the black southern sky, and everything is inside you. And you are very tired.

Finally the sun appears and you relax. Your brain feels like cotton, you think about nothing and you want nothing, only to sit there just as you are, with your gaze fixed ahead of you.

I sit on the mount of the grenade launcher and smoke. My hands are trembling slightly and the sun is already starting to beat down, warming my back and defrosting my boots enough for me even to take them off. At night they get wet, tighten and freeze to my puttees.

I am happy. Happy that I am home, that this is all over, that everything has finished and is in the past. What mountain peak is that, and where did that come from, that peak? Did I dream it? But I have never been there, so why am I dreaming about it? Or have I? I don't know. I feel clean sheets against my skin and the luxury of a warm blanket; I know I am at home and I'm happy. I smile, turn my face toward the sun and squint. It's good to be home. True, I don't know why there are mountains here, and snow, and wet boots, but it doesn't matter, I'm at home now, there's nothing to fear.

Igor appears. He is telling me something but I don't listen as I sit on the gun mount smoking and savoring this picture of home. It's good that Igor is here too, only odd that he's at my home; he surely has his own home yet he's here, but no matter. In fact it's good that he's at my place.

Ash from my cigarette falls onto the bolt of my rifle and I brush it off with my sleeve. I have to think where I'm going to stow my weapon now that I'm home. Usually I lay it under my head in the tent, but home is permanent—it's not some tent for a day.

Igor is still trying to tell me something and I am still not listening to him. Then he falls silent, looks at me strangely and says: 'Let's go!' I suddenly feel empty and cold inside. A vague thought appears but I don't allow it to register and I chase it from my head because I know what the thought is.

'Where to, Igor?'

'Let's go,' he says again, pointing behind me. I don't turn to look, I know what's there. A mountain and infantry scattered across the snow, crawling, scrabbling upward, through the gaps in the lines and toward the tracer rounds that are flying their way. But it's still quiet; the sounds of fighting are not audible. The thought in my head is now persistent but I suppress it, still not turning around to look. I cannot let it through, it's not true. I'm at home, and I won't turn around.

'No, Igor, we're at home, it's all over, have you forgotten? Come on, I'll introduce you to Olga and my mother, we'll sit down together, have a drink and talk. We dreamed about this for so long, remember?'

I am suddenly terrified—I already know what he'll reply.

'I can't, I'm dead,' he says and looks beyond me.

I turn around and see the mountain and the dots of the men and I hear the deafening, ear-splitting roar of battle. Igor is lying on the snow; his hand is shading his eyes and his chin is upturned, and this is just how people sleep when they are dead tired. He is far away, but I see him as if he is ten feet away. There is a hole in his head, just above the left eyebrow, and frozen blood and snow have formed a flat crust on his face.

'Let's go. You aren't home. We all stayed here, you know that, and there's no way out. Go on.' He motions again with his hand.

And I see myself. I am lying not far from Igor, also dead, the snow around me covered in blood, my blood, and all around me infantry are scrabbling and falling, slipping on my blood.

Damn it, such a shame. I so wanted to be home and they went and killed me. And I have to go to the mountain—I can't be one of the living if I'm dead.

Igor sets off in the direction of the mountain and I follow. I want him to let me go but I can't stay behind—how could I be alive while he's there, dead?

But then I suddenly remember. Olga! I stop, Igor stops too, and he looks at me. His face is crestfallen and I see from his eyes that he knows what I am going to say to him.

'I can't, Igor, I can't go with you. I have my Olga and I can't leave her. I have to live.'

Igor doesn't like Olga. Every night he comes to take me with him up the mountain and every night she prevents him. And this time too he leaves on his own.

His face becomes gray, dead. His teeth set in a snarl, his lips tighten in a death grimace. The bullet hole appears in his head, shrapnel holes in his jacket, it gets dark around him and the blood wells. He is no longer beside me, he is up there on the mountain, dead. I return to the realm of the living, fly away from this scene, but all the time I look back, look at him lying there on the mountain . . .

I wake up. The sheet is soaking wet and I am shaking. My soul is empty; I feel nothing, absolutely nothing. Later I come to my senses and I start to bawl. I bite the corner of the pillow so I don't wake Olga and wail and wail. Later it passes and I just lie there, clutching the pillow. I can't help it. I lie with the pillow in my teeth and I am afraid to open my jaws. I want to die.

THREE

20 / Field Deception

War always smells the same—diesel and dust tinged with sadness.

You notice it for the first time right here, in Mozdok, in the seconds after you come off the plane and stand bewildered, flaring your nostrils like a horse, absorbing the smell of the steppe. The last time I was here was a couple of years ago in 2000. I sat right here under this poplar tree where some soldiers are now sleeping as they wait to catch a flight to Moscow. I drank water at the same fountain, and over there, in the boiler house behind the road, they sold locally made raw vodka. It seems that nothing has changed since then. And there's the same smell that was here two, three and seven years ago: diesel and dust tinged with sadness . . .

I first came here as a conscript. They brought us by train from the Urals, fifteen hundred men packed into the cars like sardines after someone miscalculated the numbers.

Everything had been just the same then, the same tents, the tower, the water fountain, only there had been more people, and there was a constant flow of movement. Someone would fly in or out, the wounded waited for a flight going the right way, soldiers stole humanitarian aid. Every ten minutes, attack aircraft groaning with bombs would take off and return later without their load, while helicopters warmed their engines, sending a wave of dust over the airstrip. And we were scared.

Of the fifteen hundred men on the field, only eight stayed in North Ossetia. The rest got packed off to Chechnya right away. And the beatings we got—it wasn't just bullying but unbridled lawlessness. Soldiers with broken jaws would fly out of barracks windows onto the parade ground while they were still running up the flag in the mornings, landing at the feet of the regimental commander in the middle of the Russian anthem.

They all beat me here, including Chuk (Lieutenant Colonel Pilipchuk), a towering man with fists like shovels that he used to beat us all without distinction: the young boys, the *dembels*, the warrant officers, captains and majors. He would pin us to the wall with his huge stomach and flail at us with his fists, shouting: 'You fuckers can't hold your liquor.'

Chuk himself was no mean drinker. Once the ex-deputy chief of the army, General Shamanov, flew in to inspect discipline in the regiment. Shamanov came to headquarters, put his foot on the first step and opened the door. A body fell out onto him, drunk as a skunk—Chuk.

Now Chuk still doesn't know who shot at him, but I do. It was night and the recon were drinking vodka in the barracks. The streetlight on the square was shining through the window right into their eyes, so one of them took his silenced rifle, went to the window and aimed at the light. I was standing at the window smoking and saw Chuk walking across the square . . . Thank God they were both drunk: one missed and the other didn't notice. The bullet hit the asphalt and zipped off into the sky. Chuk disappeared into headquarters while the recon guy finally hit the light and went back to finishing his vodka. And I just carried on mopping the corridor.

*

On 12 August 1996, I waited on the field to go to Chechnya with a combined battalion that the regiment had managed to scrape together from ninety-six men. We were sitting on our backpacks when a postman ran out from headquarters, waved and ran toward us holding something up in his hand. It was a good quarter mile to the airstrip from HQ and we watched him running and shouting, each of us wondering which of us he was coming for. Turned out it was me. 'Babchenko—here. Your father died . . .' he said breathlessly, handing me a telegram. And right at that moment they gave us the signal to board and the battalion started loading its gear. The other soldiers went past me, clapping me on the back and saying: 'You're lucky.' Instead of going to Grozny I went to Moscow to my dad's funeral.

My father gave me life twice. If he had died twenty minutes later I would have missed the telegram, boarded the helicopter and died half an hour after that. The helicopter was shot to pieces as it landed in Khankala. The battalion returned a month later. Only forty-two men remained of the ninety-six. That's how the war was then.

And all that happened on this very field.

I reached Khankala only in early 2000. I was still a soldier, but this time I was under contract. It was raining. We slept beside fires beneath a railway embankment, sheltering from the wind behind doors we had removed from their hinges. We didn't stand up to our full height and didn't look over the embankment as we were being fired at by snipers.

Then the sun came out and a sniper killed Mukha. Unlike the rest of us fools he never took off his body armor, convinced that it would save him. But the bullet hit him in the side and went right through him.

'There was a little hole on his left side, but on the right there was nothing left when we tried to bandage him—even his arm had collapsed into his chest,' Sasha recounted. Mukha didn't die immediately but only later, as the boys who were looking for smoke grenades pulled him out from the line of fire.

That same day, taking advantage of the good visibility, snipers killed two more men and injured six. We began to hate the sun.

These two wars convinced me of the unshakable nature of Chechnya. Whatever happens in the world, whatever humanity might be achieved, it will always be the same here—there will always be war.

I'm a journalist these days, and now I'm back in Chechnya and I don't recognize the place. Everything is different. Khankala has grown to incredible proportions, and the republic as a whole surprises me. It has filled up with people and the smashed clay huts have been replaced with new, three-story brick cottages. You see Ladas driving along among the carriers and scheduled buses stopping outside cafés. And the towns are lit at night.

Most of all I am amazed by the airfield at Severny. The 46th brigade of the interior ministry troops is based here, and this cozy little world tucked behind concrete fences is how the army should be—neat and ordered with rows of barracks, green grass and white road surface markings.

They set up a firing range on the airfield. In accordance with regulations, red flags would be hoisted to warn people against entering. When they're not shooting, white flags flutter in the wind to signal that it's safe to cross. They built the range to teach the soldiers how to destroy the old city that's located only a stone's throw from here.

In Chechnya now there is a strong sense of duality. Wherever you go, it is more or less peacetime, but at the same time it's not. The war is never far away. In Starye-Atagi four FSB intelligence service agents have recently been killed, mines continually blow up in Grozny and there are frequent ambushes in Urus-Martan. But in Severny it's quiet. Here they shoot only when they raise the red flag.

The army in Chechnya is now in stalemate. There are no longer any large rebel bands to fight; there are no front lines, no partisan units and no field commanders. The war is generally over here, at least in the conventional sense of the word. Now there's just rampant crime. A war-hardened rebel with a bit of authority will put together a gang of three young boys to sort out feuds and extort money. He doesn't fight just federal troops. If there is a bounty on someone's head the gang will lay a booby trap to get him. If there isn't, they'll go and rob the locals or fight a neighboring gang over oil deposits in the area. It's all about money, and if they gun down a policeman in the process, it's just by the by and can even be a matter of honor.

'My husband worked in the paramilitary police,' says Khava, a trader. 'This summer their unit lost thirty-nine men. They kill them in the middle of the street with a bullet in the back of the head. Someone murdered my neighbor a week ago and then his son yesterday. Both of them worked in the militia.'

The army is incapable of fighting crime. Imagine if in Moscow they got tired of all the robbery and banditry in the back streets and stationed a regiment on Red Square to keep order with tanks, antiaircraft guns and snipers. By day the military line the Kremlin grounds with even, sandy roads and hang portraits of the president on all the corners. And at night they shut themselves into the camp, fire at the slightest sound and never venture beyond the gatehouse. Is that supposed to stop the trouble in the suburb of Tushino? And what if Tushino's neighborhood police officer and the prefect are in cahoots with the local tough guy, Shamil the Chechen, and fought on his side in the last firefight with the police?

But you can't pull the troops out either. If you do, then the same thing would happen as did after the Khasavyurt Accords of 1996, when Russia left Chechnya to the separatists, with all the chaos and violence that ensued.

'Now all we do is carry out sweep operations,' says Fidel, a task force unit commander. 'If we go through a village constantly, then it's relatively quiet. But give it two or three months without a sweep and that's it, best not to stick your head in at all. You want to go to Grozny? Here's my advice to you: don't bother. It hasn't been swept for two months. I wouldn't go there, I'd be afraid to. And don't show yourself in Shali—that's another pretty nasty place these days.'

As dusk falls we stop in Kurchaloi. It's regarded as one of the most dangerous regions, even though it's in a plain. But here too the war has slowed down. The last attack around here was on 23 December, about two and a half months ago, when a BMP combat vehicle of the 33rd brigade from St. Petersburg got blown to pieces. A shell had been buried on the road and exploded right under it.

'Sometimes they set the explosives very skillfully,' says acting brigade commander Colonel Mikhail Pedora. 'A soldier will be walking along and see a box lying there, or a kid's ball, and kick it, and then a sensor triggers a blast and half his foot's gone. They've got specialists in setting such surprises for us.

'It's bearable now,' Pedora continues. 'We haven't been fired on for a good while. And they don't bury mines so often, but our engineers still remove about three a month. Who's doing it? God knows. The locals, probably.'

A dead BMP stands at the edge of the helicopter pad, covered in tarpaulin. Its turret has been torn off and the underside has been blown up in a rose shape inside the hull. Jagged shards of torn metal bend upward at the spot where the gunners' legs would have been. Alongside it stands another vehicle that got burned out some weeks earlier. It is also covered in tarpaulin, and it looks as though there would have been dead here too. Back then, when the fighting was in full swing, they used to leave them by the side of the runway like this and cover them with tarpaulin, only there were ten times as many.

There were two familiar posters at the brigade's gatehouse: 'Soldier! Think before you touch—it could be dangerous!' and 'Soldier! Careless talk costs lives!'

There's no one better at thinking up slogans and posters than the military; in Khankala there's a poster that sees the soldiers off on their sweep operations with the words 'Have a good journey!'

I drive on and on through Chechnya. Something is wrong. Perhaps the war really is coming to an end. Maybe my soldier's nose for lousy places has deceived me and maybe it really is time to open a spa for tourists. There are unique sulphuric springs here, and you could cure every sickness in the world in the geysers of Chechnya's plains. As a soldier in Grozny this was how I cured the ulcers that broke out on my skin from the dirt, the cold and the nervous tension. You could only crawl up to the springs then; now they've built car washes beside them and the locals do a little business out of all the free hot water.

Maybe peace really is just around the corner.

*

The helicopter hovers over a small pad on a flat bald patch of the hill near Nozhai-Yurt. For a couple of seconds it hangs in the air, and then its 3,000-horsepower engine lowers a ton and a half of humanitarian aid to the ground.

The fuselage starts to rattle with the heavy trembling and the engine is palpably straining. Barely stopping, the chopper hits the ground with a thump. There's a cracking sound coming from the undercarriage and the impact sets the rotors bouncing so hard they seem liable to snap off.

'We've landed,' says the pilot, throwing the door open and lowering the little steps. 'How about that? And people wonder why they drop out of the sky. There are very few serviceable aircraft, and they all get packed to the gills. The flight payload is at its very limit and the engine is working constantly at full throttle. And each time we land, it's the same thing—we drop down. What's there to say? The aircraft are worn out. We make up to thirty flights a day . . .'

In Grozny I drop by to see some of the recon guys I met on past combat tours. The recon battalion lives separately from the rest, in a tent camp. It's a dump compared with Khankala. The recon, special forces, and the FSB are swamped with work and have no time to feather their nests. But even here they have organized some sort of life, with tables, chairs, fridges and televisions.

The recon are drinking vodka. We are glad to see each other for the first few minutes, but everyone is waiting for me to ask questions. So I do.

'So how is it here?' Their eyes grow dark and fill with pain and hatred and reflect their continual depression. A minute later they hate everything, including me. With every word they become more crazed and the conversation turns into a heated tale of woe.

'Just write, journalist, get all this down.'

'Hey, why don't you write about the casualties? In our battalion alone we had seven killed and sixteen wounded.'

'The war is still going on and we do one mission after another. We just got back from twenty-two days in the mountains.'

'And they don't pay us shit here. Look, multiply twenty-two days by three hundred men, that's already 6,600 man-days of work. Just for this mission. In a month the brigade notches up 3,000 combat days. But at headquarters they have a limit of 700. I went and found out.'

'The hardest thing will be to go home. What are we going to do there, back in the division? Write notes? No one needs us there, understand? I just want to serve my time, get the promised apartment and to hell with it all.'

Now I see myself in them. Once again I see that field before my eyes. And from somewhere outside town comes the familiar thump of a lone gun. The topics of conversation have not changed one bit either: hunger, cold and death. I wasn't wrong, nothing has changed here.

The government has erected a facade of peace that is exemplified by neat lawns and level concrete pathways. But beneath it lurks these recon men, half crazed by missions and blood, and now they are drinking themselves into a stupor for the second year in a row. They long to break the facade and climb out of here, to get back to wives and children, to go to God knows where and start life anew, without wars and killing others, and without having to bury their own. But they can't. They have been grafted onto the fabric of Chechnya. The *dedovshchina* bullying in this tent labyrinth is a well-oiled machine, and no one follows up any of the incidents that take place in the nooks and crannies, under the tarpaulins; no one pays any attention at all. Why? Because they will all die. And still they send huge bundles of rifle rounds to Grozny, and the constant gnashing of teeth is eased with gallons of vodka, and there is a nonstop supply of torn human flesh to the hospitals. Fear and hatred still rule this land.

And it still smells of diesel and dust tinged with sadness.

I am now in Mozdok again, back on the field.

Seven years, a bit less than a third of my life. A person spends a third of his life asleep, while I spent it in war. Nothing has changed on this airstrip in these seven years and nor will it change. Another seven years will pass, then seven more, and these tents will still be here, and people will crowd around the water fountain and the helicopter rotors will spin ceaselessly.

I shut my eyes and I feel like an ant. There are hundreds of thousands of men like me who stood on this field. Hundreds of thousands of lives, so different and so similar, pass before my eyes. We were here, we lived and died, and the death notices flew to all corners of Russia. I am united with them; we are all one on this field. A piece of me died in every town that received these death notices. And a piece of this field remains forever in every pair of bottomless, war-charred eyes that had seen it.

Occasionally I recognize these eyes and I approach them. Not that often, though. In summer, when a truck passes down a stuffy Moscow street, and the smell of the diesel mingles with the dust, I feel a melancholy creep over me.

'Hey, got a light, friend? Where did you fight?'

21 / The Obelisk

Pskov, northwest Russia. 1 March 2001. The cemetery.

A heavy frost grips the streets and a cold wind whips down the marble slabs and right through me, making me shiver and hunch deeper into my collar.

I light up and get told off by some colonel: 'No smoking here!'

I stand in front of the memorial, looking at the names. Six adjacent black-marble obelisks: Lieutenant Colonel Yevtyukhin, Major Dostovalov, Junior Sergeant Shwetsov, Lance Corporal Lebedev, Private Travin, Captain Talanov . . .

Exactly one year ago eighty-four of the ninety soldiers in the 6th company of the 104th paratrooper regiment were killed near Sharo-Argun. Six guys from Pskov are buried in this cemetery. It's not a big cemetery, a few rows of gray headstones and fences. A forest starts close behind it, about a hundred yards away.

Something is happening to me, some kind of delusion. The cemetery, the forest, winter. I've seen this somewhere before, but where? That's it, it was on one of those lousy hills near the place the paratroopers were wiped out. And it was also in March, just one week later. We lost twelve men or more that time.

We too ran into Khattab in the Argun Gorge, by Sharo-Argun.

He had pulled back to Ulus-Kert and then we bumped into him on a hill with a view just like this. The same woods, the same winding road. And a cemetery, just like the one in Pskov. Lord above, how it all looks so similar.

And then suddenly it's all gone: this evening, the past and present, now and then. This cemetery before me is a different one. It's very similar—gray headstones, snow—yet different. It's a clear frosty morning and the bare trees are creaking in the wind, their twigs intertwining . . .

. . . The forest is full of roaring and tracer rounds are flying through the thin trees toward us, a mass of tracers riddling the whole air, billions of them, and there's no hiding. I am crawling, burying my face in the snow, feverishly looking for a slightly deeper hole, and then I hide behind a tomb. Hard metal strikes the slabs and chips cement powder over us, whizzes five inches above our heads and smacks into the trees, and everyone is shouting, someone's been wounded, someone's getting killed . . .

Cannon fire thunders past me, so mighty that it smothers the world—nothing else exists, no love, truth, justice, bravery. The only thing that matters is to hide from the cannon fire. I wriggle across open ground like a worm, my senses dulled to everything. I dig my face into a rut on the hillock, away from the horror.

The forest is right by us, so close that we can hear their shouts: 'What are you hiding for, you Russian dogs! Come here, we'll show you hand-to-hand fighting! You shout about it enough in your newspapers!'

They have advanced to within fifty yards of us and are now raining down close-range fire on three sides, shooting figures as they writhe on the ground . . .

*

I come to my senses. It's all in the past, just a delusion. This is just a normal Russian cemetery, as you could find anywhere across the land—quiet, peaceful, familiar, melancholy. A flock of crows takes off over the crosses and somewhere someone is ringing a bell. No one is shooting or killing here.

A volley of fire erupts overhead. I jump and crouch down instinctively. Immediately there is fear, heat and one single thought: it's not a delusion, damn it, I'm really there! I don't know how this can be but I'm there, and they're shooting!

I turn around, ready to dive behind the nearest hillock . . . Oh, for God's sake. I immediately feel weak and my legs tremble—seems like I got away with it. The honor guard reload their rifles once again and salute the fallen with another volley.

I am startled again. I know there's no danger but I can't help myself. It's already in our blood, this reflexive reaction to sharp noise, like the saliva of Pavlov's dogs. Beside me a paratrooper jumps too, and I feel his shoulder twitch. He turns and I see that his eyes are racing in panic. He meets my gaze and we both look guilty for a moment, like dogs with our tails between our legs. We smile in mutual understanding.

Some mothers approach the obelisk and lay flowers. I approach with them and place two carnations on the icy marble. The mothers are crying. The cold wind beats into my face, my eyes fill with tears and everything blurs in front of me, they freeze on my cheeks and make the skin tighten. I can't see properly, and instead of the names of the paratroopers I see completely different ones, together with their portraits, other faces . . . Igor Badalov died 8 March by Sharo-Argun, Oleg Yakovlev died 15 March in Grozny, Andrei Volozhanin died 10 March in Khankala, Mukhtarov in January, Sunzha, Vaseline,

Pashka, Andy the deputy political officer, Four-Eyes the platoon commander . . . Many of them, a great many.

That's how it turned out for our generation. Many of us passed through war: Afghanistan, Nagorno-Karabakh, Abkhazia, Transdnestria, Chechnya, Yugoslavia . . . Almost all of us have our own hill somewhere.

These names blur away and the others appear. I read them, stare at them, and remember.

Greetings, 6th company. Greetings, 1st guards regiment. Greetings, 426th regiment of the Cuban Cossacks, orders of Suvorov and Bogdan Khmelnitsky. Greetings, Igor, greetings, Andy.

Hi boys.

22 / Lais

At the base of the 45th reconnaissance regiment *of the para-troop corps there stands a memorial obelisk. The names of the paratroopers who died in the two Chechen wars are inlaid in the black marble. One of the last names to be added was that of Alexander Lais.*

When Captain Vladimir Shabalin comes here, he brings with him the only remaining picture of Alexander and a bunch of flowers. In keeping with tradition, he places a glass of vodka by the grave, covered with a piece of black bread, and then stands for a long time by the memorial, looking at those who did not return from the war.

'Here you go, all of his info,' Deputy Battalion Commander Major Agapov says, handing me the roll of the 2nd company. I read: 'Lais, Alexander Viktorovich, guards private, machine gunner. Born in the village of Neninka, 1982–2001.'

Alexander Viktorovich. Back in 2001 he was just eighteen years old. Everybody called him Sasha. Sasha Lais. He died on 7 August, one week after he arrived at the front.

'I only saw him once,' says Major Agapov, 'in Khankala. I was the receiving officer then and his team was just arriving in Chechnya. I can't say that he immediately stood out, no. He was an ordinary guy, nothing heroic about him, he was just another soldier. But for some reason he stuck in my mind, because of his name I suppose. Or maybe because he seemed like a pleasant sort of fellow. Here, you can use his photo—make sure you give it back.'

Lais went off to war from a small village in the Altai, Siberia. He had lived there for ten years. For the year before he went into the army he lived with his grandmother and grandfather. His mother and his little sister went to live in Germany with his stepfather, a descendant of deported Germans. They were sure that their son would come and join them when he finished high school in the town of Biisk. But then the second Chechen war began and Sasha made his choice. He didn't try to wriggle out of army service, although he could have; he was willing to do his duty.

His teacher Natalya Kashirina remembers how Sasha actually wanted to join the army, unlike most of his peers:

'You know, he went into the army quite happily. Sasha was one of those people who are very aware of concepts like "duty" and "Motherland."'

His grandparents Yelena Ivanova and Alexander Ivanovich received letters and photos from him almost every week. They kept them and would read them in the evening over tea. His grandfather knew by heart the last letter they got from Moscow, where Alexander was serving.

Hello Grandma and Grandpa. How are you both? How's the weather? I'm fine, although the heat here is unbearable. In a week we are supposed to fly to Chechnya but send your letters to my unit, they'll forward them to us. Everything's pretty OK here. A couple of days ago I sent you three letters at the same time, with twelve photos. Please write and let me know if you got them. And before that I sent you a roll of film in a letter. Anyway, don't worry about me. I'll stay in

touch. When you get this letter I'll already be in Chechnya—
we're due to go 24 July. OK, bye, your grandson.

He died two weeks later.
Excerpt from a list of commendations for Private A. V. Lais:

On 07.08.2001 the recon unit carried out a search for
bunkers and arms caches in the course of reconnaissance
operations near the village of Khatuni. While on the move
the point man detected an enemy unit of about fifteen men
heading in the direction of Kirov-Yurt to the Agishty road to
set up an ambush for a supply column. At the order of
Group Commander Captain V. V. Shabalin the recon went
straight into battle, hitting the enemy from the flank . . .

I run into Captain Shabalin in the smoking area of the 2nd
company.
'Can you tell me about that firefight?' I ask.
Vladimir frowns.
'I don't care to think about that.'
'Maybe a few words?'
'Well, on that day, 7 August 2001, the group was assigned to
set up an ambush on one of the trails used by the Chechens. At
this time they were pretty active in the area, and command
presumed they would try to hit a column in the rear that was
supposed to be delivering food and water to our unit. And
that's when we got wind of the ambush.
'We decided to use this column as bait to draw the Chechens
down from the hill,' says Shabalin. 'Otherwise we'd never flush
them out of there. Selmentausen is the sort of place where
we'll never be able to enforce our authority. It's not far from
the Georgian border, with mountain ridges on all sides. The

place has some very handy routes for evacuating the wounded and bringing in munitions without being noticed.'

His group moved out at daybreak, long before the column itself. According to the plan, the unit was supposed to outmaneuver the rebels and set up a counterambush. Looking at the map, there was only one place where they could do this.

During the first half of the day, everything went as planned. The column moved out at the designated time and the unit was already on its way to the area. In turn, the rebels took the bait and began to prepare an ambush. It seemed that the column and the Chechens and the paratroopers would all meet in the right place at the right time. But it wasn't to be.

The thing about warfare is that fighting doesn't usually start just because someone gives the command. For every action there are a thousand opposite reactions, like snow that falls at the wrong time, or something devised by the enemy. You can dig fortifications and mine the undergrowth for months; you can shell positions and pore over the maps and cook up intricate plans, but all to no avail. Because as soon as you stop in the most inconvenient place at the most inappropriate time, like if you need to drop your pants behind a bush, then some bearded bastard will shoot at you.

Shabalin's group went ahead of the unit. They left the departure point twenty minutes before the bulk of the forces. The Chechens didn't see them and let them right through. But the paratroopers missed the Chechens too and kept moving.

They stumbled into the rebels from the flank and everything happened very fast. Private Kuzin, who was at the front of the group, raised his arm, bent at the elbow, signaling that there were Chechens ahead, and then flapped it downward a few times, meaning 'Lots of them.' And that's when the shooting started.

'We ran right into them,' Shabalin recalls. 'They hadn't expected us to come so early and they were getting ready to meet the unit that was due there twenty minutes later. Meanwhile, their commander was positioning his fighters. Kuzin picked him off with the first shot from his silenced rifle and winged another. Of course we'd expected to encounter them, but in the event it happened in such an awkward place, between two hills, as exposed as your palm. The path there was in the shape of a G and we came out around the bend. There wasn't even any grass for shelter.'

The Chechen commander had managed to position his men well. They pinned down the group with just three weapons from the high ground, while the rest started to shoot up the recon from some nameless hill to the right. Another small group of Chechens had taken up positions beyond the precipice and cut off their withdrawal route. The paratroopers had walked into a trap.

The fire was so heavy that they could barely raise their heads. Nor could they withdraw—they couldn't leave the two pointmen, Sagdeyev and Kuzin.

Sagdeyev was badly hit in the first exchange of fire. His jaw got smashed, his right hand was torn apart and his waist was shot up. There was no way he could shoot himself out of that one.

'He lay right on the path, on his back, and every one of those bastards felt he had to fire a burst at him,' says Shabalin.

After the firefight, they found eleven holes in Sagdeyev. One of the bullets had struck an F-1 grenade that was hanging on his belt but didn't penetrate its casing.

They pinned the Chechens down with fire as best they could, but it couldn't go on like that for long, so the captain called up artillery support by radio. The first shells landed too far away, and as he corrected the guns Shabalin began to draw the Chechens toward him. The rebels decided to retreat from the artillery fire and moved closer to the Russian recon, and the paratroopers prepared for hand-to-hand combat.

'They came so close that they even started commenting on the messages they heard on my radio. We'd hear our guys say, "Hold on, we're coming," and the Chechens would shout back, "Why don't you hurry up, we'll give you a taste of action at close quarters!" There were perhaps fifteen yards separating us.'

Wounded Sagdeyev was still lying out in the open. The rebels were telling them to surrender, but Kuzin shouted back that Russians don't surrender and threw some grenades.

'They worked out that I was the group commander and started shooting right at me,' says Shabalin. 'I remember they were firing from the underbarrel grenade launchers, but every time I was saved by this rut in front of my head—the shells hit it and glanced off. It was a pretty serious situation—we couldn't stay there getting shot up for long, but nor could we move out. If we had, the Chechens would have killed both Sagdeyev and Kuzin. I told Lais to get ready to make a dash for it.'

A moment later, Alexander Lais performed a heroic feat.

Did he realize this would mean his death? Probably. There's no way he couldn't have known. There are no feats like this that aren't carried out consciously. But he didn't think about death. He was just doing his duty. There was no time to feel afraid, and there was less than a second's worth of life left, only as much time as a sniper needs to move his finger in the bushes.

And then Lais got up on his knees and began to cover his commander.

'I didn't know what was going on,' Shabalin continues. 'Lais was to my right and I told him to get ready to make a dash for it, and before I knew it he was half kneeling, half lying and firing long bursts. Then he sat up for a moment and slumped down again, turned to me and said: "I've been hit." I remember blood on his lips and telling him: "Hang on while we get you out of here." Then he started to fire again, loosed off another four bursts I suppose.'

Eventually a medic pulled Sasha out of the line of fire and started to bandage him.

A bullet had hit him in the throat. He stayed conscious for a while after that and Shabalin began to think the injuries weren't so serious and he'd make it. The doctor tugged at Shabalin's sleeve and told him he couldn't stem the blood—Sasha had internal bleeding. He died quickly.

'The Chechens came so close we prepared to fight hand-to-hand. If I'd had hair on my neck it would have stood on end, not with fear but with a sort of fury, mixed with fear, of course,' says Shabalin.

It didn't come to it in the end. After they'd collected their dead and wounded, the rebels pulled back. No one bothered to give chase; we had our own wounded to evacuate, as well as the body of machine gunner Alexander Lais.

As I write these lines I catch myself thinking that I can't call him Alexander. To me he's just Sasha. We might have met somewhere on the roads of Chechnya. Maybe he was on one of those carriers escorting the column of journalists I was in. We might have lit cigarettes off each other, and I would have called him brother and used the familiar form of Russian speech, just like we all do there. And that's why Alexander can only be Sasha to me.

The rebels left suddenly, as if ordered, and the fighting ended as unexpectedly as it had begun. Two men lay on the

path: Sagdeyev, miraculously still alive, and dead Lais who paid
for this courage with his life. Some of his fellow soldiers who
were next to him when he was shooting said that he managed
to kill the sniper that had wounded him. Later, after the battle,
it was announced that the paratroopers had killed five rebels.
At least that's how many fresh graves appeared at the edge of
the village the next morning.

Excerpt from a list of commendations:

> For exemplary performance of his duty, exceptional courage
> and heroism, and for services to the state and the people,
> performed during the counterterrorist operation on the
> territory of the North Caucasus in hazardous conditions,
> Private Lais, Alexander Viktorovich merits the Gold Star of
> Hero of the Russian Federation.

Today Vladimir Shabalin is calm as he remembers that fight.
Only his hands give away his agitation; he cannot keep them
still and constantly wrings his blue paratrooper's beret.

'Could that have been a stray bullet? No. He knew he shouldn't
stand up like that. And basically there's no point in discussing
what should or shouldn't have happened. He didn't have to cover
me, but he got up and did it anyway, just like that. Even if he
hadn't done it, the group wouldn't have been destroyed; the second in command was still there alive and the other soldiers were
at the ready. It's not like we all idolize the commander and protect him as our only hope. Everything was organized quite normally. The soldier simply acted as he saw fit—that's the kind of
guy he was. None of them showed any cowardice: Kuzin fought
them off as long as he could, threw all seven of his grenades
although he could have just kept his head down and even

surrendered. My radioman, the medic and the deputy commander, all of them fought. And so did Lais.'

Alexander Lais was posthumously awarded the Gold Star of Hero of the Russian Federation, but that's all the state did. For some reason, no one from the president's administration took the trouble to track down Alexander's parents and give them the medal. Only two years later did the paratroopers and journalists from the *Forgotten Regiment* TV program bring Sasha's mother over from Germany to the unit and present her with the Gold Star.

Vladimir Shabalin met with her too.

'I saw this film *Scorched by Kandahar*,' he says. 'There's a part when a wounded officer takes home the body of a soldier who saved him, and the relatives ask, "Why are you alive and our boy is dead?" So I was really afraid that I'd hear the same. But we got along well and are still in touch. I probably became one of the family to them. Seems I now have to live two lives . . .'

Suddenly he throws his blue beret down on the bench and looks straight into my eyes.

'You know, he's not the first soldier I've lost in this war. And that fight wasn't the worst I've been in either. But even so, it was different that time. Guys died in battle and they didn't have a choice, but this . . . it was self-sacrifice. Today, though, I think he shouldn't have done it. It would probably have been better if that sniper had got me. Don't think I have a death wish. I very much value my life. But I just don't like this life the way it is. I have nothing under my belt: no home, no money, no health. Just three combat tours and four stars on my shoulders. And I have no future. My whole life is right there, on my epaulettes. So what now?'

Shabalin doesn't like to remember that he probably owes his life to someone. On 7 August he doesn't mark an anniversary, but rather a day that commemorates a soldier he didn't manage to keep safe. It's a day of mourning for him, and each year he brings the photo here to the memorial and stands beside the glass of vodka and bread for a long time as he looks at the faces.

Postscript: After Sasha's death, a brother was born to Alexander Lais. The family also called him Alexander and had him christened by the priest of the paratroopers corps, Father Mikhail. And Captain Vladimir Shabalin became his godfather.

23/ Hello Sister

'Put the woman in the truck with the humanitarian aid,' barked Colonel Kotenochkin, looking pensively at the female medic who was riding in the convoy with us. He frowned in annoyance, spat and climbed onto the lead carrier.

When I first went to war in June 1996 as a nineteen-year-old conscript, we drove out of Mozdok in a small column with two escort carriers and Ural trucks loaded with humanitarian aid. The attack on this convoy and my first taste of action are detailed earlier.

I was feeling lousy, plagued by fear, sadness, loneliness and the inevitability of something imminent, something unknown and terrible. Since I had entered the draft office as a conscript, my situation had gone from bad to worse. First, there was the constant lack of sleep and starvation that reduced us to eating toothpaste during training in the Urals. Then came the period of frenzied beatings by the older conscripts in Mozdok, when my blood was spattered up the storeroom walls and my knocked-out teeth scattered on the floor. And now, this terrifying journey into the unknown, where things would only deteriorate further.

Cowed to an impossible, hopeless state, with eyes that just begged for someone to spare me any more suffering and finish me off, I was being thrown around on top of the carrier, clutching my rifle in my hands. As instructed, I was watching to the front and right, but couldn't help also glancing behind me at the truck where the woman was riding in her flak jacket.

No one got any peace because of her. Everybody made a point of ignoring her, while all the time she was subconsciously egging them on. The soldiers moved with manly abandon, their caps tipped back jauntily on their heads, and cockiness in their eyes. Boots, dirty puttees and exhaustion were forgotten in a moment, as basic instincts made us fluff up our feathers and dig the earth with our hooves in the presence of this female.

I had very mixed feelings toward her. I wanted to be strong, and yet weak at the same time. Strong so that she would admire my manliness and courage, and how I was fearlessly going to war, regardless of the hardships. I daydreamed about how the column would get ambushed and the commander would get killed, but I would save everybody, take over and single-handedly cover our withdrawal under the withering fire of superior enemy forces. I'd get wounded, of course, and she would lean over me, crying as she bandaged me, and I would hug her and wipe away her tears. And then I'd light up a cigarette and say something like: 'Don't cry, honey, I'm here.'

But at the same time I wanted to rest my head on her lap and cry so that this woman—who might well be the last I'd ever meet in my life—would shed tears over me too, understanding how bad it is to die when you're only nineteen, when you've barely let go of your mother's apron strings and haven't yet seen anything of life. You'd inhaled its heady aroma as it beckoned you with promises of a world of new experiences, which were still forbidden fruit but definitely within reach—all it needed was a little time.

After we arrived at Achkhoi-Martan, she and I went our separate ways and I didn't see her for a few weeks. She was a nurse and the medical corps wasn't exactly one of my main concerns at the time. For me it was trenches, dugouts, the kitchen, the constant need to steal water, the torment of lighting a stove in the freezing wet mornings, and messy nighttime firefights when you didn't have a clue what was going on and all you could see were streams of tracers in the sky. After a few days and weeks of that, death became simple and didn't frighten us any more. Weapons lost their magical aura and became just another instrument for performing a task.

I saw that woman only one more time.

It was about five in the morning and just getting light. The sun hadn't yet risen and a cool morning mist was crawling across the depression, making me shiver. I was on guard, with my back pressed against the wall of the trench and huddled into my jacket. My eyes were closed; all senses apart from my hearing were shut down. Night-vision sights were no use, and to stare into the darkness for three or four hours was a waste of time anyway. So I entrusted myself to my hearing, which grew razor sharp from the nervous tension. I wasn't particularly worried because there was a minefield just over the top, and if something happened I couldn't fail to hear it.

My left shoulder had gone numb and I shifted around, straightened my flak jacket and opened my eyes. In front of me, about fifty yards away, two people were walking right through the minefield. They moved absolutely soundlessly, as if they were floating on the mist, above the mined ground where death lurked at every step. It was the nurse and a young doctor from the medical battalion. They were walking as if they were all alone in Chechnya, and all that surrounded them was peace. He was telling her something as he wiped his glasses and

368 / One Soldier's War

she was listening, holding his hand. They emanated peace and love, and they were far removed from the war, the minefield, and me watching, holding my breath, afraid to scare them with a careless movement that might destroy this surreal picture. In their blissful ignorance they wandered clean through, and not one single trip wire or mine exploded. They reached the positions of the recon company, he did a few pull-ups on a horizontal bar someone had set up there, she smiled and took his hand and they went into a trench and disappeared. Like they'd never been there. The mist just kept creeping across the depression and under my jacket, making me shrink deeper into it.

Years have passed since then, and I never saw her or the doctor again. I don't know their names or what happened to them, whether they died in the Grozny meat grinder or, if they made it, what became of them after that.

But in the summer sometimes, not too often, I dream of two people walking silently across a minefield in the mist, and that feeling of duality returns—I'm afraid to startle or bother them and yet I'm confident that nothing on earth can shatter their idyll.

When they pulled our battalion down from the mountains in March there were already three new medics: two women and a young man. We weren't so interested in the man—after three months of living in a completely male company we'd had quite enough of our own unshaven mugs. But we showed great interest in the other two, Olga and Rita, who tended our various injuries and ailments at Argun. You'll recall how I took a liking to Olga, when she used to change the dressings on my ulcer-covered thighs. My feet had started to rot from the unsanitary living conditions, the cold, the hunger and the constant nervous exertion. She didn't say much; she bandaged me quickly and very deftly, and always asked if my condition had improved since the last dressing, if I was in pain and if the bandage was too tight. My mood always brightened after she did my dressing. We had become brutalized in the long months of fighting, fused into a single entity with the war; we had forgotten about our past lives and our own world. The presence of a woman revived us, and reminded us that apart from fighting there was also love, home, warmth. Just by being there, Olga had returned us to the world of the living. Whenever I talked to her, I was even more drawn to the idea of going home. I wanted to live, drink vodka in Taganka Park and chat up girls. I liked her for pulling me back from the filth of war to normal life.

In mid-March they moved our battalion to Gikalovsky, which is not far from Chernorechye, one of Grozny's suburbs. It's the same place where Shamil Basayev got his leg blown off. It was at the end of winter, when the storming of Grozny was coming to an end and the Russians had clearly taken the city. Basayev, who had no wish to die in a city that was surrounded, took fifteen hundred of his men and left Grozny via a dried-up riverbed. The wadi was mined so well that not even one person stood much chance of getting through, let alone a group of fifteen hundred. They'd just dumped antipersonnel mines out of helicopters, nasty little things that don't kill but tear off your foot, or just half of it, crippling you instead. But Basayev made it through. Some say a warrant officer in the FSB sold him a map showing the path through the minefields for about two thousand dollars.

They were moving at night, carrying all their stuff, weapons and wounded with them. They moved in absolute silence, right under the noses of the federal forces, slipping between two army units and passing within one hundred yards of our positions. They would have passed by entirely unnoticed if they'd been a tiny bit luckier. But near Chernorechye, where the gap was only a yard or so wide, one of the rebels stepped on a mine. A burst of automatic rifle fire echoed from the nearby infantry positions, although they had no idea yet what they were firing at. The Chechens walked right into it, and then there was another blast. Realizing they had been spotted, the rebels tried to regroup, and then the mines started going off one after the other. Seeing a crowd of rebels illuminated in the light of the explosions right under their noses, our infantry sounded the alarm and brought down a hail of fire. Some self-propelled guns joined in from up on the heights, and then came the mortars, creating an inferno on the river plain that lasted the whole night. Basayev managed to escape, but he lost half of his men in the valley.

I had heard about this but hadn't seen the place until one day my platoon leader and his deputy supply officer came up with the idea of going fishing around there. They'd heard rumors that the fishing was excellent, and that the mountain streams were packed with yard-long trout, fattened up in the absence of anglers and multiplying in unbelievable numbers. We decided to go the very next morning in two carriers, and instead of rods we'd take rocket launchers, the best fishing equipment there is—one shot upstream and you get a bucket full of stunned fish right away; you just have to make sure you scoop them out in time. Olga decided to go with us.

But things went wrong from the beginning. After we'd created Armageddon upstream, using up a week's supply of rockets, we caught a grand total of two fish the size of a finger. As we cavorted between the Chechen lakes and streams we didn't even notice that we'd ended up in Chernorechye. And in an instant, our happy vacation mood died like the wind.

There was no earth under our feet, just metal; everywhere was strewn with shards of different-caliber shells, from little pea-sized ones, tiny splinters of underbarrel grenades, to enormous casings the size of two fists from 152mm self-propelled guns. There wasn't a single tree left standing; all of them had had their tops cut off and been shredded, and their branches were scattered like torn-off arms, the white flesh of the wood showing at their stubs. And craters, craters and more craters. The whole river valley was made up of craters as far as you could see.

And between the craters, on the other riverbank . . . we couldn't make it out at first, what was that? Had there been a trash dump here or something? There were rags and bits of junk strewn all over it among the boughs of trees and bushes churned up from the soil by the explosions.

Looking closer we realized that these weren't rags; this wasn't a garbage dump. The rags weren't rags at all, but people. They lay a long way off, maybe three hundred yards away, and they were hard to make out. It's hard to distinguish what's what or who's who in the jumble left behind by a shelling, but some of the corpses were pretty clearly visible. One was sitting up, his dead arms hugging a wide tree stump that had been blown apart by a direct hit. His head was missing; it had rolled down the slope and was lying about fifty feet to one side. Another hung headfirst from a small precipice, his arms dangling into the water, playing in the current, bending and flexing at the elbow. Beside him lay his legs, just two torn-off legs, one in an army boot and the other bare.

It started to get a bit creepy, and an unpleasant chill appeared at the back of my stomach. The sense of death in this valley was so strong, almost palpable, and weighed heavily on our minds. We felt a kind of listless fatigue. These dead people were the enemy and we didn't feel any kind of pity for them, nor could we, but we still felt wretched at the realization of what can happen to the human body. And the knowledge that we were no exception, that we too could be scattered in a valley like this with our entrails hanging out and our heads rolled down slopes, had a shocking effect.

We jumped down from the carriers and walked across to the dam that blocked the river. We stepped carefully as it had not yet been de-mined, and none of us wanted to join the Chechens lying here. As it was, the death rate was way above the norm, even by military standards. Try as they might, the engineers could not remove all the charges. They had worked at night and hurried, and it had ended with one of them blowing himself up. His bloodied hat and bits of his belt were still lying beside the crater. The blast had detonated the grenades that hung from his belt and there was nothing else left of him.

As we stepped onto the dam we felt a pleasant sense of relaxation in our muscles; we were no longer standing on the treacherous earth, where death lurked beneath the surface. Beneath our feet now there was just plain, honest concrete, and we knew we could cross the smooth hardness without danger.

We had gone only a few yards when we came across the remains of two women. I had heard of them; they were Russians who'd become snipers for Basayev and had left Grozny with the rear guard. They were both over thirty, and I remembered that one was from Volgograd and the other from St. Petersburg.

The woman from Volgograd was named Olga. She was identified by a young infantryman, and when he came out on the dam and saw her, his hair stood on end. He said later that he'd never have believed it if he hadn't seen it for himself. The woman had lived on the same floor of his building, and he had been a guest in her home more than once.

The women lay next to each other. Death hadn't disfigured

them too badly; even now they were still different than men. Their poses were coquettish and their long hair was spread on the concrete. We stood over them and looked at their dead female bodies. Then Olga came over to us. I don't know if this was a coincidence or not, or if she felt something, but she went straight to the one from Volgograd, the one named Olga, and paid no attention to the other. She stood silently over her, not saying anything, just standing and looking, and at that moment her eyes acquired an incredible depth; all the secrets of the universe were mirrored in them, as if she had suddenly understood the meaning of life.

I looked at these women, the living and the dead, and thought that they were very similar. Both were petite, both in camouflage, both had chestnut-colored hair, both sharing the same name. It was as if Olga were standing above herself, like in dreams when you see yourself from the outside. Then she silently turned and went back to the carrier without looking at anyone. We all just stood there by the dead women and watched the living one walk off, and none of us made a single sound.

24/ Traitors

They also fought in the Chechen war, only on the other side.

In war a person doesn't get better or worse. War is like an emery board—it strips off everything that's affected and superficial and exposes the core, the real you. And if the core is strong to start with, then it becomes stronger in wartime, it toughens up. That sort of person can take anything and won't break. If the core was rotten, like a wormy nut, then war will destroy him once and for all, crush him and abandon him to the rot of fear. And in order to save his life he will go to any lengths.

From criminal case documents:

On 21 November 1995, Private K. M. Limonchenko deserted combat positions in the region of Orekhovo in the Chechen republic. On 22 November Limonchenko, in agreement with one Kryuchkov, stole a box of 7.62mm cartridges and ten RGD-5 grenades and defected to the rebels.

Konstantin Limonchenko had been thinking about deserting for quite a while. He badly wanted to live, not die in this unnecessary and corrupt war. If the generals wanted to fight, let them do so—he wanted to go home. But it wasn't so easy to go home. Konstantin's health was excellent; this native Siberian hadn't been ill since he was a kid, and faking pneumonia or dysentery so that he could serve out his time in the hospital hadn't worked out for him. Of course, he could have inflicted an injury on himself, he could have shot himself in the arm or leg, but he was terrified of pain and loved himself too much to resort to that. Maybe he'd run away? But if he got caught he'd be jailed for desertion. Recently the deputy political officer had read them the criminal code and dwelled on this article in particular. There was nowhere to run to anyway. There were just Chechens and more Chechens all around. Of course, why hadn't he thought about that before?

His decision to cross over to the side of the rebels came unexpectedly, of its own accord. Limonchenko immediately understood that this was his only real chance to save his life, with just a little blood and without self-mutilation or prison. The Chechens are strong and they always win, and when Chechnya gets its independence he will be in another country altogether. True, he'd probably have to bloody his hands, but that wasn't so bad—it'd be someone else's blood, not his.

That same night Limonchenko and Kryuchkov, another guy who thought it was too soon for him to die, grabbed a box of cartridges and grenades, vaulted over the front of the trench and headed in the direction of Stary Achkhoi.

From the criminal case documents:

In August 1996, during the interrogation of soldier
Vladimir Denisov who escaped from Chechen captivity, we
received information that he had been held in a school
building in the village of Stary Achkhoi, guarded by two
Russian soldiers of the parachute corps. One had changed
his name from Konstantin to Kazbek (sometimes they called

him Limon), the other was called Ruslan. Both voluntarily converted to Islam.

Private Roman Makarov, former prisoner of war:

I knew Limonchenko and Kryuchkov. I met them in Stary Achkhoi when I was a prisoner there, in the dugout where they kept us. They were also prisoners at first, but later, in February, they converted to Islam.

Limon was pissed off. The Chechens had not welcomed him quite as he had expected, and at the beginning they'd stuck him in a big pit with the other prisoners and construction workers who'd been taken hostage. Later they'd noted his servility and let him out of the pit, and before long they'd singled out this respectful Russian from the rest of the prisoners, brought him closer to them and allowed him to convert to Islam. They even gave him a machine gun and let him guard the other prisoners. But the Chechens still didn't trust him like one of their own, and Limon understood that they would betray him at the drop of a hat, casually expending him if the need arose. He gave the matter some thought. 'I'll have to show these damned Chechens that I can be useful, merge with their herd; I really have to become Kazbek, and not Konstantin,' he concluded.

But how? Go to the front lines and prove himself by fighting? No thanks, he could have stayed with the Russians—front lines are the same on both sides. His position as a guard in the rear was good enough for him. So he decided to perform a 'feat of valor' back there in the rear, far away from all the shooting.

As his first victim he chose a captured lieutenant colonel of the FSB. He had nothing against him personally; the colonel was simply the most suitable candidate—the Chechens especially hated the FSB.

At first he didn't get any particular pleasure out of tormenting the man and beat him without enthusiasm, simply because he had to. But then Limon started getting into it. He liked this feeling of control over someone else's life. He began to derive pleasure from the beating, and even cut a small club off a tree so he could spare his fingers. He punched and kicked him, and then held him while two Chechens, Isa and Aslambek, worked him over, and then he took over again. When the colonel died from a brain hemorrhage, he turned his attentions to another FSB prisoner, a warrant officer.

From the criminal case documents:

In mid-March they gave Limonchenko a weapon with which to guard the prisoners and mete out punishment at his discretion. Together with a Chechen called Isa he beat unconscious a builder from Saratov, who showed signs of psychological disturbance, so that he would be quiet and not shout.

Beating up this scrawny builder gave him particular pleasure. He was so ridiculous when he ran away, cowering from the club and squealing so amusingly, shielding his head with his arms when Limon threw him to the ground and started to kick him in the stomach. It would buck up his mood every time and he couldn't stop laughing. The builder was his favorite toy, and Limon played with him a lot as he wrestled with boredom in the camp. When the builder's head swelled up massively, Isa banned people from beating him because he was becoming unfit for work. Limon was to leave the guy in peace. But when Isa wasn't watching, Limon would allow himself to smack him around a bit—not hard, just a couple of blows to knock him over, although that wasn't as much fun.

Private Oleg Vasiliyev, former prisoner of war:

I was taken prisoner in December 1996. When they brought us to Stary Achkhoi, Limonchenko and Kryuchkov were already there. They had gone over to the Chechens and converted to Islam. They wanted me to convert too, but I refused. The Chechens stopped feeding me after that, so I ate what I could find—ramsons, nettles—and survived.

How did Limonchenko look? Burly, about six feet tall, strong as a wild boar. But he didn't beat me, maybe because he was a conscript himself. He generally beat the conscripts less than the contract soldiers, officers or civilians. But the young boys died faster anyway. The contract soldiers got it worst of all; they were beaten with extreme cruelty, told that they had come to Chechnya to kill for money. I spent nine months in captivity, and Limonchenko and Kryuchkov were with us the whole time, guarding us. Occasionally they went off on trips somewhere but I don't know where they went.

One day at the start of June 1996, these new mujahideen with Russian faces went off to shoot some prisoners.

Limonchenko, Kryuchkov and a Chechen named Zelimkhan took sixteen contract soldiers and a Chechen teacher from the prisoners in Stary Achkhoi, put them in a truck and drove them out of the camp. In the steppe Limon ordered them to get out of the vehicle and dig graves.

'Put your backs into it, you are working for yourselves,' he said, mocking his victims.

The stony ground was hard to dig and the prisoners were

happy about this. A sunny June day, full of the intoxicating aromas of the steppe, was too beautiful for death, and every stone they had to loosen from the earth prolonged their existence. They worked at their leisure, with fatalistic indifference, no longer paying any attention to the shouts of their guards.

When the graves were ready, Limon gave each of them a knife. Not understanding what he wanted from them, the men twirled the long wide-bladed Caucasian daggers and waited tensely. Limon spat and pronounced their sentence: 'So bastards, do you want to live? Is that what you want, you animals? We'll give you a chance. You will now kill each other, and whoever refuses will be shot. Whichever one of you survives will be set free.'

They wouldn't kill each other. So Limon, Kryuchkov and Zelimkhan shot them as promised. They told the Chechen teacher to bury the bodies, having spared him for the task.

Before the war, the teacher had worked in Stary Achkhoi where he was now being held hostage. They tortured him in the same classroom in which he'd taught kids reading and writing. The Chechens called him an FSB spy, beat him and demanded that he tell them who could pay a ransom for him, and how much.

Recently he'd been feeling ill. Three weeks earlier the rebels had taken them to a fortified site in the mountains that had been destroyed by Russian planes. Limon had ordered them all to get out of the bunker and form up outside, adding: 'If you don't manage to get out in thirty seconds you're going to get a good beating.'

The teacher didn't make it in time, and Limon set on him while he was still in the bunker and continued outside, in the fresh air, as he put it. First, he beat him with his fists, trying to hit him in the jaw every time, and then, when the teacher lost consciousness and fell, he kicked him and clubbed him in the stomach, in the kidneys and the groin, so that he could no longer move and his kidneys were damaged. The teacher didn't recover from that session; he limped and started to forget who he was and what he was doing there.

Once he'd buried the prisoners, the teacher went over to the truck where Limon was smoking on the cab step. Seeing that the work was finished, Limon told him to go and collect the shovels. When the teacher turned around, Limon shot him in the back of the head.

Dmitry Groznetsky, former prisoner of war:

In August they exchanged me and some other prisoners in Grozny for some Chechens the federals had been holding. Limonchenko and Kryuchkov were riding with us then, but refused to be exchanged. Their parents came and visited them and talked to them, begging them to come home, but they went back with the Chechens.

Limon had been right. He didn't become one of the Chechens, the Caucasian name Kazbek didn't stick and they did give him up in the end, forcefully turning him over to the FSB in exchange for one of their field commanders. The exchange took place in October 1996 in Grozny.

Oleg Vasiliyev, former prisoner of war:

I don't think they'll go to jail. Going to the crime scene to carry out a test investigation was impossible and the evidence had all remained there. Moreover, Limonchenko found a good lawyer and paid him a lot of money. They summoned me as a witness in this case, but that was a long time ago, maybe two years. Since then, I haven't heard a word.

The criminal case opened by the Moscow military district prosecutor's office under article 338, clause 2 (desertion), and article 226, clause 3 (theft of munitions), was halted through a strange coincidence of circumstances. Because of the amnesty for Chechen rebels announced by the State Duma, Privates Limonchenko and Kryuchkov were released on a written promise not to leave town. Even though it was written in black and white that the amnesty did not extend to people who had stolen munitions. It was not possible to find the investigator in charge of this case; he had been either discharged or transferred to Moscow. After a two-year interval the case was sent for completion to the regional prosecutor's office of the North Caucasus military district.

'No comment. The case is in the final stages,' say the military prosecutors. 'All we can say is that we have ample grounds on which to press charges and it falls to a court to pronounce them guilty or not.'

25 / Chechen Penal Battalion

No one liked them, not in the first war or the second.

The Chechens hated them for the robbery, rape and murder they perpetrated; they never took them prisoner but killed them on the spot after first cutting off their ears and ripping out their tongues.

Our soldiers hated them for wriggling out of combat, for saving their own skins and for their lies. 'We do the same work as them but do it better,' the conscripts complained, 'so why do they get paid more?'

And the officers hated them for being uncontrollable, for their drunkenness and stealing, and for shooting them in the back at night.

They always got sent right into the thick of it. The storming companies who had to attack in the first wave and who got killed first were formed from their ranks. Not because they fought better than anyone else, but because no one minded much about using them as cannon fodder. If someone has to die, then let it be the worst people you can find.

They called these combined units penal battalions. At least half of the contract soldiers in them had been ex-criminals who had served time in prison camps.

Ex-criminals serving in the army are nothing new, all the

more so in Chechnya. From the very start of the Caucasus wars the scum of the earth would flock here from all over Russia. The stench of robbery and impunity around them was so strong that it blotted out even the fear of death. How many criminals went to Chechnya back then no one could count even now. It was quite normal for contract soldiers to have a criminal record. Many of them had sentences hanging over them, and you would meet individuals who had signed a written oath not to leave wherever they came from.

'Back in 1995 the situation in the contract-based army service was about the same as it is now with alternative army service. There was no mechanism in place and there was no question of any kind of professional selection,' says Major Petrenko, a commander of Moscow's draft commissions. 'They took anyone they got and only demanded reference documents from the police as a matter of procedure—it didn't mean anything. Do you want to go and join the slaughter? Be our guest, off you go to die. It was better than sending conscripted boys.'

Making the most of this opportunity, a wave of assorted dregs washed into the army, causing the military to howl with dismay. They immediately hated the contract soldiers, every last one of them. I remember how one battalion commander frowned when the helicopter brought him long-awaited replacements from Khankala.

'What the hell do I need this bunch for? They'll drink vodka for two weeks and scavenge in the ruins, and there's enough looting going on as it is. And they'll start dumping their rifles and applying for discharge. They'll take all their looted junk back home, drink away the money they've earned and then come back to Chechnya again.'

They stole everything they could lay their hands on, even in battle. Here's a typical scene during an attack: the platoon occupies an apartment building and scatters among the floors. Five minutes later the unit is already dispersed throughout the building. The conscripts are on the second floor, which is the optimum height: grenades won't reach you, and if you have to get out you're not too high up. From the third floor up the looters are busy. With their weapons slung over their backs, they rummage through abandoned trunks in strangers' apartments. Greed burns in their eyes, and they have no time for any fighting. Nothing deters them. The most sought-after items were of course jewelry, but tape recorders, crystal, sets of china and quality clothing disappeared just as readily. One came up to me once with a folded handkerchief in his hand.

'Hey, you're from Moscow, you're educated. Tell me, is this gold?' he asked, producing several lumps of heavy metal from the cloth.

It was gold. Dental crowns, several of them, one for three teeth in the lower jaw.

There persists a romantic notion that the most reckless acts of heroism are pulled off by ex-criminals, as if life in the camps had taught them the toughest laws of survival.

But that's a long way from the truth. Malice and bravery are different things. In order to be a good soldier you can have no fear of death. You have to be ready to lay down your life for a comrade, or crawl for a wounded man in an open space under sniper fire. But the morality of the criminal world teaches you something else: to save your own skin.

You can't force that kind of guy into battle with a rifle butt. He will always find a thousand reasons to stay behind and stoke the stove for the oatmeal, and if you really go for him he'll start wailing about a violation of his constitutional rights and apply for a discharge. Fortunately for him, there's a clause in his contract that says it can be annulled at any time, even in the midst of battle.

Over the years, the army forces in Chechnya have become a magnet for former camp inmates, only now they don't go there to loot. There's nothing left to steal, apart from maybe a few barrels of crude oil. Now it's the threat of a new prison sentence that drives them there. If you want to lie low there is no better place than Chechnya. And the best thing is that it's totally legal to avoid prison this way. The criminal code says that the statute of limitations for a crime applies only if the suspect has not evaded the investigation. So what happens if he is also serving the state? And what if he even earns himself a medal? It's the medals that attract the criminals to Chechnya. Once, when we stopped near Shatoi, I had a smoke with an infantryman. He introduced himself as Anton, a sniper from St. Petersburg.

'Like hell do I need Chechnya—all you can earn is pennies here now. I'm actually an investigator. I've collected so much money in bribes that I could buy myself a house abroad. I have a nice apartment and a foreign car. But there's a sentence hanging over me. I need to get a medal, and then I'll qualify for the amnesty.'

Not only rank and file escape court by going to Chechnya, there are regimental commanders who have done the same thing. Once I was talking to a staff officer from the Moscow district's military prosecutor's office. The conversation turned to Chechnya and we tried to list mutual acquaintances.

'What did you say his name was, Dvornikov?' he asked. 'Yeah, of course I know him, a colonel, commands a regiment. He's one of our clients. We've been working on him for some time. But we're very unlikely to finish his case because he got promoted in Chechnya and has some medals now.'

*

The ex-criminals bring cruelty with them to the army, and their main characteristics are bitterness and greed. I remember how they made a captured Chechen run across the minefield in Chernorechye. It was the same field that was littered with the bodies of hundreds of Basayev's men after their ill-fated exit from Grozny. The Chechen brought the infantry weapons, drugs and money, and they sent him out into the field again and again to go through the pockets of the dead. The prisoner made three trips, enriching his captors by thirty thousand dollars, and then an antipersonnel mine tore off half his foot. They shot him after that.

The worst thing is that the ex-criminals infect the others. We had a conscript who killed a Chechen for effect, took him to the dam and shot him. Later he boasted, 'I just shot down a Chechen,' failing to understand that killing a one-legged prisoner doesn't make you a soldier.

Another soldier in my regiment, Sanya Darykin, was just a normal guy when we got called up. We served together, defended ourselves together from the *dembels*, and mopped the floors side by side. Then after three months he went absent without leave and stole a car. Seventy days in a disciplinary battalion turned him into a completely different person. He no longer acknowledged us, his fellow soldiers, and nor did he acknowledge the *dembels*. He gathered a little gang of others who had done time like him and associated only with them. His favorite entertainment was to make young soldiers crawl through the heating pipe under the barrack ceiling after lights-out. Those who didn't make it through in fifteen seconds took a beating.

After four months Sanya went down the tube completely. The next time he went absent without leave, he and another guy robbed a man after they'd first smashed him unconscious with a metal pipe.

*

People think that *dedovshchina* is a symptom of a broadly conscript-based army and that you can avoid it by switching to a contract-based system. But units that consist entirely of contract soldiers have existed for a long time now, and there it's exactly the same. Only it's the criminal elements rather than the older recruits who assume the role of bully.

I saw with my own eyes how an orderly, a former engineer with a graduate degree, mopped the barracks with a rag, getting ready for the next detail, while some tattooed 'Granddad' soldier spurred him on with kicks.

The army has been living according to prison-camp rules for a long time. A male collective in a confined space inevitably assumes a prison's model of existence. It's a universal truth—the strong always push around the weak, and, anyway, someone has to mop the latrines.

To create an army with a human rather than a criminal face, you have to apply a few axioms that are as obvious as they are impossible to apply. A soldier should serve, and cleaning the latrines should be the job of voluntarily employed cleaners. A soldier should be well paid and afraid to lose his job. There should be professional selection, just as occurs in cosmonauts' schools, and a speeding fine should be a black mark on a soldier's career. A soldier is inviolable, and any violence against him should be punishable by law. Just as any act of violence by a soldier outside of his duty should be punished with a jail sentence too.

But this is clearly a utopia.

26/ Operation 'Life' Continues

No one returns from the war. Ever. Mothers get back a sad semblance of their sons—embittered, aggressive beasts, hardened against the whole world and believing in nothing except death. Yesterday's soldiers no longer belong to their parents. They belong to war, and only their body returns from war. Their soul stays there.

But the body still comes home. And the war within it dies gradually, shedding itself in layers, scale by scale. Slowly, very slowly, yesterday's soldier, sergeant or captain transforms from a soulless dummy with empty eyes and a burned-out soul into something like a human being. The unbearable nervous tension ebbs away, the aggression simmers down, the hatred passes, the loneliness abates. It's the fear that lingers longest of all, an animal fear of death, but that too passes with time.

And you start to learn to live in this life again. You learn to walk without checking the ground beneath your feet for mines and trip wires, and step on manholes on the road without fear, and stand at your full height in open ground. And you go shopping, talk on the phone and sleep on a bed. You learn to take for granted the hot water in the taps, the electricity and the central heating. You no longer jump at loud noises.

You start to live. At first because that's how it's worked out and you have stayed alive, you do it without gaining much joy from life; you look at everything as a windfall that came your way through some whim of fate. You lived your life from cover to cover in those hundred and eighty days you were there, and the remaining fifty-odd years can't add anything to that time, or detract from it.

Then you start to get drawn into life. You get interested in this game, which isn't for real. You pass yourself off as a fully fledged member of society, and the mask of a normal person grows onto you, no longer rejected by your body. And those around you think you are just the same as everyone else.

But no one knows your real face, and no one knows that you are no longer a person. Happy, laughing people walk around you, accepting you as one of their own, and no one knows where you have been.

But that doesn't bother you any more. You now remember the war as some cartoon horror movie you once saw, but you no longer recognize yourself as one of its characters.

You don't tell anyone the truth any more. You can't explain what war really is to someone who has never been there, just as you can't explain green to a blind person or a man can't know what it's like to give birth. They simply don't have the necessary sensory organs. You can't explain or understand war—all you can do is experience it.

You're still waiting for something all these years. God knows what, though, you simply can't believe that it ends just like that, without any consequences. You're probably waiting for someone to shed some light on it all, for someone to come up to you and say, 'Brother, I know where you've been. I know what war is. I know what you've been fighting for.'

That's very important, to know why and what for. Why the

brothers the war gave you had to die? Why people were killed, why they fired on goodwill, justice, faith and love, crushed children and bombed women? Why the world needed to lose that girl I saw back on the runway in Mozdok, with her smashed head and a bit of her brain lying in an ammo box next to her? Why?

But no one tells you. And then you, yesterday's soldier, sergeant or captain, start to explain it to yourself. You take a pen and paper and produce the first phrase as you start to write. You still don't know what it will be, a short story, a poem or a song. The lines come with difficulty, each letter tearing your body like a shard being pulled from a wound. You feel this pain physically as the war comes out of you and onto paper, shaking you so that you can't see the letters. You are back there again and death once more rules everything, the room fills with moaning and fear, and once again you hear the big guns, the screams of the wounded and people being burned alive, and the whistle of mortar shells falling toward your prone back.

A drum beats and a band on a sultry parade ground plays 'Farewell, Slavs,' and the dead rise from their graves and form up, a great number of them, everyone who was dear to you and was killed, and you can already spot familiar faces: Igor, Vaseline, Four-Eyes the platoon commander . . . They lean toward you and their whispering fills the room: 'Go on, brother, tell them how we burned in the carriers! Tell them how we cried in surrounded checkpoints in August 1996, how we whimpered and begged them not to kill us as they pinned us to the ground with their feet and slit our throats! Tell them how boys' bodies twitch when bullets hit them. You survived only because we died there. Go on, they should know all this! No one should die before they know what war is!'

And tinged with blood, the written pints appear one after

the other. Vodka is downed by the pint while death and madness sit beside you, nudging you and correcting your pen.

And there you are, yesterday's soldier, sergeant or captain, concussed a hundred times, shot to pieces, patched up and reassembled, half crazed and stupefied, and you write and write and whine with helplessness and sorrow, and tears pour down your face and stick in your stubble. And you realize that you should not have returned from the war.

27/ I Am a Reminder

About a million military personnel passed through Chechnya in the ten years after the start of the first war in 1994. That's the population of a large city. Fifty divisions of seasoned soldiers who bring their philosophy, the philosophy of war, back to civilian life with them when they return.

Ave Caesar, morituri te salutant!—Hail Caesar, those who are about to die salute you!

At the age of eighteen they had already killed men who were sometimes older than their fathers, and they saw how these grown men died from the bullets unleashed by their hands. There were no voices of authority, and there was no God either. They were ready for anything. There were no women in their world, no children, no old men, no sick people, no cripples. There were just goals: dangerous ones, safe ones and ones with potential.

Three of them meet and sit in the subway near my metro station every morning. They have five medals between them, six crutches, two artificial limbs and one leg. And a common hatred for the whole world. They've been coming here for a few years now to sing songs, and they are always the same songs in the same order. They sing terribly, but that doesn't bother them. They hate the people they are singing for.

They see the world from below, and not just because they have only half of their bodies left, but because half of their souls are gone too. They're closer to the spit-drenched asphalt than to people's faces. They no longer have the strength to get up and start a new life on plastic legs, and no longer wish to. These young men don't want to try to keep up with life any more. All they want is for the war to last forever, and for them to be part of it.

I sit on the ground with them in the subway. On the scratched marble stand a bottle of vodka and a soldier's mug, and beside them a pack of cigarettes and some matches. For 'furnishings,' one of them brought a traveling rug, a small cushion to sit on and a tape player. When his two comrades leave, he stays there on his own and plays one cassette of Afghan and Chechen songs until evening. He doesn't look homeless; he's clean and shaven, his hair is neatly cut and his camouflage fatigues are washed and pressed. Nor is he begging. There's a small bowl in front of him but it just kind of lies there on its own. If people want to they can drop a coin in; if not, they just carry on. He couldn't care less. He doesn't say thanks to the first type and he doesn't abuse the second. He just sits there, listens to music and smokes. He's not here. His column left five years ago and he stayed with it.

I don't know his name and it doesn't matter. He is my brother, they all are, brothers given to me by the war. The whole of Moscow is full of such brothers; there's at least one in each subway.

He spoke first.

'Where did you fight then, brother?'

I told him. Then he started to remember stuff—where, when, how. He told me about getting his leg torn off when his carrier got ambushed. A shell hit the armor right by his hip. He didn't lose consciousness, and he even saw his ripped-off leg jerking, and the boot scraping on the rivets. I didn't ask him anything, just listened in silence. And he spoke calmly and without any hysterics, just discussing life.

'I don't understand this world. These people. Why are they alive? What for? They were given life at birth and didn't have to pry it away from death—Have a good life, people! But how do they spend it? Do they want to invent a cure for AIDS and build the world's most beautiful bridge, or make everyone happy? No. They want to rip everyone off, stash away as much money as they can, and that's it. So many boys died, real kids, and these people here fritter their lives away as ignorantly as a kitten playing with a ball and have no idea why they are alive. Pointless people. A whole world full of pointless people. A lost generation. It's not we who are the lost generation, it's them, those who didn't fight, they are. If their deaths could bring back just one of those boys then I'd kill all of them without hesitating. Every single one of them is my personal enemy.'

He lights a new cigarette from the stub of his last and pours a shot of vodka. And then he laughs evilly, and his eyes flash with hatred.

'Did you ever think the Dubrovka Theater siege in Moscow was payback? And then collapse of the Transvaal aqua park there too? You can't go enjoying yourself while two hours' flight away people are killing each other! Children are still dying there and there's starvation, and yet these people were willing to pay seven hundred rubles for a theater ticket—that's two thousand for the family—just to amuse themselves. You can live for two months in Chechnya on that money. I must be concussed, because I don't understand this. I just can't get my head around it! There's a war going on in their country and they don't give a damn. So in that case we shouldn't give a damn about them either. Not one of them should ever die without knowing what war is. I want for them too to cry out at night and cry in their sleep, and without waking to dive under the bed when New Year's fireworks are exploding in the yard, and whine there from terror like we did. They are as guilty of our deaths as those who killed us, who sent us to this slaughter. Why weren't they striking in Moscow and blocking the roads when we were being killed in Grozny? Why? Why weren't they screaming and tearing their hair out when they saw on TV how dogs fed off the flesh of their boys? Why was there no revolution, uprising or civil unrest? How could they send their sons off to this slaughter and then go and have fun, live, drink beer and earn money while they were dying down there? While jets were flattening the mountains and tearing apart children and women, when wounded Chechen kids rotted in cellars, wrapping the stumps of their limbs in rags and infection crept across the wounds? They're also guilty of these deaths. We are here to get what's ours, and we are ready to kill.'

His hatred abates as suddenly as it had welled over. His eyes recede once again behind a film of indifference.

'Half-truths everywhere, half-sincerity, half-friendship. I can't accept that. Here in civilian life they have only half-truths. And the small measure of truth we had in war was a big lie. So many boys died and I survived. The whole time I used to wonder what for. They were better than I was, but I survived. Surely this is not pure chance. Maybe I lived so that others remember us? I am a reminder,' he says with another evil-sounding laugh.

I get up silently and leave him cigarettes, matches and vodka. There's nothing else I can give him apart from money. I walk away without saying anything and he doesn't even look at me. For him I am also 'one of them.' Which means whatever I say is a half-truth.

Military Abbreviations

AGS	automatic grenade launcher
PTUR	guided anti-tank missile
OMON	special purpose police unit (paramilitary)
NURS	unguided rocket
BMP	tracked infantry combat vehicle
RPG	Rocket Propelled Grenade
FSB	federal security service (the main successor to the Soviet KGB)
BTP	armored personnel carrier
RGD	anti-personnel hand grenade

355